Homersham Cox

A History of the Reform Bills of 1866 and 1867

Homersham Cox
A History of the Reform Bills of 1866 and 1867
ISBN/EAN: 9783337295394

Printed in Europe, USA, Canada, Australia, Japan

Cover: Foto ©ninafisch / pixelio.de

More available books at **www.hansebooks.com**

A HISTORY

OF

THE REFORM BILLS

OF

1866 AND 1867.

PRESENTED BY THE AUTHOR.

49 CHANCERY LANE, *Feb.* 19, 1868.

'The next remove must be to the study of politics; to know the beginning, end, and reasons of political societies; that they may not, in a dangerous fit of the Commonwealth, be such poor, shaken, uncertain reeds, of such a tottering conscience as many of our great counsellors have of late shown themselves, but steadfast pillars of the State.'   MILTON'S *Epistle to Hartlib on Education.*

LONDON:
LONGMANS, GREEN, AND CO.
1868.

CONTENTS.

CHAPTER I.

THE REFORM QUESTION SINCE 1832.

Transfer of power from the Working to the Middle Classes in 1832, page 7.
—Reform Bills of 1852 and 1854, 8.—Conservative Reform Bill in 1859,
9.—Lord Palmerston's accession to office, 20.—The Reform Bill introduced by Lord John Russell in 1860, 20.

CHAPTER II.

THE FRANCHISE BILL OF 1866.

Mr. Baines's Franchise Bill, page 26.—Dissolution of Parliament in 1865, 27.
Demise of Lord Palmerston; Earl Russell, Premier, 29.—Franchise
Bill introduced by Mr. Gladstone in 1866, 31.—The computed number
of new voters, 36.—The Bill opposed by Mr. Lowe, 38.—Second reading, 43.

CHAPTER III.

THE REDISTRIBUTION OF SEATS BILL, 1866.

Lord Grosvenor's amendment, page 45.—Redistribution of Seats Bill, 50.—
Second reading of Redistribution Bill, 53.—Sir Rainald Knightley's
'Instruction' with reference to the Bribery Laws, 56.—Captain Hayter's amendment condemning the Redistribution scheme, 57.

CHAPTER IV.

THE REFORM BILLS OF 1866 IN COMMITTEE.

The Franchise Bill and Seats Bill consolidated, page 60.—Lord Stanley's motion to postpone the clauses relating to the suffrage, 61.—Mr. Walpole's amendment to raise the county suffrage, 64.—Motions to base the suffrage on rateable value, 67.—Resignation of Earl Russell's ministry, 79.

CHAPTER V.

ACCESSION OF THE CONSERVATIVE MINISTRY IN 1866.

The causes of Earl Russell's resignation, page 80.—Mr. Bright's position and opinions, 83.—Influence of Lord Grosvenor and Mr. Lowe, 85.—The Conservative ministry of 1866, 86.

CHAPTER VI.

THE GOVERNMENT REFORM RESOLUTIONS OF 1867.

Reform Resolutions proposed by Mr. Disraeli, February 1867, page 91.—His error as to the electoral rights of freemen, 92.—The Resolutions opposed by Mr. Lowe and Mr. Bright, 95.

CHAPTER VII.

THE FIRST PROJECT OF A REFORM BILL IN 1867.

The Resolutions abandoned, page 97.—Another scheme selected at a meeting of the Conservative party, 97.—The scheme submitted to the House of Commons, but speedily relinquished, 99.—Resignation of three Secretaries of State, 100.—Their explanations of their reasons for retiring, 103.

CHAPTER VIII.

THE REFORM BILL PRESENTED, MARCH 1867.

A Bill to amend the Representation introduced, page 106.—Mr. Disraeli's erroneous statistics, 107.—Extension of the borough franchise less under this Bill than under that of 1866, 108.—The Bill of 1867 would have increased the voting power of the wealthier classes, 118.—The irregular operation of the Bill, 120.—Mr. Gladstone's strictures on the scheme, 124.—The compound householders fined for their votes, 126.—Resolution of the Liberal party not to oppose the second reading, 133.

CHAPTER IX.

THE SECOND READING OF THE REFORM BILL, 1867.

Ten objections to the Bill enumerated by Mr. Gladstone, page 134.—Examples of irregular operation of the proposed franchise, 137.—Mr. Hardy's defence of the measure, 139.—Right of compound householders to be repaid rates paid by them, 143.—Comparison of Mr. Bright's Bill and that of the Government, 143.—The Government abandon the dual vote, and offer other concessions, 150.

CHAPTER X.

THE REFORM BILL OF 1867 IN COMMITTEE: BOROUGH SUFFRAGE.

Three classes of amendments of the proposed borough franchise, page 156.—The ministerial amendments affecting compound householders, 159.—Meeting of the Liberal party—Mr. Coleridge's 'instruction,' 160.—The 'tea room' schism: part of the Instruction abandoned, and the rest accepted by the Government, 162.—Mr. Gladstone's amendment to enfranchise non-rated tenants, 165.—The principle of 'personal payment' is not embodied in the Bill, 169.—Public meetings; addresses to Mr. Gladstone, 173.

CHAPTER XI.

THE REFORM BILL OF 1867 IN COMMITTEE. CLAUSES RELATING TO RESIDENCE AND PAYMENT OF RATES.

Amendment respecting residence of borough voters, page 175.—Mr. Hibbert's amendment to enfranchise compound householders on payment of reduced rates, 177.—Conference between the Secretary to the Treasury and Liberal members, 178.—The Government insist on the enfranchised compound householder paying full rates, 181.—And on 'personal payment,' 187.

CHAPTER XII.

GENERAL ENFRANCHISEMENT OF HOUSEHOLDERS IN BOROUGHS.

Exclusion of compound householders from the suffrage, page 190.—Mr. Hodgkinson's method of enfranchising them, 194.—Accepted by the Government, 196.—Influence of public opinion in procuring this concession, 199.—Its extensive effect, 200.—Lord Cranbourne and Mr. Lowe oppose the democratic amendment, 204.—Mr. Disraeli tries to modify it, 207.—The amendment has established household suffrage in boroughs, 209.

CHAPTER XIII.

The County Suffrage.

Reduction of the copyholders' and leaseholders' qualification, page 211.— Restriction as to land in boroughs, 212.—Attempt to make the occupiers' qualification depend on residence, 213.—Estimate of number of new county voters, 215.

CHAPTER XIV.

The Distribution of Seats.

Amendment to increase the number of partially disfranchised boroughs, page 217.—Unsuccessful motion to give additional members to six large boroughs, 219.—Subsequent concession with respect to four of them, 224. —The schedules finally adopted, 225.—Statistics of their effects; preponderance of the power of small boroughs, 227.

CHAPTER XV.

Distinction of Borough and County Franchises; Boundaries.

Attempts to exclude owners of property in towns from the county franchise, page 220.—Townsmen anciently voted in county elections, 230.—Restriction of this right by the Reform Act of 1832, 232.—Mr. Colville's motion to abrogate the restriction with respect to copyholders, 233.—Similar motion by Mr. Hussey Vivian with respect to householders, 234. —The boundary commission, 240.—Comparison of the methods of rectifying boundaries adopted in the Reform Bills of 1866 and 1867.

CHAPTER XVI.

The Reform Bill of 1867. The Third Reading in the House of Commons.

Lord Cranbourne and Mr. Lowe strongly condemn the Bill, page 244. Objections to it generally expressed in the debate, 248.—Mr. Disraeli's statement that the Conservative government was in favour of household suffrage in 1859, 253.—The statement contradicted by the Earl of Carnarvon, 255.

CHAPTER XVII.

The Reform Bill of 1867 in the House of Lords.

Two nights' debate on the second reading in the House of Lords, page 256. Lord Cairns's argument for enfranchising householders of all classes, 59.—Series of speeches condemning the Bill, 261.

CHAPTER XVIII.

THE LORDS' AMENDMENTS OF THE REFORM BILL OF 1867.

Amendments with respect to copyholders' qualification, voting papers, and representation of minorities, page 268.—All these amendments rejected by the Commons, excepting those relating to the representation of minorities, 270.—Arguments for and against such a system of representation, 271.

CHAPTER XIX.

THE FINAL STAGES OF THE REFORM BILL OF 1867.

The Premier's description of the Bill, page 277.—The Reform Act of 1832 and that of 1867 contrasted, 281.

APPENDIX.

An Abstract of the Reform Act of 1867, showing the additions to and material variations from the original Bill of March 1867, under the clauses borrowed from the Franchise Bill and Redistribution of Seats Bill of 1866, page 283.

The original Reform Bill of 1867; (showing the omitted and altered clauses, and the clauses borrowed from the Franchise Bill and Redistribution of Seats Bill of 1866,) page 289.

A HISTORY

OF THE

REFORM BILLS OF 1866 AND 1867.

INTRODUCTION.

A CONCISE HISTORY of English civilisation might be deciphered from the Statute Book alone. That venerable record, it is true, is silent respecting many subjects which make up the bulk of ordinary annals, and takes but little note of foreign wars, the intricacies of diplomacy, enterprises and exploits of warriors and politicians, or the intrigues of Courts, and the lives of Kings. But the principal epochs in the social progress of the English people are very distinctly and most authentically traced in the great collection which narrates the transactions of their Parliaments and National Councils from the time of the Conquest. How vividly do the Constitutions of Clarendon, for example, represent the issues of the momentous struggle in the reign of Henry II. between the Church and State, and the resolution with which the nation, even at that early period, resisted ecclesiastical domination! The great charters of John and his successors, frequently violated, and as often renewed with more stringent provisions, mark, with equal precision, another characteristic principle of English polity, the limitation of the royal prerogative. The wonderful series of statutes passed in the reign of the great lawgiver, Edward I., show

B

plainly that England had then commenced a new era of its civilisation, had outgrown the feudal policy suited only for the infancy of a nation, and had replaced it by the systematic institutions and jurisprudence of a people capable of self-government. We might, in like manner, trace out from the Statute Book other great social changes. Thus the Statutes of Provisors in the reign of Edward III. record the resistance of this kingdom to the papal thraldom. The electoral laws in the reign of Henry IV. demonstrate the established power of the House of Commons. The sudden and violent restriction of the county suffrage in the time of Henry VI. proves that the liberties of the people were, in that lawless and corrupt age, overwhelmed by the internecine struggles of two aristocratical factions, and the fury of civil war. The consequent degradation of the power of Parliament is clearly discernible in the legislation of the following age, and notably in the statute which, in the reign of Henry VII., authorised the Star Chamber, and in the enactment by which his successor obtained the prerogatives of an autocrat. Similarly, the Acts passed in the time of Elizabeth and under the Stuart dynasty, denote that revival of the popular power which, after the Revolution of 1688, culminated in the Bill of Rights.

The method of investigation here suggested might easily be continued to our own times. How distinctly do the Catholic Emancipation Act of 1829, and the Reform Acts passed three years later, show the commencement of a new chapter in the social history of this country! Those great legislative measures declared the abandonment of a policy of repression which had been observed during the whole of the previous century, and with especial severity after the French Revolution. Roman Catholic Emancipation and Reform were each the complement of the other. The one decreed religious toleration; the other restored to the people a large portion of their ancient political rights.

It is not, of course, contended that Acts of Parliament always correctly represent the national will at the period when they are passed. We know, on the contrary, that many of the statutes—for example, the Acts of the reign of George III. directed against public meetings and the press—were in the highest degree distasteful to the majority of the people. But even the most unpopular decrees of Parliament illustrate the condition of. society in successive ages, because they show the evils or dangers which the Legislature attempted to remedy or obviate. To obtain however, the full benefit of the historical information which statutes afford, we must examine them with their context—the conduct of politicians, the debates in and out of Parliament, and the manifestations of public opinion respecting them. In some cases the mere legal effect of an Act of Parliament is of less interest and importance than the mode in which its enactment has been accomplished. The defects of a faulty statute may be cured by later legislation, but precedents of political temerity or faithlessness have a longer life. They tend to lower the standard of political morality, to destroy public confidence in the Legislature, and to degrade statesmanship to the level of Parliamentary strategy.

Of the effects of the Reform of 1867, we can at present speak only in the language of conjecture or prediction. We know, indeed, that it increases largely the democratic influence in the constitution, but cannot yet estimate with precision the extent of the change. With respect, however, to the manner in which this important measure was passed, and the methods adopted in order to mould it into its present shape, ample means already exist for arriving at just conclusions. All the data for a sound judgment upon these points are before us, and we possess the information necessary for a comparison of the statesmanship of the past session with other great political performances. The objects of the following pages are to present these materials in a connected form, and to explain the place which the new Reform Act occupies in English Electoral Law.

CHAPTER I.

THE REFORM QUESTION SINCE THE YEAR 1832.

Transfer of Power from the Working to the Middle Classes in 1832, 7.—*Reform Bills of* 1852 *and* 1854, 8.—*Conservative Reform Bill in* 1859, 9. —*Lord Palmerston's accession to office,* 20.—*The Reform Bill introduced by Lord John Russell in* 1860, 20.

THE REFORM ACT of 1832 greatly increased the power of the middle classes. It is now well ascertained that the original right of suffrage, when Parliaments were first established six centuries ago, included almost every rank of the free community. The elections of knights of the shire took place in the County Court—an open Court, to which everybody who chose might resort; and we have, beside other evidences, the unmistakable testimony of two statutes of Henry IV., declaring that all persons who were present at these elections were to take part in them, and that this practice was the ancient usage. In boroughs, all the resident householders were burgesses qualified to vote for members of Parliament. Elections, both of knights and burgesses, were taken by the 'view' or show of hands, and not by the 'poll.' The suffrage in both towns and counties was almost universal; and not until the time of Henry VI. was any attempt made to restrict it. In that reign, during a period of great corruption and violent civil discord, a law was passed limiting the right of voting to the class commonly designated as the forty shilling freeholders, and the county suffrage remained in the almost exclusive possession of this class for several centuries subsequently. The borough franchise became narrowed by various causes, principally by the gradual establishment of select or self-elective municipal corporations, which by usurpation acquired the power of choosing the representatives of towns, to the exclusion of the inhabitants at large. The great Reform Act of 1832 was passed at a period when the representation had fallen into a state of the utmost disorder. Many great towns which had acquired wealth and importance in modern times did not send members to Parliament, while the right of sending them was possessed by an enormous number of insignificant decayed boroughs, which in many instances had scarcely a score of inhabitants.

Undoubtedly the greatest and most difficult achievement of the Reformers of 1832 was the redress of these anomalies. The 'Act to amend the Representation of the People in England and Wales' entirely disfranchised fifty-six boroughs, which had collectively returned 111 members, and in thirty other places the franchise was reduced to the return of one member instead of two. The vacancies thus created were supplied by constituting many new Parliamentary boroughs, and by increasing the number of knights of the shire. In England alone, 141 seats in the House of Commons were transferred from deserted villages to great constituencies. This was a great change in the balance of political power. But another almost equally important was the general effect of the Reform Acts, to give a predominating power to the middle classes. In boroughs an entirely new class of voters was created—'the ten-pound householders,' as they are popularly designated. Subject to certain restrictions, every male occupier of a tenement within a borough worth ten pounds a year was rendered entitled to vote, provided that he duly paid rates and assessed taxes, and resided within seven miles of the borough. The large majority of the persons who came under this description belonged to the middle class. It is not practicable to ascertain with absolute precision the proportion which their number bore to the other classes immediately before and after the Reform Act of 1832. But there are sufficient data to warrant the conclusion that the distribution of political power among different classes of society was most materially altered by that measure. In the aggregate the working classes were a majority of the voters, though in consequence of the number of nomination boroughs and those in which the right of election was confined to close corporations, a large proportion of the House of Commons was chosen by a very small oligarchy. For the reasons given in the subjoined note it may be inferred that before the Reform Act the working classes constituted a majority of the aggregate number of borough electors; and immediately after that Act was passed were outnumbered in a proportion greater than two to one.* And this disproportion in after times continually increased; for that statute not

---

* The following calculation is submitted as an approximately correct estimate of the effect of the Reform Act of 1832, in adding to the relative power of the middle classes.

At the first registration 1832-3 there were on the borough registers, in round numbers—

Ten-pound householders	174,000
Freemen, scot and lot voters, and other ancient-right voters	108,000

(See *Electoral Returns*, 1866, page 8.) The latter number must have nearly represented the borough constituency immediately before the Reform Act. Also it appears by the *Electoral Returns* of 1866 that in that year 55 per cent. of the freemen belonged to the working classes. We may fairly suppose that the same proportion obtained immediately before 1832. But of the 174,000 added by the Reform Act nearly all were of the middle and higher classes. Probably not more than 15 per cent. belonged to the lower class. (See Mr. Gladstone's speech on the introduction of the Reform Bill, 1866: *Hansard*, vol. 182, col. 30.)

Hence the number of artisan voters immediately after the Reform Act were 15 per cent. of 174,000 and 55 per cent. of 108,000; the middle and higher class of voters were 85 per cent. of 174,000 and 45 per cent. of 108,000. The result is, that immediately after the Reform Act the borough voters included—

Working men	85,500
Middle and higher classes . . .	196,500

In other words, the working men, instead of being more than one-half the borough constituency, became less than one-third of it; instead of having the majority, they were outnumbered more than two to one.

only created a new property qualification, which by its nature excluded, and was intended to exclude, the poorer inhabitants of towns, but also provided for the gradual extinction of the electoral rights of scot and lot voters, and several other ancient rights which were possessed for the most part by persons in the lowest ranks of life.

In counties, also, the tendency of the Legislation of 1832 was undoubtedly to confer political power upon a class occupying an intermediate position in the social scale. The new qualifications of electors in shires were given almost exclusively to such persons—to the possessors of copyholds of the annual value of ten pounds, various classes of leaseholders, and, above all, to annual tenants occupying lands at a rent of 50l. or upwards.

Several Bills have been introduced into Parliament since 1832, by which it has been proposed to make further changes in the distribution of the franchise of returning members of the House of Commons, and in the qualifications of voters. Lord John Russell's Bill of 1852 proposed to extend the borough franchise to occupiers of houses of 5l. annual value, and the county franchise to tenants rated at 20l. The measure introduced by the same statesman in 1854 fixed the borough qualification at 6l. rated value. Both Bills introduced various new electoral qualifications. That of 1854 included among them an income of ten pounds annually arising from dividends, the payment of forty shillings annually in direct taxes, and an academical degree of any University. Provision was also made in both Bills for the disfranchisement of some places and the enfranchisement of others.

Both these measures failed. That of 1852 was not pressed, in consequence of the change of Ministry which took place in that year. The Bill brought in two years later by Lord John Russell was withdrawn because the Ministry considered that the attention of Parliament would be so much absorbed by the Russian War then pending, that sufficient attention could not be given to the subject of the representation of the people.

In 1859 a Ministry, of which the Earl of Derby was chief, was in power, and Mr. Disraeli was Chancellor of the Exchequer. In the Speech from the Throne, the attention of Parliament was again directed to the defects of the representative system, and very soon after the commencement of the Session Mr. Disraeli introduced a Bill upon the subject. Some of the arguments which he used upon this occasion present a remarkable contrast with the doctrines espoused by him a few years later. In 1866 he earnestly supported a motion which involved the fate of the Russell-Gladstone Cabinet, and which recommended a suffrage qualification founded upon the rateable value of the qualifying tenements. In 1859 he insisted with equal earnestness that such a scheme was impracticable and unjust. The following is an extract from his speech of Feb. 28, 1859:—

Notwithstanding the Parochial Assessment Act, the rating of this country is most unequal; and it is only those whose business it has been to examine into this subject in its minute details who can be aware of the preposterous consequences which would arise from a rating instead of a value qualification. Take the present qualification of 10*l.* value, which it is very generally and popularly supposed might be supplied by an 8*l.* rating. Now let us see what would be the consequence upon the present constituency of adopting an 8*l.* rating instead of a 10*l.* rental. I will take the instance of Boston, represented by my hon. and learned friend behind me (Mr. Adams). The borough of Boston consists of two parishes; the rating of one of them is upon half the value, and of the other upon two-thirds of the value. The practical consequence of having an 8*l.* rating in Boston would be to disfranchise 400 of the electors of that borough. The House will see that the idea of establishing a franchise based upon rating instead of value is by no means the simple process it is by some persons supposed to be. The great objection to such a measure, which led us to relinquish all idea of adopting it, is its tendency to disfranchise many of the constituencies.*

* *Hansard*, vol. 152, col. 983.

It is worthy of note that at this time Mr. Disraeli's views on the subject of a rating franchise were in complete accord with those of Lord John Russell, who had adopted such a franchise in his Bills of 1852 and 1854; but now, in the debates of 1859, acknowledged his error. He said, ' I doubt whether the propositions I formerly made, founded upon rating, were based upon a very sound foundation, for I have certainly found that rating varies very much. . . . I believe that any change you may make in the 10*l.* franchise should be of the same nature as the franchise established by the Reform Act—namely, based upon annual value.' *

In 1866 the very question here considered was raised by Lord Dunkellin's amendment to the Reform Bill, introduced in that year by Mr. Gladstone. Lord Dunkellin proposed that the 'rateable' value of property should be made the basis of occupiers' qualification in boroughs. This proposal, which involved, as was well understood, the fate of the Whig Ministry, was supported by all the influence of Mr. Disraeli and the Conservative party. The very arguments which Mr. Disraeli had used in 1859 respecting the variable character of 'rateable' value were repeated in various forms in this great party debate. In 1859 he strenuously opposed ' the idea of establishing a franchise based upon rating.' In 1866, the temptation to adopt that idea as a means of ousting his political opponents was irresistible.

The chief characteristic of the Reform Bill of 1859 was the establishment of an identity between the borough and county suffrage. Various qualifications were defined, which were to give titles to vote in boroughs or counties, according as the elector or his property were within the limits of the one or the other, and the occupier's qualification in shires was brought to the same level as in towns—ten pounds clear yearly value.

* March 21, 1859. *Hansard,* vol. 153, col. 399.

Among other qualifications which were to have a similar effect was the possession of an estate of inheritance in copyholds worth five pounds per annum, the qualification of lodgers paying eight shillings weekly rent, of graduates in the Universities, and members of various professions.*

In his exposition of this scheme, Mr. Disraeli admitted that there were many persons capable of exercising the suffrage who do not live in 10*l.* houses; but expressed himself adverse to the admission of them 'by the coarse and common expedient which is recommended, of what is called "lowering the franchise in towns."' Some of the arguments which he used upon this subject afford a ludicrous contrast to his later concessions in favour of household suffrage. For instance—

I beg the House to consider for a moment what must be the effect of lowering the franchise in towns. Suppose that instead of a 10*l.* borough qualification you had a 5*l.* borough qualification. Well, the moment you had a 5*l.* borough qualification, you would realise all those inconvenient results which are erroneously ascribed to the 10*l.* qualification. You would then have a monotonous constituency. You would then have a constituency whose predominant opinions would be identical. You would then have a constituency who would return to Parliament members holding the same ideas, the same opinions, the same sentiments. . . It certainly would be most injudicious, not to say intolerable, when we are guarding ourselves against the predominance of a territorial aristocracy, that we should reform Parliament by securing the predominance of a household democracy.

'Household democracy' was an object of very safe invective eight years ago, and within a much more recent period. The Chancellor of the Exchequer perfectly understood his audience when he denounced 'household democracy' and the 'coarse and common expedient' of lowering the suffrage in towns. His plan of extension of the suffrage in boroughs, as at a subsequent date, contemplated lateral extension only; for instance, it

* A copy of the Bill of 1859 is given as an appendix to vol. 153 of *Hansard's Debates.*

included the possessors of funded property to the amount of 10*l.* per annum, or of a pension in the civil, military, or naval service to the amount of 20*l.* per annum. He estimated that 200,000 would be added to the number of county votes by the reduction of the tenants' qualification in shires to 10*l.* annual rental.

The Bill materially affected the rights of freeholders in towns. It proposed that the electors should vote in the places in which they resided, or, if their qualifications were real property, in the place in which it was situated. Consequently, a considerable number of freeholders of land in towns who had hitherto voted for knights of the shire were proposed to be transferred to the borough registers.

On the 10th of March, 1859, Lord John Russell gave notice that on the motion for the second reading of the Bill he should move—

That this House is of opinion that it is neither just nor politic to interfere in the manner proposed in this Bill with the freehold franchise as hitherto exercised in the counties in England and Wales;

And that no readjustment of the franchise will satisfy this House or the country which does not provide for a greater extension of the suffrage in cities and boroughs than is contemplated in the present measure.

This resolution, after a protracted debate of seven nights, was carried (March 31, 1859) by a considerable majority (39), in one of the fullest Houses ever known. On the motion for the second reading of the Ministerial Bill, the numbers on the division were: ayes, 291; noes, 330.* In consequence of this defeat Lord Derby advised Her Majesty to sanction a dissolution of Parliament; and the proclamation dissolving it was issued on the 23rd of April following.

The new Parliament assembled at the end of May. Upon the Address in answer to the Speech from the

* *Hansard*, vol. 153, col. 1257.

Throne an amendment was moved in the House of Commons, declaring that the confidence of the House and country 'is not reposed in the present advisers of Her Majesty.' This motion was carried, June 10, by a majority of 13 (ayes, 323; noes, 310);* and in consequence of this defeat, Lord Derby and his colleagues shortly afterwards resigned their offices. A new Ministry was thereupon formed, in which Lord Palmerston became First Lord of the Treasury, Lord John Russell, Secretary of State for the Foreign Department, and Mr. Gladstone, Chancellor of the Exchequer. Lord Palmerston announced (June 30) that it was not the intention of the new Administration to bring in a Reform Bill during that Session, but that they would do so in the following year.†

At this stage of the narrative it will be convenient to take a retrospect of the position which up to this time the two principal political parties had assumed with reference to the Reform question. The main issue between them related to the borough suffrage. Was it to be lowered or merely extended laterally? The phrases 'lateral extension' and 'vertical extension' had not then been invented, but the distinction was already well recognised. The only Reform Bill which the Conservatives had hitherto supported offered lateral extension only. Mr. Disraeli maintained the 10*l*. qualification of householders in boroughs; and the new classes of voters whom he proposed to enfranchise were persons of the same social rank, such as lodgers paying 20*l*. annual rent, and persons in the receipt of Government pensions to the same amount. On the other hand, the two Reform Bills which had been projected by Lord John Russell in 1852 and 1854 were based on the assumption that the occupiers' qualification in boroughs

* *Hansard*, vol. 154, col. 416. † *Ibid.* col. 478.

ought to be reduced. On the first occasion he recommended 5*l*. rated value, and on the second 6*l*. rated value as the limit of this qualification.

The issue was also distinctly raised by his successful amendment with reference to the Conservative Bill of 1859. In moving that amendment Lord John Russell complained bitterly that the Bill, while it subverted rights of freeholders which had existed for centuries, and threatened to entirely change the character of the county constituencies, made no substantial addition to those of boroughs.

While (he said) there is a total alteration in the basis of our representative system, such as no one ever proposed, and such as Earl Grey and his colleagues were praised for not attempting in 1831, no change is made in regard to that which I own appears to me to be a necessary provision in any Reform Bill. You destroy what is ancient, but do you make provision for what is new? By no means. Every man will admit that since the Reform Bill, which, with great and not overdue caution, placed the franchise for boroughs and cities in the occupants of 10*l*. houses, great progress in knowledge and capacity has been made by the working classes. . . . Can you say that since the period of the Reform Act there are not persons below the class of 10*l*. householders thoroughly fitted for the suffrage? Are there not numbers of persons who are perfectly capable of judging, and in circumstances sufficiently independent to qualify them to vote at elections? For my own part I have no hesitation in answering that question in the affirmative; and I confess it has appeared to me for some years, that such is the growth of intelligence, such the improvement of the people, that you ought not to confine yourselves to the limit of 10*l*. *

Lord Stanley, then Secretary of State for India, followed Lord John Russell in the debate, and strongly supported the maintenance of the 10*l*. limit in boroughs. Lord Stanley allowed that additions to the number of working men on the electoral register might properly be made, but contended that such additions were provided by the proposed savings' bank franchise,

* *Hansard*, vol. 153, col. 396-398.

the enfranchisement of lodgers paying a rent of 20*l.* per annum, and the possessors of funded property worth 10*l.* per annum. These three franchises were enumerated by the noble Lord—and these alone—as means of increasing the number of artisan electors. He said expressly that he spoke on the part of the Ministry, and his language must be taken as an authoritative exposition of the views of the Conservative Government respecting the reduction of the occupation franchise in boroughs. One extract from this speech is well worth consideration as a perspicuous statement of the determination of his colleagues upon this vital point of any Reform Bill.

When it is said, that by retaining the borough franchise at 10*l.* the working classes are excluded, I apprehend that what is intended is, that they are not admitted in a body. It is not a question whether they should be shut out altogether—no one wishes for that—but whether they should be admitted indiscriminately—the ignorant with the educated, the idle with the industrious, the man who spends as well as the man who saves. . . . . We think that the possession of some property in the hands of a man who has earned it by his labour is evidence of industry, of self-control, of good moral character. With the details of the machinery employed you are not now dealing. If the machinery we have adopted is good, employ it; if defective, amend it; but upon the principle laid down by us we confidently ask the verdict of this House, namely, the admission of the working classes by some principle of selection, and not at hap-hazard.*

But the lowering of the occupation franchise was obviously not a mere matter of 'detail' or of 'machinery.' It constituted the first and most important test of any Bill for the amendment of the representation. It was the very backbone of the Reform which the Liberal party demanded. The Conservative Ministry of 1859 prepared a measure which did not contain any concession to that demand, and even under the pressure of Lord John Russell's menacing amendment could not bring themselves to offer any such concession.

* *Hansard*, vol. 153, col. 413–415.

Two eminent members of the Government, Mr. Henley, the President of the Board of Trade, and Mr. Walpole, the Home Secretary, had both seceded from the Cabinet a few days before the commencement of the Session, because they disapproved of the contemplated Reform Bill. In their explanations in the House of Commons, March 1, 1859, they adverted to the equalisation of the borough and county qualifications, and the maintenance of the 10*l.* standard in the boroughs as their principal objections to the Bill.* In his speech on Lord John Russell's amendment, Mr. Walpole recommended the 6*l.* rating franchise in towns:—

I believe that you might find another resting-place in boroughs by going to a 6*l.* rating, which would be equivalent to an 8*l.* value; because that is the point where the landlord by law is permitted to compound for the tenants' rates, at a lower rate than that which is paid by others. There is the line therefore where dependence ends and independence begins. †

And in the course of the same debate the other seceder from the Ministry, Mr. Henley, advocated a similar extension of the suffrage. He computed that a 6*l.* rating would increase the number of voters by not more than 100,000, and expressed his belief that 'this addition to the borough voters might have been very safely made.' ‡

Lord Palmerston and Mr. Gladstone on the same occasion both avowed that the proper time for lowering the urban occupiers' qualification had arrived.

Those, said Lord Palmerston, who have no property ought not to be the persons to direct the legislation applicable to those who have property; subject to those conditions, I am convinced that a reduction might be made, and I think ought to be made, in the amount of the borough occupancy franchise.§

And Mr. Gladstone avowed his adhesion to the measure of a 6*l.* franchise recommended by Mr. Henley and Mr. Walpole. In reference to the embarrassments of the

* *Hansard*, vol. 152, col. 1058. † *Ibid.* vol. 153, col. 771.
‡ *Ibid.* col. 1218. § *Ibid.* col. 877.

Government occasioned by their secession, Mr. Gladstone observed:—

I cannot deny that the first cause of these embarrassments, so far as I am able to perceive, is the most unfortunate error committed by the Government in the construction of their Bill in opposition to the wise advice of two most distinguished members of the Cabinet. I believe that the Government are now as well aware as any hon. gentleman who sits on either side of the House, that in all probability if they had taken the wise advice of their two colleagues, while their counsels were still unknown to the public, and had presented a plan framed on the basis of the suggestions of those right hon. gentlemen, the Bill would then have met with very general acceptance.*

The great seven nights' debate of March, 1859, was, in the language of the Chancellor of the Exchequer (Mr. Disraeli), conducted with a vigour and variety which sustained the reputation of the House of Commons; and certainly that remarkable discussion deserved the encomium. Whatever may be said of the imperfect constitution of the representative assembly, no one can deny that upon great occasions it affords noble examples of rhetorical ability. The opinions of the principal speakers upon Lord John Russell's amendment have a peculiar interest and importance at the present time, because they serve to illustrate the history of the Reform Act passed eight years subsequently, and to test the political fidelity of most of the chief actors in the parliamentary struggle of the last two years. Few persons have suffered more frequently from misrepresentation of their political opinions than Mr. Bright. It has been constantly assumed, without a tittle of proof, that he is the advocate of extreme democratic doctrines and an apostle of universal suffrage. His moderation during the discussions of 1866 and 1867 have been regarded as inconsistent and simulated; but the sentiments which he expressed during that period are perfectly in accord

* *Hansard*, vol. 153, col. 1040.

with the views which he adopted in 1859. In the debate on Lord John Russell's amendment, Mr. Walpole directed attention to a speech then recently delivered by Mr. Bright at Rochdale, in the following terms:—

He recently made a speech of great power at Rochdale, in which he showed, and I think conclusively, that you cannot have manhood suffrage, and that you cannot have, strictly speaking, household suffrage, if you desire that your electors should be independent. The honourable gentleman also showed, conclusively in my opinion, that in regard to those living in small tenements, some by scores, some by hundreds, and some by thousands, they were so little independent of those around them that they could hardly be said to have a free will of their own.*

This language, addressed, be it remembered, to a popular meeting, is not that of a mere demagogue who appeals only to the passions and sympathies of an unreasoning mob. In his speech in the House of Commons immediately following Mr. Walpole, Mr. Bright argued with great power against the proposal in Mr. Disraeli's Bill with respect to the exclusion of the freeholders in towns from the county register. 'The proposition of the Bill,' he said, 'is, first of all, to get rid from the county of one-fourth, or 25 per cent., of the whole, or 100,000 freeholders of the independent class. I am not now speaking of disfranchising them, but of getting rid of them in counties and putting them into another class of electors. But every one will see at a glance, that if 100,000 of the most independent class of electors be taken from the county list the less independent must be made more powerful.' †

It was this feature of the Conservative Reform Bill of 1859—the apparent attempt to remove independent urban influence in county elections—and the determination of the Ministry to maintain the borough occupation franchise, which principally excited public reprobation and caused the rejection of the Bill. In closing the

* *Hansard*, vol. 153, col. 702. † *Ibid.* col. 775.

debate, the Chancellor of the Exchequer distinctly avowed the determination of the Government not to lower the borough occupiers' qualification. He enumerated three principles which he considered essential parts of the Bill. The first was the increase of the county constituencies. The second, the enfranchisement of large communities of which the wealth and population have been developed since 1832:—

The third principle is that the Bill maintains generally the present borough system of representation in this country, on the ground that no efficient substitute has yet been offered for it; and on the ground also that it is the only means by which you can obtain an adequate representation of the various interests and classes of the country, and that all other proposed changes would only lead to the predominance of a numerical majority of the population. Now, Sir, these are the three great principles upon which this Bill is founded. All the rest, however important – all the rest, is matter of detail which ought to be and can only be sufficiently discussed in Committee.*

There could be no mistake about this declaration. It was a distinct avowal that the Conservative Government would not recede from the 'hard and fast line' of the 10l. qualification ; would not adopt any measure for the further enfranchisement of the working classes beyond the insignificant addition to the number of artisan electors resulting from the qualifications respecting money in the savings' banks or stocks. The manner in which this scheme perished has been already stated. The House of Commons rejected it, and the country upon appeal ratified the rejection. The result of the general election of 1859 showed that the Government of Lord Derby did not possess the confidence of the nation. In the new Parliament they were defeated upon an amendment to the Address, declaring that 'confidence is not reposed in the present advisers of her Majesty.' The amendment was moved June 7, 1859. The Chancellor of the Exchequer's speech on this occasion contains

* *Hansard,* vol. 153, col. 1231.

the following passage, in which he announced that the Government was prepared to make fresh concessions:—

We are perfectly prepared to deal with that question of the borough franchise and the introduction of the working classes, by lowering the franchise in boroughs, and by acting in that direction with sincerity, because, as I ventured to observe in the debate upon our measure, if you intend to admit the working classes to the franchise by lowering the suffrage in boroughs, you must not keep the promise to the ear and break it to the hope. The lowering of the suffrage must be done in a manner which satisfactorily and completely effects your object, and is at the same time consistent with maintaining the institutions of the country.*

But the offer came too late; and the Derby Ministry was compelled to make way for a Cabinet in which Lord Palmerston was chief.

The Reform Bill of 1860 not merely differed from that of 1859, but was conceived in a directly contrary spirit. The Conservative scheme contemplated an entire segregation of the political interests of counties from those of boroughs, and in the latter offered only a lateral and not a vertical extension of the franchise. The measure proposed by Lord John Russell in the following year under the auspices of the Palmerston Administration, carefully preserved the rights of urban electors in counties, and greatly reduced the occupier's qualification in the towns. On March 1, 1860, the veteran reformer, then Secretary of State for the Foreign Department, asked leave to bring in a Bill to amend the laws relating to the representation of the people in England and Wales.† One of the principal clauses was that which conferred the right of voting for burgesses upon occupiers of 'premises' of the clear yearly value of not less than 6*l*. Lord John Russell referred to the 'great variety in the proportions of the rating franchise to the true value of houses,' and concluded that it would be

* *Hansard*, vol. 154, col. 140.
† A copy of the Bill is given as an appendix to vol. 157 of *Hansard's Debates*.

practically inconvenient, and, in point of abstract right, unjust, to fix upon a franchise that should be dependent on rating. He computed that the 6*l.* franchise would make an addition of 194,199 voters.* In the counties, following the example of the preceding Ministry, he proposed to reduce the occupiers' qualification to 10*l.* per annum, with the proviso that the holding should comprise a dwelling-house or building worth 5*l.* per annum.

The redistribution scheme was much less extensive than that which had been proposed in 1854 by Lord John Russell. He then recommended that upwards of sixty seats should be taken from the smaller boroughs and transferred to the larger towns, but now with Lord Palmerston for his political chief he was compelled to adopt much more moderate counsels. The Reform Bill of 1860 proposed that twenty-five boroughs, then returning two members each, should for the future return one only, and that the vacated seats should be transferred, fifteen to counties, nine to boroughs, and one to the University of London.

The Bill had a provision for the representation of minorities—that where there were three members, electors should have only two votes. The noble lord in his speech introducing the measure said—

> I have observed that when there are three members and there is a division of parties, one being the majority but the others comprising a very large number of electors, there is a growing tendency arising from a sense of fairness and justice that the minority, though it be the weaker party, shall not be altogether excluded from the representation but that the third member shall be given to it.†

His Lordship did not, however, explain, and nobody has yet explained, why this peculiar relief was to be given to suffering minorities only in the constituencies which have three members. The alleged wrongs of

---

* *Hansard*, vol. 156, col. 2056. † *Ibid.* vol. 166, p. 2002.

all other minorities were left without redress, or any attempt at redress.

Among the many defects of this measure of 1860, was the total neglect of the rights of the 'compound householders,' as they are commonly called, i. e., the tenants in towns whose rates under various local and general Acts are paid, not by themselves but by their landlords. One of the conditions of burgess suffrage under the Reform Act of 1832 was payment of rates. Consequently, those tenants who by the effect of the Small Tenements Acts were prevented from being rate-payers, were debarred from the right of electors.

The injustice of the ratepaying clauses of the statute of 1832 had long been felt by the comparatively small class of politicians who took the trouble to study the intricacies of our electoral laws and their practical operation. In the debate of March 1, 1860, Mr. Walpole asked, 'whether the payment of rates must be made by the tenant himself, or by any other person on his behalf.'* And in a subsequent stage of the discussion, Mr. Bright very clearly explained the grievance under which the compound householder suffered, as follows:—

> The overseers refuse in the majority of cases to put anybody's name on the register who does not pay his own rates. They put the landlord on, who pays the rates of a street; but the tenant's name is not entered. Therefore when they come to make out the list of voters from their rate books, they find the names of the landlords of course but do not find the names of the tenants; and the tenants under those circumstances are left off the list and actually disfranchised. What I propose is that the noble lord should by some clause to be introduced into this Bill insist upon it that the names of all tenants shall be upon the rate-book.†

Mr. Gladstone acknowledged the justice of the complaint in the debate on the second reading of the Representation Bill.

* *Hansard*, vol. 156, col. 2006. † *Ibid.* vol. 157, col. 907.

Besides your actual constituency (he said) you have an immense and what I may call potential constituency in a great many towns consisting of persons who are kept off the register simply by the fact that they do not pay the rate which the landlord pays for them, but who might claim to be put upon it at any period. I confess I think it undesirable to have a large number of persons, who might at any moment, under the influence of some local motive, or from passion or temporary excitement be brought upon the register and thereby suddenly alter the character of the electoral body. Whatever may be the character of the constituency, be it large or small, it is desirable that the character should be marked and permanent and not subject to sudden and violent changes.*

These objections to the anomalous position of the compound householder were as reasonable in 1860, when they were received with impatience or indifference, as in 1867, when after immense struggle and controversy they finally prevailed. Neither the Ministry nor the Parliament of 1860 was inclined to redress the enormous grievance upon which Mr. Gladstone and Mr. Bright then insisted.

In the debate on the second reading of Lord John Russell's Bill, Mr. Disraeli principally objected that the borough franchise was proposed to be extended to persons nearly all of the same class. 'The noble lord,' he said, 'under this Bill proposed to add 248,000 who are all of the same class, and whose opinions, feelings, and habits are identical.' The same objection to the apprehended predominance of the working classes was elaborated by the speaker in various ways. It was indeed the staple of his objection to the Bill.

It is said that the working classes are exceedingly intelligent and educated, and therefore likely to appreciate the possession of the franchise. But these are reasons why you should take care in legislating on this subject that you do not give them a predominance. What has been the object of our legislative labours for many years past but to put an end to a class legislation which was much complained of? But you are now pro-

* *Hansard*, vol. 158, col. 635.

posing to establish a class legislation of a kind which may be well viewed with apprehension. It is highly necessary in dealing with this subject, and in attempting to confer the franchise on the working classes, that you should not establish by that means a class legislation with which, considering its power and probable consequences, no class legislation that has hitherto though only partially prevailed, can for a moment be compared. It was obvious policy that while you attempted to introduce the working classes to the exercise of the franchise, you should counteract the tendency to this class domination by giving a variety of franchises and by effecting a natural counterpoise to consequences which all must deprecate. This was attempted in the Bill brought forward last year, and how were the propositions contained in that measure met? They were called 'fancy franchises,' and that was considered an answer.*

Thus the burden of Mr. Disraeli's complaint against the Reform Bill of 1860 was the *homogeneity* of the class proposed to be enfranchised, and the absence of such compensations as the 'fancy franchise.' These professions, as we shall hereafter see, were abandoned in the course of the debate of 1867, when Mr. Disraeli relinquished these safeguards, formerly deemed indispensable, and consented to a uniform and uncompensated enfranchisement of the artisan population in boroughs.

But in 1860 his Conservative supporters believed, as they were taught, that the indiscriminate extension of the suffrage would be fatal to the British Constitution, that it would produce class legislation, a destruction of the rights of property, and various other calamities. That was the primary article of their leader's faith, or at least creed, and it answered its intended purpose. The Reform Bill introduced by Lord John Russell was opposed, not directly, but by what lawyers term 'dilatory pleas.' To the motion for going into committee an amendment was moved to the effect that it would be inexpedient to proceed with the measure until the House had before it 'the result of the census authorized by the

---

* *Hansard*, vol. 158, col. 844.

Bill.'* The whole Conservative party rallied in support of this amendment. In a very full House it was rejected by a narrow majority, the numbers being, ayes 248, noes 261. Four days afterwards Lord John Russell announced that in the face of the opposition which he encountered he found it impossible to carry the measure through both Houses of Parliament, and accordingly withdrew it.†

This failure was due primarily to the opposition of the Tories, but secondarily to the known indifference of Lord Palmerston,‡ who took no part in the debate until after the second reading, and only spoke in favour of the Bill when a motion was proposed which threatened the existence of his Ministry. Moreover, many of the more earnest Reformers were dissatisfied with the inadequacy of the Bill, especially in the provisions relating to the redistribution of seats. Lord John Russell himself had expressly stated on introducing the measure, that he preferred the larger scheme of disfranchisement which he had proposed in 1854. His earnest efforts to effect a moderate Reform were defeated by the lukewarmness of the Prime Minister and the direct hostility of the Opposition. Not the less honour is due to the veteran Whig statesman, who with rare courage, good temper, and conscientious zeal made three separate efforts in the course of eight years to carry forward the work begun in 1832, and to provide for a gradual and cautious extension of the principles then established.

* *Hansard*, vol. 159, col. 26. † *Ibid.* vol. 159, col. 29.
‡ In a speech in the House of Lords, July 23, 1867, Earl Russell said, 'Mr. Brand went to Lord Palmerston after the measure of 1860 had failed, and told him that he thought he could not succeed in dealing with the redistribution of seats together with the settlement of the franchise. He advised Lord Palmerston, therefore, to bring in a Bill dealing with the franchise only. Lord Palmerston replied that he did not think either one measure or the other could be carried in the then existing House of Commons, and declined to accept the advice so offered him.'—*Hansard*, vol. 188, col. 2016.

CHAPTER II.

THE FRANCHISE BILL OF 1866.

Mr. Baines's Franchise Bill, 26.—*Dissolution of Parliament in* 1865, 27.— *Demise of Lord Palmerston; Earl Russell Premier*, 29.—*Franchise Bill introduced by Mr. Gladstone in* 1866, 31.—*The computed number of New Voters*, 36.—*The Bill opposed by Mr. Lowe*, 38.—*Second Reading*, 43.

AFTER the withdrawal of Lord John Russell's Reform Bill of 1860, no similar measure was proposed to Parliament during the life of Lord Palmerston. In 1865, the eighteenth Parliament of the United Kingdom having existed for nearly seven years, was dissolved. During the Session preceding that event the battle of Reform was renewed by Mr. Baines, the member for Leeds, who, in May, 1865, moved the second reading of what was derisively termed a 'single-barrelled' Franchise Bill, by which he proposed to reduce the borough occupiers' qualification to £6. annual value. Lord Elcho opposed the second reading, and moved the previous question. This motion was carried (May 8th, 1865,) by a large majority of 74, the numbers being: for the previous question, 288; against it, 214; and so the Bill was lost. Sir George Grey, who spoke on behalf and in the name of the Government, gave only a qualified support to the measure:—

Upon this occasion (he said) the Government will, as we have hitherto done, affirm the principle that there ought to be a reduction in the borough franchise, by voting for the second reading of this Bill. But I wish this vote to go for no more than it is worth. I wish it to be distinctly understood that if the Bill proposed by my honourable friend—a Bill for a 6l. franchise in boroughs—is to be applied as a political test at the elections now not far distant—to such a test her Majesty's

Government object, and we are not bound without further consideration to the 6*l.* franchise.

At the commencement of July, the long Parliament, which had immediately after its commencement placed Lord Palmerston in office, and retained him there, died a natural death. The septennial period, the utmost legal span of its existence, was anticipated by only a few months. The elections which followed in the month of July resulted very much in Lord Palmerston's favour, and gave him, as it was computed, a majority of about seventy in the House of Commons. In his election address to the electors of Tiverton he summed up the results of his six years' administration by referring to the preservation of peace with foreign nations, 'the additional freedom given to the employment of capital, and the exercise of productive industry,' the great reductions which had been effected in the taxation, the efficiency of naval and military defences, and improvements in the government of India. These were no small benefits. The country fully appreciated them, and willingly acquiesced in the continuance of his power. But it had come to be generally understood that during the probably short period of active life which remained to him—he had nearly attained his eighty-second year—the struggle of Reform would be suspended. In the address just quoted, and in his subsequent speech to the electors of Tiverton, he made no reference to the subject. Mr. Disraeli observed a similar reticence. The leader of the Opposition, in a style peculiarly his own, informed the constituency of Buckinghamshire, 'that on the complexion of the new Parliament, the character of our future policy for years, and that of our institutions, perhaps for ever, will mainly depend.' The mode in which a 'character' could 'depend' upon a 'complexion' was not explained. He also announced the nature of his prayers—or one of them—as follows:—' I fervently pray, therefore, that the country will unmistakably decide on securing our happy constitution in Church and State.' The phrase and the idea were not absolutely novel, but they sufficed for the occasion.

The election speeches of July, 1865, were, however, generally very different from those of the leaders of the two parties in the House of Commons. Almost every speaker at the hustings referred to an amendment of the representation—referred to it as something which, if not actually imminent, could not long be deferred. Tories as well as the Liberals adopted this language. The state of political feeling upon this subject was thus expressed by Mr. Bright at the nomination of representatives for Birmingham:—

> I take that question to be the one great question of the hour, and that really it may be said at this moment to include every other question. The Prime Minister in his address to the electors of Tiverton says nothing about it. That I think was wise, considering what he has done with regard to it. But passing that address we find that both among Liberal and Tory candidates the question of Reform is mentioned in some way or other either in their written or spoken addresses to constituents at the present election. I do not know who mentioned it oftenest —Whigs or Tories. I know in the county from whence I came there are three Tory candidates, and in their recent speeches they say that they think the question of Reform is one that must soon be considered and soon settled.

Upon examination of the addresses to which Mr. Bright refers, it will be found that he has given an accurate account of them. They do, in general, advert to the amendment of the representation, but in terms so vague that it is frequently impossible to ascertain the opinions of the candidates. The prominent question before the country was—not Reform—but confidence in Lord Palmerston. Many of the professions of Liberalism amounted to nothing more than adhesion to a popular statesman whose political faith was certainly not that of a zealous sectarian. The cross-examination of speakers at the hustings is not very effective, and accordingly many of them managed to produce a general impression in the minds of their auditors that they were Reformers, without really pledging themselves to the popular doctrines upon that subject. The result was that the people unwittingly elected a number of political Erastians—men, who like the followers of Erastus in the sixteenth century, thought they could be on both sides at once, and strove to import into politics that principle of universal communion and toleration which he advocated in matters of religion. Such mistakes as the electors committed at the general election of 1865 will be of constant recurrence as long as they are satisfied with the vague empty election addresses which are usually issued on such occasions—as long as the common platitudes about 'well-considered progressive improvements' and 'respect for our time-honoured institutions' are considered sufficient substitutes for definite language. It was not until six months after the general election that the mistake was discovered. When the test of parliamentary divisions came to be applied in the following Session, many constituencies learned with amazement and mortification that they had utterly misunderstood the opinions of their representatives.

The death of Lord Palmerston which occurred on October 18, 1865, made an immense change in the relations of political parties and the prospects of Reform. Earl Russell, by her Majesty's command, immediately formed a new Ministry in which he became Prime Minister, and Mr. Gladstone retained his office of Chancellor of the Exchequer. The leadership of these two statesmen in the House of Lords and Commons respectively was, of itself, a guarantee that Parliament would be forthwith called upon to amend the representation. The country instantly became aware, without any formal announcement, that the often-deferred question would constitute the chief work of the ensuing Session.

In the course of the autumn the Government was actively engaged in procuring electoral statistics as a basis of future legislation. Returns were obtained from the various Poor Law Unions throughout England and Wales, for the purpose of affording information with respect to the borough and county constituencies, and the probable addition to the number of electors which would result from an extension of the franchise. The agency of the Poor Law Board was employed for the purpose of collecting the materials, and the arrangement of them was, by a happy selection, entrusted to Mr. Lambert, a very able statistician, thoroughly versed in the intricacies of the law and practice respecting local rating and registration of electors. During the autumn and winter, circulars were issued to Union clerks and parochial officers, and from their returns the blue book of electoral statistics of 1866 was compiled. Among other valuable information, this work showed the operation of Small Tenement Rating Acts, in excluding large numbers of 'compound householders' in various towns from the suffrage. The results with respect to the proportion of artisans on the register occasioned considerable surprise. It appeared from the statistics, that out of the 488,920 persons entitled to vote in English and Welsh boroughs, 128,603, or about twenty-six per cent.* were electors who come within the description of mechanics, artisans and other persons maintaining themselves by daily manual labour. This part of the statistics gave rise to much controversy, and, with respect to many towns, it was contended that the Union officers had greatly overrated the proportion

* In a speech in the House of Commons, April 12, 1866, Mr. Gladstone said, 'After the best examination I can make, it is a moderate estimate to put the income of the working classes at *five-twelfths* of the aggregate income of the country, whereas they are put off under the present law with, at the outside, only *one-seventh* of the electoral power.' In this estimate the populations of counties and towns are reckoned together.

of working men possessed of votes. Obviously, it would be impossible to ascertain in very large towns, with absolute accuracy, the mode in which all the poorer electors gain their subsistence; and it is apparent from the returns, that in many instances small shopkeepers and other persons who did not support themselves by manual labour exclusively were returned as artisans.

The ' Bill to extend the Rights of Voting at Elections of Members of Parliament in England and Wales,' was brought in by Mr. Gladstone in March, 1866. This measure of Reform appears by contrast with what has followed almost timidly moderate. In some respects it was less liberal than Lord John Russell's Bill of 1860. That measure would have extended the borough franchise to persons occupying houses of the clear annual value of 6*l*. The corresponding figure adopted by Mr. Gladstone in 1866 was 7*l*. The reason for preferring the higher figure was thus explained by him. After some computations of the relative numbers of the middle class and artisan voters, he continued:—

> If a 6*l*. rental were added I find that this would be the result. A 6*l*. rental calculated upon the most careful investigation, and after making every allowance and deduction that ought to be made, would give 242,000 new voters whom I should take as all belonging to the working class. I should thus arrive at a gross total of 428,000 persons, which would in fact probably place the working classes in a clear majority upon the constituency. Well, that has never been the intention of any Bill proposed in this House. I do not think it is a proposal that Parliament would ever adopt. I cannot say I think it would be attended with great danger, but I am sure it is not according to the present view or expectation of Parliament. . . I fully admit that upon general ground of political prudence it it is not well to make sudden and extensive changes in the disposition of political power. I do not think that we are called upon by any overruling or sufficient consideration under the circumstances to give over the majority of the town constituencies into the hands of the working class. We therefore

propose to take the figure next above that which I have named —namely, a clear annual value of 7*l*.*

Mr. Gladstone computed that this reduction of the franchise would bring about 144,000 voters, all of the working class, upon the register. Besides this, he proposed to enfranchise 60,000 other borough voters by various means, principally by a lodger franchise extended to persons occupying rooms of the annual value of 10*l*., by the abolition of the ratepaying clauses of the Reform Act of 1832, and by registration of 'compound householders.' These two latter subjects have subsequently acquired so much interest that it is desirable to explain briefly the law which Mr. Gladstone proposed to alter.

The subject in its broad outlines is simple enough. One of the conditions which the Reform Act of 1832 annexed to the possession of the electoral right in boroughs was the payment of rates. No occupier was to be registered unless he was rated to the poor rate, and had paid his rates and taxes up to a certain period before the time of registration.† This provision excluded a considerable number of persons, occupiers of 10*l*. houses whose rates were paid, not by themselves, but by their landlords. In many parishes, either under the various Acts relating to the collection of rates, or by private arrangements with landlords, the rates were paid by them, and the tenants' names did not appear upon the rate books; consequently, though they occupied houses of more than sufficient value to qualify them, they were excluded from the franchise.

This state of the law was for years a subject of complaint among practical politicians. But it is quite evident now that the subject was one of which a large section of the House of Commons was profoundly ignorant, not only in 1866, but even in 1867, after

* *Hansard*, vol. 182, col. 52. † 2 Will. IV. c. 45, s. 38.

several attempts to direct their attention to this branch of the Reform question. They could make flashy speeches about our admirable constitution in Church and State, and utter platitudes at the hustings about the progressive improvement of our time-honoured institutions; but they could not take the trouble to examine certain Acts of Parliament and dry details of parochial administration, which materially affected the state of the suffrage. The probability is, that when the compound householder assumed a sudden and unexpected importance in 1867, half the House of Commons knew nothing of his history and mystery.

Mr. Gladstone and Mr. Bright, as we have seen, called attention, so long before as 1860, to the unsatisfactory operation of the ratepaying clauses. These provisions operated very severely with respect to the 10l. householders; but, of course, the disfranchising effect would be still more felt with reference to any lower class of occupiers. There are various Acts of Parliament, some general, some local, under which parishes are enabled to arrange that the landlords of small tenements shall pay not the full rates, but a composition or reduced sum. The reduction is often 25 per cent., and sometimes as high as 50 per cent. The parishes content themselves with this reduced payment from the landlord in consideration of the facility of collection, and the promptness and regularity of payment, secured by this method. Another way of looking at the matter is to regard the 25 or 50 per cent., or other discount, as a bonus paid to the landlord for collecting the rates of his own tenants. He, of course, recoups himself by a corresponding increase of his rents. The tenants for whose rates he compounds have, by a barbarous metonymy, acquired the designation 'compound householders.'

This system of composition prevails most extensively with respect to the lowest class of houses. Of persons rented at 10*l.* and upwards a considerable majority pay their own rates. But below the 10*l.* line, the practice of vicarious payment by the landlord is very general. Hence any provision for reducing the occupation franchise would be almost neutralised in some districts unless the disqualifications of the compound householders were removed. Mr. Gladstone, as we have seen, had, in 1860, perceived the necessity of improving their position. In his Bill of 1866, simple but effectual means were taken for the purpose.

In the first place, the Bill provided that the ratepaying clause in the English Reform Act of 1832 should be abolished. This abolition would have enfranchised more than 25,000 persons belonging chiefly to the middle classes—tenants above the 10*l.* line. They were not properly *compound* householders, for no composition was paid for their rates under any of the Small Tenements' Acts, but by arrangement with the parish officers the rates were regularly collected from their landlords.* In Liverpool alone, Mr. Gladstone stated that there were 6,000 to 7,000 occupiers in this position. By no fault of their own they were disfranchised by the conflict between the ratepaying clause and the local practice of rate collectors. It would seem almost superfluous to argue that such a state of the law was indefensible; but in 1867, Mr. Disraeli discovered that it was one of the bulwarks of the British Constitution.

The next provision under this head in the Bill of 1866 related to the compound householder especially. Henceforth his name was to appear in the rate-book just as if he paid the rates *in propriâ personâ;* and thence it would be transferred in due course to the

* A return issued January, 1868, shows that in the Parliamentary cities and boroughs of England and Wales there are 98,598 dwelling-houses not included in a composition under any general or local Act, but on account of which the owners pay the poor-rates by agreement with the overseers or other authority, or by agreement with the occupiers.

list of claims of votes. Mr. Gladstone computed that 35,000 persons above the 10l. line would thus be added to the register. Below that line the new provision would obviously operate extensively by giving effect to the proposed 7l. franchise. In truth, without such an arrangement, the reduction from 10l. to 7l. would have been almost nugatory.

With the additional knowledge which we now possess it seems to be somewhat a matter of regret that the Chancellor of the Exchequer did not in the exposition of his Bill of 1866 dwell more forcibly and fully upon the anomalies which he thus proposed to rectify. It is obvious now that the majority of his hearers were not acquainted even with the rudiments of the subject: this was certainly Mr. Disraeli's predicament more than twelve months later, as will be demonstrated in the proper place. The explanation which Mr. Gladstone gave in 1866 respecting the effect of the ratepaying clause attracted but little attention even from that portion of the public press which sympathised with him. Other commentators altogether overlooked the very reasonable amendment which he proposed, simply because they were wholly ignorant of the subject. Possibly a more emphatic and popular exposition at the time when he introduced the Bill might have prevented the absurd blunders of the measure introduced by Mr. Disraeli just one year later.

By the alterations just mentioned, Mr. Gladstone computed that 204,000 persons would be added to the borough constituencies. Besides these additions, he proposed a franchise in respect of the occupation of lodgings of the clear annual value of 10l.; also the deposit of 50l. in the Savings' Bank for a given period was to constitute a qualification either in counties or towns.

In counties, the tenants' qualification was to be

reduced from 50*l.* to 14*l.* annual value. Also the possessors of leasehold and copyhold property of a certain value in towns were to have votes for the counties where the tenure did not give them a borough qualification.

Under the Reform Act of 1832, the owner of a *freehold* in a borough might vote in respect of it for the county, provided that it did not confer on *him* the right to vote for the borough. But the owners of *leasehold* or *copyhold* property in a borough could not vote in the county if the property conferred on him or *anyone else* a right to vote for the towns.* Now it was proposed to alter this rule and simply provide in lieu of it, that either freeholders, copyholders, or leaseholders of property of sufficient value in boroughs might vote for the county, provided that they themselves had not the right to be registered in respect of it for the borough.† It would frequently happen that, from not being rated and resident in a town, they could not be registered there. The present measure put these persons on the same footing as freeholders, leaseholders, and copyholders whose property was situated outside the municipal boundaries.

The estimated numbers of new voters under this Reform Bill are shown in the following tabular statement—

In Boroughs.
Above the 10*l.* line; compound householders, &c. . 60,000
Below the 10*l.* line; 7*l.* householders . . 144,000

In Counties.
Fourteen-pound tenants 172,000

In either Counties or Boroughs.
Depositors in savings' banks, lodgers, copyholders and leaseholders in towns; in all, probably . . 24,000

Total . . 400,000

Of these 400,000 new electors, Mr. Gladstone com-

* 2 Will. IV. c. 45, s. 24, 25.   † Reform Bill, 1866, s. 15.

puted that about one-half would belong to the working and one-half to the middle classes.

The measure of Reform which he thus introduced related only to the extension of the franchise, and did not deal with the distribution of seats. He justified this course by the argument that a single Session was not sufficient for a complete review of the representative system. Referring to the Reform debates of 1831 and 1832, he said:—

A single one of the three Bills out of which the Reform Act finally grew occupied fifty nights of the House of Commons. But I feel that I should understate the case if I were to say that 100 nights at least were required for the review of the electoral system which was achieved in the years 1831–2.

A comparison of the Bill of 1831* with the statute actually passed in the following year supports this argument. The two measures are identical in all their principal characteristics. The English Reform Act of 1832 was in fact the work of two years.

This precedent sufficiently illustrated the difficulty of entirely reviewing the representative system in a single Session. But, as we shall presently see, Mr. Gladstone's omission to include the distribution of seats in his Reform Bill was speedily made the occasion of a Parliamentary attack, and he was compelled to yield to the demand for a complete measure. Yet the wisdom of the course which he at first proposed was proved experimentally in 1867, when, notwithstanding the unusual frequency and duration of the sittings, one half of the statute passed during the Conservative Administration was scrambled through hastily, and the work of distributing seats left confessedly incomplete. In 1867, the House of Commons got through their work imper-

* A copy of this Bill is given in the appendix to Roebuck's *History of the Whig Ministry of* 1830, vol. 2.

fectly, though they were induced to devote much more time to it, than they would have given up in the preceding year, when their zeal for Reform was much less fervent.

From the very commencement of its course, Mr. Gladstone's measure encountered fierce opposition. His introductory statement (March 12, 1866) was subject to an adverse criticism by many speakers on both sides of the House. It is quite evident now that Parliamentary Reform was utterly distasteful to the majority of the body affected by it. Mr. Laing, the Liberal Member for the Wick Boroughs, contended that the proposed alteration of the borough franchise would not be permanent; and that if it were reduced to 7*l.*, a demand would immediately be made for a still further reduction. The conclusion of his speech is worth quoting, for it shows very distinctly the position assumed by many of the members who were included in the supposed majority of 70 returned at the general election:—

For himself, he had given no pledge on entering Parliament but a promise generally to support Lord Palmerston's Administration, and he did not feel disposed to violate that pledge either in the letter or the spirit. Would Lord Palmerston have consented in the face of the Returns recently presented to the House to introduce a measure proposing to lower the franchise without redistributing the seats, to re-open an agitation, the issue of which none could foresee, to offer them a Reform Bill which was not final, and contained no element of security? *

Mr. Lowe, the member for Calne, who had held office during Lord Palmerston's Administration,† now commenced the series of attacks which were among the principal means of overthrowing the Reform Bill of 1866. His animadversions were directed not so much against that measure in particular—as against Reform

* *Hansard*, vol. 182, col. 84.

† Mr. Lowe had been Vice-President of the Committee of Council for Education, from 1859 to 1864.

altogether. Consequently his position was at least self-consistent. In the philippics to which he gave utterance it is easy to discover now a want of foresight and political sagacity. Indeed, he himself, as we shall see hereafter, publicly admitted in 1867, that he had, by assisting the Tories to gain power, unwittingly promoted a much more democratic scheme than that which he opposed in the previous year. But his arguments were, at least, free from the offences against logic committed by the Tories who acknowledged the necessity of Reform. A single sentence in Mr. Lowe's speech in the introduction of the Bill is a key to his conduct during the remainder of the Session. After commenting upon the minute manner in which the Chancellor of the Exchequer had explained the nature of various proposed qualifications, he observes:—

But although he ably entered into these matters, and with a detail which reminds me more of a speech on the Budget than on Reform, he did not find—he was so pinched for time—a moment to say a single word why the Constitution which we have lived so long under might not be left to us a little longer.*

That is, Mr. Lowe disputed entirely the necessity for a Reform. In a subsequent part of his speech he said—and said truly—that the question whether there should be a Reform Bill *solvitur ambulando*: 'The plan is to assume there are reasons. Bring in the Bill, *solvitur ambulando*, by walking into the subject.'

This was meant as a reproach. But surely it was unnecessary to prove that which everybody but himself admitted. To politicians generally the necessity for Reform was and had been for years axiomatic. Whigs and Tories had both produced their Bills to amend the representation. At the recent general election of 1865, candidates had universally, or almost

* *Hansard*, vol. 182, col. 144.

universally, treated it as a subject which should no longer be deferred. They must have known tolerably well the feelings of the constituencies when they chose this topic for their addresses; must have known that in the opinion of the voters there were large numbers of their countrymen excluded from the franchise who might properly be admitted to it. This was just the case in which the testimony of a multitude was to be preferred to the opinion of one man, however able and eminent. The electors knew from social intercourse with their unenfranchised fellow-townsmen and neighbours, that many of them were worthy of being trusted with the right of suffrage. This local and minute knowledge of a cloud of witnesses was more reliable evidence than the individual researches of any one statesman.

In this speech of March 13, 1866, occurs the celebrated passage respecting the venality, ignorance and drunkenness observable in the lower 'stratum' of constituencies:—

If you want venality, if you want ignorance, if you want drunkenness and facility for being intimidated; or if, on the other hand, you want impulsive, unreflecting and violent people, where do you look for them in the constituencies? Do you go to the top or to the bottom? It is ridiculous for us to allege that since the Reform Bill the sins of the constituencies or the voters are mainly comprised between 20*l*. and 10*l*. But then it has been said the 10*l*. shopkeepers and lodging-house keepers and beerhouse keepers are an indifferent class of people; but go to the artisan, and there you will see the difference. . . . . We know what those persons are that live in small houses, we have had experience of them under the name of freemen—and no better law I think could have been passed than that which disfranchised them altogether. The Government are proposing to enfranchise one class of men who have been disfranchised heretofore. This class dying out under one name, the Government propose to bring back under another. That being so, I ask the House to consider what good we are to get for the country at large by this reduction of the franchise. The effect will manifestly be to add a large number of persons to our constituencies of the class from which, if there is to be anything wrong going on, we may naturally expect to find it. *

Two parts of this statement, at all events, were not correct. Mr. Lowe said the Reform Act of 1832 disfranchised freemen 'altogether;' this was not the case. He asserted, further, that the present Bill renewed the suffrage of that class; most distinctly it did not. The freemen included among their number persons who deserved all his severe epithets—persons who, as the experience of the former elections showed, could be bribed with money or beer. The Whigs in 1831 had tried their utmost to get rid of this class of electors. The first Reform Bill of that year abrogated their franchise, saving only the rights of persons then living. In 1832 the Reformers were compelled by the urgency of the Tories to retain prospectively the qualifications of various classes of freemen and burgesses—and to give the suffrage generally to everyone who 'shall hereafter become a burgess or freeman in respect of birth or servitude.' †

The policy which favoured the electoral power of 'freemen' was that which in many ages and countries has induced the patricians to ally themselves with the lowest of the population against the more intelligent and independent classes. But Mr. Gladstone's Bill of

* *Hansard*, vol. 182, col. 147.
† 2 & 3 William IV. c. 45, s. 32. Lord Althorp, on the part of the Government, stated that the alteration was a concession to the opponents of Reform. *Hansard*, vol. 10, col. 52.

In many constituencies the freemen and ancient-right voters bear at the present time a large proportion to the other electors. In London, they are nearly one-third of the electoral body: of 17,534 persons on the register, 5,514 are freemen. In Coventry, nearly 80 per cent, or four-fifths are of this class; the total number registered being 4,967, and of these 3,911 are freemen. In Beverley, out of 1,474 electors, 885 are freemen. In Lancaster, of 1,473 electors, 1,006 are returned as freemen. In Norwich, out of 5,682 electors, 3,243 or 57 per cent. are either freemen or other ancient-right voters. These statistics are taken from Return A in the Electoral Returns, 1865-66.

1866 was framed on the directly opposite principle. The
property qualification which he proposed was intended
to exclude the venal class which Mr. Lowe dreaded.
Whether the 7*l.* line were too high or too low might be
a matter of controversy, but the statement of the eloquent member for Calne, that the Government proposed
to bring back the freeman class was manifestly incorrect.
A 7*l.* franchise, as Mr. Gladstone very clearly showed,
indicated the possession of an income considerably larger than that of the peasant or mere hand labourer :—

Adding 60 per cent. as in the other cases for rates and furniture to the sum of 7*l.* it would come in the gross to 11*l.* 4*s.*,
which would represent an income of 67*l.* 4*s.*, a little under
26*s.* a week. Now, 26*s.* a week is an income which is undoubtedly unattainable by the peasant or mere hand labourer
except under very favourable circumstances.*

These moderate counsels failed to obtain acceptance
from a House of Commons which twelve months later
adopted household suffrage. A year's debate and agitation were needed to resuscitate the reforming zeal
which had waxed feebler and feebler during Lord Palmerston's Administration. The coldness or hostility
with which Mr. Gladstone's proposals were received in
Parliament contrasted strangely with their popularity
out of doors. Almost immediately after the introduction of the Bill, public meetings began to be held all
over the kingdom in which resolutions were passed in
support of the Government. It was a fashion with a
portion of the public press to disparage those meetings.
But the frequency of them and the numbers assembled
were ample indications of the opinion of the community.
In Manchester, Liverpool and the other great towns of
the north, assemblies of many thousands of persons declared themselves in favour of the Bill. In Manchester,
on the 27th March, 1,000 delegates of the National

* *Hansard*, vol. 182, col. 54.

Reform Union met together and pronounced a general approval of the Ministerial measure. In Rochdale a meeting of 12,000 persons was held with the like result on the 4th April. In Leeds a similar demonstration on the part of the West Riding occurred on the previous day, and the attendance was equally large. The metropolis and the southern counties exhibited a similar feeling. Large meetings were held in Lambeth, Marylebone, the Tower Hamlets and elsewhere in London, and at Bristol, Brighton, Norwich and in a vast number of other towns. From the lists of these assemblies which have been collected it appears that all the great towns of England, with scarcely a single exception, had large public meetings in which resolutions were passed in favour of the Reform Bill.

One of the strongest arguments for adopting it was or ought to have been this general acceptance. It fell short of the desires of extreme Reformers, but they approved of it, and declared their assent to it, as an honestly intended compromise.

In moving the second reading of the Franchise Bill (April 12, 1866) Mr. Gladstone strenuously insisted upon the moderate character of the measure—that it gave a smaller share of power to the working classes than they possessed before the last great Reform Act. In 1830 they were in the majority in sixty-five boroughs returning in all 130 members, whereas under the proposed system there would be only 101 representatives of constituencies in which artisans predominated. He added:—

> We now therefore stand to a certain extent upon the firm ground of history and experience for the purpose of comparison. Was there among those 130 members at any period of our history developed a character in any degree dangerous to the institutions of the country?*

* *Hansard*, vol. 182, col. 1138.

In the course of this speech an amusing episode occurred. The Chancellor of the Exchequer appealed to the character of the constituencies which elect the Town Councils and governing offices of municipal boroughs. Comparing those towns of which the corporate and parliamentary limits are alike, he showed that of the 346,000 *municipal* voters 224,000 are working men. He continued:—

Is not this a dreadful state of things? Yet there has been no explosion, no antagonism between classes, no question has been raised about property, nor indeed has any even the slightest attempt been made to give a political character to municipal institutions. Yes, but when the municipal franchise was discussed in 1835 the party who occupied the seats of hon. gentlemen opposite—

Mr. Disraeli: Where were you sitting then?

Mr. Gladstone: If, however, such questions are relevant to the matter in hand, I was sitting on the benches of that party, but I was not one of those who supported the argument. Where was the right hon. gentleman sitting at that time? He was not sitting indeed, for he did not sit at all; but he was standing somewhere or other in the interests of the 'Mountain' far above the benches behind me.*

* *Hansard*, vol. 132, col. 1136. Mr. Gladstone first sat in Parliament in 1832, as representative of Newark.

CHAPTER III.

THE REDISTRIBUTION OF SEATS BILL, 1866.

Lord Grosvenor's Amendment, 45.—Redistribution of Seats' Bill, 50.—Second Reading of Redistribution Bill, 53.—Sir Rainald Knightley's 'Instruction' with reference to the Bribery Laws, 56.—Captain Hayter's Amendment condemning the Redistribution Scheme, 57.

THE opponents of the Franchise Bill, conscious of the popular feeling in favour of it which had been manifested at large and numerous public meetings held in almost every great town all over the country, adopted an ingeniously obstructive policy in order to escape the obloquy of direct hostility to Reform. Deeming it imprudent to commence a direct assault upon the Bill— they attacked it in the flank and rear. They professed willingness to amend the representation, but, like Felix the Roman governor of Judea, wished to evade a disagreeable subject by postponing it to 'a convenient season.' On the motion for the second reading of the Bill, Earl Grosvenor proposed an amendment declaring that the House was ready to consider the question of Parliamentary Reform, but would not discuss the Franchise Bill 'until the House has before it the entire scheme contemplated by the Government for the amendment of the representation of the people.' Earl Grosvenor considered it necessary to explain that this resolution had not been 'framed or worded by a Tory hand, as has been suggested.' He said that he was aware that he laid himself open 'not only to the imputation of deserting the Government but also the party of which I have hitherto been a member.' He met the charge as follows:—

Does not the accusation of deserting their party attach more properly to the members of the Government than to some of the members of that party? And are not the Government, in disregarding the feelings and opinions of the great majority of the Whig party, and forsaking the old traditions of that party and allowing themselves to be guided by the opinions of hon. gentlemen below the gangway, really deserting their party?*

Hinc illæ lachrymæ. The Ministers had committed an offence the most heinous in Lord Grosvenor's political decalogue—they had forsaken the old traditions of the Whig party; i.e., they had not sufficiently consulted and shown deference to the wealthy Whig aristocracy. This was all that could be implied by the reference to the 'hon. gentlemen below the gangway.' It is not often that personal jealousy is so plainly confessed in a Parliamentary debate. His amendment merely objected to the separation of the two questions of suffrage and the distribution of seats; but his arguments were mainly directed against the proposed lowering of the borough occupiers' qualification. His Lordship believed 'the tendency of this Bill, if passed, will be to give a preponderance of power to the working classes.' He insisted that the electoral returns showed the working classes to be possessed of a much larger share in the representation than was generally supposed, and he deprecated legislation 'on one of the most vital questions that can engage our attention upon imperfect data and inaccurate information.' Rather inconsistently with the first part of his speech, Lord Grosvenor declared there was not 'any possibility of a Reform Bill passing until the question be taken out of the domain of party.' It is not easy to reconcile this sentiment with the censure of the Government for forsaking the 'old traditions' of the Whig party.

The amendment was seconded by Lord Stanley.

Mr. Gladstone had, about a fortnight previously to this debate, announced in the House of Commons

* *Hansard*, vol. 182, col. 1154.

(March 23) the intention of the Government to lay on the table a Bill for the redistribution of seats as soon as the second reading of the Franchise Bill had determined the principle of that measure. That he thus placed the two subjects in their logical order seems almost indisputable.

The debate on Lord Grosvenor's amendment lasted eight nights. Ostensibly the discussion was upon a question of procedure merely: in reality the fate of the Bill itself was in suspense. The two parties in the House had arrayed themselves in pitched battle, and the struggle was carried on certainly with very great ability upon both sides. Among the Conservative speakers there were differences of opinion as wide as among their opponents. Lord Stanley virtually admitted the claim of the working classes to a larger share of power. On the other hand, General Peel, in an honest, out-spoken, soldierlike fashion which extorted the admiration of the Radicals whom he abhorred, declared that he did not wish 'the working classes to have a majority of that House,' and that he 'would not under any circumstances vote for an indiscriminate reduction of the franchise in boroughs to $7l$.'* Mr. Bank Stanhope in like manner denounced the threatened inroads of democracy, and implored 'that the House of Commons would not and should not be dictated to by the Member for Birmingham.'

These denunciations and warnings produced upon the susceptible audience the same effect as a ghost story upon children. But the fears seem rather ludicrous now, after the Conservative party has itself broken down the much-lauded bulwarks of the Constitution, and admitted the working men in a fashion far more wholesale than Mr. Gladstone or even Mr. Bright recommended.

Among the ablest of the many remarkable speeches

* *Hansard*, vol. 182, col. 1211.

delivered in the course of the debate was that of Mr. John Stuart Mill, the Member for Westminster. In a very effective manner he dealt with an argument which had made much impression in the House—that the proportion of artisan voters appeared by the recent electoral returns to be unexpectedly large.

It has just come to light to the astonishment of everybody, that these classes actually form 26 per cent. of the borough constituencies. They kept the secret so well—it required so much research to detect their presence on the register—their votes were so devoid of any traceable consequences—they had all this power of shaking our institutions and so obstinately persisted in not doing it—that hon. gentlemen are quite alarmed and recoil in terror from the abyss into which they have not fallen. . . . A class may have a great number of votes in every constituency of the kingdom and not obtain a single representative in the House. Their right of voting may be only the right of being everywhere outvoted . . . 26 per cent. concentrated would be a considerable representation but 26 per cent. diffused may be almost the same as none at all.*

The result of reducing the borough occupiers' franchise by the sum of 3*l.* was in 1866 invested with peculiar horrors; but no one else portrayed the tremendous consequences of that change in language so fervid as that of Mr. Lowe. The House must have been very much excited to have been able to listen gravely to such a peroration as the following:—

Surely the heroic work of so many centuries, the matchless achievements of so many wise heads and strong hands, deserve a nobler consummation than to be sacrificed at the shrine of revolutionary passion or the maudlin enthusiasm of humanity? But if we do fall, we shall fall deservedly. Uncoerced by any external force, not borne down by any internal calamity, but in the full plethora of our wealth and the surfeit of our too exuberant prosperity, with our own rash and inconsiderate hands we are about to pluck down on our own heads the venerable temple of our liberty and glory.

Mr. Disraeli was less poetical, but equally confident

* *Hansard*, vol. 182, col. 1256. † *Ibid.* col. 2118.

that the British Constitution was about to be destroyed. Referring to Mr. Gladstone's estimate of the number of voters proposed to be enfranchised, he said:—

> Well, there may or may not be good reasons for introducing 400,000 additional voters, but we have never yet argued that matter. We can do that indeed in Committee if we ever get there. But if your views of the English Constitution are the same as mine it is a very great addition to the present constituency.*

We shall see hereafter that the hon. gentleman's views upon this point became greatly enlarged after his accession to office. He concluded his speech by citing a speech of the late Sir George Lewis, and added:—

> Sir George Lewis would not have built up the constituent body on the rights of man. He would not have intrusted the destiny of this country to the judgment of a numerical majority. He would not have counselled the Whig party to reconstruct their famous institutions on the American model and to profit in time by the wisdom of the children of their loins. Sir, it is because I wish to avert from this country such calamities and disasters that I shall vote for the amendment of the noble lord.†

It is generally difficult to find definite statements of Mr. Disraeli's opinions. His *forte* is judicious obscurity. On the present occasion he was unusually distinct. He declared plainly that the proposed addition to the number of voters would have the effect of 'Americanising' the Constitution, and of producing 'calamities and disasters.' This avowal ought to be carefully borne in mind when we come to examine Mr. Disraeli's political conduct in the following year, when he assented to a much more democratic measure. Mr. Gladstone, who knew by experience the difficulty of pinning his opponent to any exact statement of principles, promptly availed himself of this admission, and instantly commenced his reply with these words:—

* *Hansard*, vol. 183, col. 111.   † *Ibid.* col. 113.

At last, Sir, we have obtained a clear declaration from an authoritative source; and we now know that a Bill which in a country of 5,000,000 of adult males proposes to add to its present limited constituency 200,000 of the middle class and 200,000 of the working class, is, in the judgment of the leader of the Tory party, a Bill to reconstruct the Constitution upon American principles.

Upon a division, the amendment of Lord Grosvenor was rejected by the narrow majority of 5; the numbers were—against it, 318; for it, 313. The number of members (631) who voted was nearly unprecedented. Immediately afterwards the Bill was read a second time without a further division.

In accordance with his previous pledge, the Chancellor of the Exchequer introduced (May 7th, 1866) a Bill for the Redistribution of Seats in Parliament. The principal characteristic of this measure was the mode in which it proposed to reduce the electoral power of small boroughs by grouping them together. In lieu of absolute disfranchisement of any, it was proposed that certain small constituencies which had hitherto been represented separately, should be henceforth associated in the election of their members. For instance, the small towns of Devizes and Marlborough, in Wiltshire, which had each of them two representatives, were for the future to return only one jointly. Eight pairs of boroughs were thus coupled together, in seven other instances three boroughs were similarly grouped, and in one case the group consisted of four small towns.

The proposed system affected all those boroughs having a population of less than 8,000 each which could be joined together with geographical convenience. None of the stars of the political firmament were to be extinguished; but some of those of the least magnitude were to be collected into constellations. Some precedents for this arrangement exist in the English Reform Act of 1832. Weymouth is associated with Melcombe Regis, Penryn with Falmouth, and the borough of Sandwich is extended for Parliamentary purposes to Deal and Walmer.* In Scotland the system of grouping has been carried out much more extensively. It was introduced by the Act of Union of the two Kingdoms in Queen Anne's reign, and adopted in the Scotch Reform Act of 1832; which establishes fourteen groups, including in all sixty-nine towns, each set returning one member.† Again, Schedule E of the English Act enumerates eleven Welsh groups containing from two to eight towns in each.‡

It is well to remember some of the arguments in favour of this system. For assuredly the question of the partial or total disfranchisement of the smallest parliamentary towns or rather villages of England has not yet been disposed of; and the time will come when the merits of Mr. Gladstone's plan will have to be rediscussed. It is beyond dispute that the system of grouping had been found an almost insuperable obstacle to bribery. The plurality of places at which the election is conducted simultaneously effectually baffles the most skilful adepts in the art of corruption. They cannot work together with the requisite secrecy and unity of design, nor ascertain the market value of votes. In only one, or at the most two instances, has a return from a Scotch group of boroughs been questioned by a petition to the House of Commons.

The Seats Redistribution Bill of 1866 proposed also with respect to certain small towns having two members

---

* 2 & 3 Will. IV. c. 45, s. 6. † 2 & 3 Will. IV. c. 65, schedule E.
‡ For example, Rhyddlan, Overton, Caerwis, Caergwrley, St. Asaph, Holywell, and Mold, share with Flint in returning one member; 2 Will. IV. c. 45, schedule E.

to reduce the electoral franchise to the return of one member only. In all forty-nine seats were to be vacated. The vacancies were to be supplied by giving twenty-six additional members to English counties, a third member to each of the four boroughs, Liverpool, Birmingham, Manchester, and Leeds, four more members to metropolitan constituencies (Chelsea and the Tower Hamlets), one member to the University of London, an additional member to Salford, six members to as many newly enfranchised boroughs, and seven additional members to Scotland.

At the conclusion of his exposition of the Redistribution Bill, Mr. Gladstone stated that though the Government originally feared that Parliament would not accord the time required for the complete revision of the representation in a single Session, he would be very glad if the House would consent to that course, and added:—

If it be proposed to combine the subjects whether by consolidation of the two Bills into one, or by any other method less stringent, but still satisfactory to the House, we shall give a willing consideration to the proposal, if only it be understood that we adhere to our original proposition and that we have no intention to advise the prorogation of Parliament until the whole subject—meaning by the whole subject nothing less than the question of the franchise and the question of the redistribution of seats—shall have been disposed of by the judgment of the House.*

The Government distinctly pledged itself to assent either to a consolidation of the two Bills, or to a separate consideration of them, as the House might prefer. But it did not suit Mr. Disraeli's views to accept this unqualified submission to the previous demands of his own party. He objected that—

It is generally considered the duty of a private member of the

* *Hansard*, vol. 183, col. 506.

House when he brings forward a Bill, or proposes a measure for our consideration, that he should at least indicate the mode in which he intends to invite the opinion of the House and the time at which he thinks it may be convenient to ask for that opinion. But, as I could collect from the right hon. gentleman's observations, he has not supplied any means to the House by which we can arrive at a conclusion as to the course which the Government proposes that the House should adopt.*

A fortnight previously he had accused the Chancellor of the Exchequer of domineering and attempting to dictate the course in which Parliament should consider the two branches of the subject; now when the option is presented to him of choosing the order of procedure Mr. Disraeli charges the Government with an abdication of its functions. The truth was that while professing anxiety to get the question settled, and protesting repeatedly that it ought not to be discussed in a party spirit, he was determined to give his opponent no help whatever even in matters of mere procedure. He would rely upon every technical objection, every chance of a slip in the routine. Old Bailey barristers are astute in the discovery of flaws in indictments; yet even they sometimes make mutual concessions and arrangements to get a case tried on its merits. But Mr. Disraeli's parliamentary tactics are free from such displays of weakness; they are essentially unchivalrous. In his view debates are struggles for victory, not mutual consultations for the benefit of the nation; and generosity towards an opponent is as little to be expected from him as from a special pleader of the days of Eldon and Ellenborough.

The motion for the second reading of the Redistribution Bill was fixed for the week after it was introduced. In an elaborate speech (May 14, 1866) Mr. Disraeli severely criticised the scheme. Some of his

* *Hansard*, vol. 182, col. 508.

objections seem amusing now that we are able to compare them with the Reform Act of 1867. For instance, he thought the plan of giving three members severally to Leeds, Manchester, and other large towns was to be looked upon with 'doubt and suspicion.' To each of those same towns he himself assigned a third member in 1867.

Again, he stated that our electoral system recoils from a plurality of votes, and added 'that a man shall have only one vote is, I think, the right principle. . . . The law of England recognises, and I hold, nobly recognises equality not of the man—but of the political citizen, who is invested with duties and privileges for the public good.' * Of the Bill, which he introduced in March 1867, one of the principal features was a provision entitling the wealthier section of the borough constituencies to double votes.

His principal strictures were however directed to the system of 'grouping.' He said it was 'altogether foreign to this country'†—a statement contradicted by political history. Weymouth returned members to Parliament from the time of Edward II. ‡ Melcombe Regis, or Melecumbe as the name was more anciently spelled, was a 'King's town,' and elected representatives in the same reign. § These two towns were united by an Act of Parliament in the reign of Elizabeth. ‖ The ancient town of Deal and the old cinque port of Sandwich have each its own mayor and municipality. The Reform Act united them for representative purposes. Another precedent of precisely the same kind is the association of the ancient parliamentary borough of Penryn with Falmouth, which was incorporated as a separate

* *Hansard*, vol. 183, col. 882. † *Ibid.* col. 880.
‡ *Merewether, History of Boroughs*, p. 000.
§ *Madox, Firma Burgi*, p. 11.
‖ 13 Eliz. c. 0. See *Hutchins' History of Dorset*, vol. ii. 607.

borough by Charles II. in 1661. Beaumaris, Cardigan, Caernarvon, and seven or eight other Welsh towns were made parliamentary boroughs in the reign of Henry VIII. by the Act* for the incorporation of Wales. To these boroughs a large number of other towns were annexed for electoral purposes by the Reform Act of 1832.

Another objection to Mr. Gladstone's system of grouping was the distance between various boroughs which he proposed to connect. But in Scotland, many of the associated towns are 80 to 100 miles asunder, and are separated by wide stretches of sea, mountain, moor, and loch; while in England, the distances in almost every case are under 20 miles.†

The leader of the Opposition explained that he did not object to grouping *in toto*. It might, he thought, be applied to new parliamentary boroughs. In other words, political bigamy or polygamy was to be the rule with the new boroughs, celibacy with respect to the old. The reason of this distinction it is not easy to discover, and, indeed, it appears to be principally of a sentimental kind.

Why should all these terrible disasters ensue in the old boroughs and not in the new ? Why should jealousies rage between Maldon and Harwich, which Mr. Gladstone proposed to associate; and Dartford and Gravesend, which Mr. Disraeli would link together, be exempt from the baleful passion ? Why should heterogeneity be more mischievous and corruption more probable in the one case than in the other ? This necessary step in his argument Mr. Disraeli omits altogether.

The Redistribution of Seats Bill was read a second time without a division (May 14, 1866). The next

* 27 Henry VIII. c. 28.
† Return to House of Commons, Session 1866, No. 297.

attack upon the Franchise Bill was a motion (May 28) by Sir Rainald Knightley, the Conservative member for Northamptonshire, as follows:—

That it be an instruction to the Committee that they have power to make provision for the better prevention of bribery and corruption.*

The object of this motion was rendered more palpable from the circumstance that it followed immediately after an instruction empowering the Committee to consolidate the Franchise and the Seats Bills. As if that were not work enough for one Session, the Tories now proposed to load the Reform Bill with another heavy burden—a revision of the laws relating to electoral corruption. The Government declared its readiness to deal with the subject—the Bribery Laws, but urged reasonably enough that it would be intolerably inconvenient to incorporate that extensive subject with the Reform Bill. There are multitudes of statutes against electoral malpractices passed both before and after 1832, but the Reform Acts of that year have not a word on the subject. There could be no real reason for mixing it up with the distinct questions of the franchise and distribution of seats. But the motion of Sir Rainald Knightley was a convenient means of obstruction and attack, and it was therefore supported by the leader of the Opposition. The instruction was carried by a majority of ten, the numbers being—Ayes, 248; Noes, 238. What makes the factiousness of this motion more palpable now than in 1866 is the circumstance that when Mr. Disraeli introduced his Reform Bill in 1867 he was obliged to acknowledge the expediency of treating the question of bribery separately; and the Reform Act of 1867 has been passed in accordance with that suggestion.

The next great onslaught on the Government mea-

---

* *Hansard*, vol. 183, col. 1320.

sure was Captain Hayter's amendment (April 28, 1866):—

That the House, while ready to consider the general subject of a Redistribution of Seats, is of opinion that the system of grouping proposed by Her Majesty's Government is neither convenient nor equitable, and that the scheme is otherwise not sufficiently matured to form the basis of a satisfactory measure.*

Of the reasoning by which Captain Hayter supported his amendment the following will be a sufficient specimen:—

The analogy of the Welsh boroughs does not hold, they being always in the same county so as to admit of united action.

As if the invisible boundary of a county created by law were an obstacle to 'united action'—whatever may be meant by that phrase!

The debate was continued at great length for several nights. One of the speeches which attracted the most attention was that of Mr. Lowe. Everybody said it was very eloquent; this at least is certain, that it contained a great number of poetical quotations. The peroration was as follows:—

To precipitate a decision in the case of a single human life would be cruel. It is more than cruel—it is parricide in the case of the Constitution, which is the life and soul of this great nation. If it is to perish, as all human things must perish, give it at any rate time to gather its robes about it and to fall with decency and deliberation.

> To-morrow! Oh that's sudden! Spare it! spare it!
> It ought not so to die.

The House of Commons was almost moved to tears at the idea that it was about to commit murder. The final quotation was especially effective. Here is another somewhat like it:—

* *Hansard*, vol. 183, col. 1357.

To-morrow ? O, that's sudden! Spare him! spare him!
He's not prepared for death!

The passage occurs in a play called 'Measure for
Measure,' written by an author not altogether unknown
in the House of Commons. It is a speech by Isabella,
pleading for her brother Claudio, who had been condemned to death for the seduction of Juliet, in Vienna.
The connection between that subject and the electoral franchise in England is not immediately apparent. Claudio condemned to die stands for the British
Constitution, Isabella, the pleader, is represented by
Mr. Lowe, but it would be difficult to find any analogue
for Juliet, or to suggest an offence resembling seduction which can be imputed to the British Constitution.
The difficulty is not diminished by the misquotation to
which the orator has been compelled to resort, in order
to conceal the inapplicability of the original passage.

Earl Grosvenor on this occasion supported the Government. In all the critical divisions* except one (Sir
R. Knightley's motion) he voted against the Ministers.
But when the existence of the Government was directly
assailed by Captain Hayter's amendment, the opposition
of Lord Grosvenor to the Cabinet was for a short time
intermitted. He held it 'of the utmost importance that
the Government should not resign office at this moment,'
and especially referred to the state of foreign affairs.
But at the same time Lord Grosvenor repeated his objections to the Reform Bill, and expressed a hope that
the Chancellor of the Exchequer would not persevere
with it.

Captain Hayter's amendment was not pressed to a
division. In consequence of Lord Grosvenor's announcement that he should vote with the Government, the

* These were: Lord Grosvenor's motion, April 27; Sir Rainald Knightley's, May 28; Lord Stanley's, June 7; Mr. Walpole's, June 7; Mr. Hunt's,
June 14; Lord Dunkellin's, June 18.

Opposition perceived that it would be hopeless to persevere with the amendment, and it was accordingly negatived without a division. Thereupon the House resolved itself into Committee (June 4, 1866) upon the two Bills relating to the suffrage and the redistribution of seats.*

* *Hansard,* vol. 184, col. 1910.

CHAPTER IV.

THE REFORM BILLS OF 1866 IN COMMITTEE.

The Franchise Bill and Seats Bill consolidated, 60.—Lord Stanley's Motion to postpone the Clauses relating to the Suffrage, 61.—Mr. Walpole's Amendment to raise the County Suffrage, 64.—Motions to base the Suffrage on Rateable Value, 67.—Resignation of Lord Russell's Ministry, 79.

By this time it had become sufficiently evident that the Ministerial measures of Reform were in great peril. In one critical division (upon Lord Grosvenor's motion) the Government had obtained a narrow majority of five. In another—on Sir Rainald Knightley's motion—they had been defeated by a majority of ten. Captain Hayter's amendment probably would have succeeded but for the temporary support given to the Ministry by Lord Grosvenor. A boat so crank that his weight could trim it was not likely to live long on the rough sea of politics. There were about forty members returned to Parliament on the supposition that they were Liberals, who generally voted against the Government on the Reform question. The Tories were united; their leaders astute and ready to avail themselves of all the arts of Parliamentary strategy. A section of the press deprecated the ruinous effects of democracy in language which, read again after the Reform Act of 1867, seems preposterous. Against combined opposition Mr. Gladstone struggled manfully as long as there was any hope of success, and he had the constant, unswerving support of between 250 and 300 Liberal members, whose loyalty to their professed principles has scarcely received the honourable recognition which it deserves.*

The next determined attack upon the Reform Bill occurred in Committee upon the fourth clause, June 7, 1866. Upon that day the preamble and first two clauses were adopted without discussion, and the third clause (the interpretation clause) was postponed at the suggestion of Mr. Hunt.† The Chancellor of the Exchequer then proceeded to move the fourth clause, evidently without the slightest suspicion of the surprise prepared for him. In a speech of considerable length he supported the 14*l.* occupation franchise in counties, and explained why he could not assent to an amendment of which Mr. Walpole had given notice for that evening, by which this franchise was to be raised to 20*l.*

As soon as Mr. Gladstone had finished his speech Lord Stanley advanced quietly to the table, and, to the amazement of every one but a very few who were in the secret, said that he did not rise to reply to the speech of the Chancellor, but to propose 'that the portion of the joint Bill which relates to the distribution of seats shall be taken first.' To give effect to this proposal, he moved the postponement of the clause under consideration.

This brief speech had the effect of a *coup de théâtre.* Even the Tories were quite unprepared for it—so well had the plot been veiled. There was a full attendance, especially of the Opposition, on account of Mr. Walpole's anticipated motion; and from the aspect of the House Lord Stanley and his two or three confidential advisers calculated that they could snatch a sudden victory from the unprepared Ministerialists. Of the

---

* On Sir Rainald Knightley's motion, 238 voted with the Government. On Lord Dunkellin's, 305 Liberals and one Conservative voted with the Government.

† *Hansard,* vol. 183, col. 2042.

proposal to postpone the clauses of the franchise scheme there had not been the slightest warning. On a previous day, as we have seen, Mr. Gladstone had offered to consult the wishes of the House, by either consolidating the two measures or taking them separately. When he thus offered to be guided by the wishes of his opponents, Mr. Disraeli retorted that he was deserting 'his duty to regulate the general course of business,' * and called upon him to fix a day for the future proceedings. In answer to this remonstrance and appeal, Mr. Gladstone had appointed a time for proceeding with each Bill.† This promise had been kept in every tittle. The Redistribution Bill had been read a second time, and an instruction given (without opposition) to consolidate it with the Franchise Bill. The 7th of June had been fixed by vote of the House for the Committee on the Franchise Bill. At that day the Committee actually sat, and disposed of three clauses, when at the fourth Lord Stanley intervened, in the manner above described. His pretexts for inverting the previously arranged order of procedure were, first, a fear of the Government 'contenting themselves with the passing of that portion of the Bill which disposes of the franchise question, and dropping the rest of the measure, and thus reverting to their original proposal'—a suggestion which came naturally enough from an adept in strategy. The other reason offered by Lord Stanley was this:—

The franchise question, although exceedingly important, is one comparatively simple and lying within narrow limits. It is a question which may probably be disposed of in two or three nights.

To which observation Mr. Bright made the obvious reply:—

If that be so, and if honourable gentlemen opposite will

* *Hansard*, vol. 183, col. 508. † *Ibid.* vol. 515.
‡ *Ibid.* col. 2068.

follow the moderate lead of the noble lord in respect of the franchise clauses, and let us get through them in the course of next week, there can be no kind of difficulty in proceeding with the clauses relating to the distribution of seats.

This affected solicitude about the redistribution of seats was a mere pretext. The House would in any case have retained the power of rejecting the Franchise Bill on the third reading, if the clauses respecting seats were omitted, or, rather, it would have been impossible for the Bill to reach that stage with such omission, unless the House consented. It was utterly inconsistent with the conduct of Lord Stanley's party in former years that they should yearn for the transfer of power from small to large constituencies. The device intended to defeat the Reform Bill altogether was described by Mr. Gladstone in language certainly not unduly severe:—

> Sir, whatever may be said about fighting in open day and upon an open field, I cannot but congratulate hon. gentlemen opposite upon their perfect mastery of the art of ambush. Ten days have elapsed since the motion for going into Committee on this Bill has been under discussion, and not till the moment when the noble lord rose was the gallant party opposite able to make up its mind as to the next step it should take. . . . . At last, after many efforts, having got nearer the time when something like decisive issues are to be taken, this new strategy comes in, having been locked up in the breasts of those who concealed it, lest it should suffer from exposure to the open air.*

Lord Stanley's motion was defeated on this occasion by a larger majority (27) than at any time previously during the Session supported the Reform Bill. The numbers were—Ayes, 260; Noes, 287.† Many Liberal members who on former occasions had opposed the Ministers now voted with them, and refused to abet a scheme which offended their sense of honour and fair play. The engineer for once was hoist with his own

* *Hansard*, vol. 183, col. 2069.   † *Ibid.* col. 2071.

petard, very much to the satisfaction of honest men who think that the legislation of a great kingdom ought not to depend on the success or failure of ingenious manœuvres.

Immediately after the failure of Lord Stanley's motion, Mr. Walpole proposed an amendment, which had been fixed for discussion the same evening, to the effect that the occupation franchise in counties should be raised from 14l., as proposed by the Bill, to 20l. It has been already mentioned that Mr. Walpole had seceded from the Conservative Ministry of 1859, principally from objections to their proposal to reduce the occupation franchise in counties to 10l. He was therefore at least consistent in now endeavouring to raise the qualification above the standard proposed in the pending Bill, and he argued the question in a straightforward and legitimate manner. He contended for the necessity of maintaining a wide distinction between the borough and county constituencies:—

> The character of the rural population was much less active and much less stirring, and they were far less easily combined together for agitating purposes than the population of towns, being entirely devoted to their own business—the cultivation of the soil. The town population was the reverse of all this. They were more active and stirring, and could more easily be brought together by combinations, by means of which they could make their voices more fully heard and their opinions more distinctly understood and appreciated. The reason, therefore, for keeping the two constituencies distinct is as clear to my mind as the fact that they were distinct.*

But surely this argument involved a *non sequitur*. The fact of the distinction could not be a reason for it. If the country population were 'less stirring,' it might derive advantage from an intermixture of the urban element. If the town constituencies were too 'active and stirring,' their superabundant activity might

---

* *Hansard*, vol. 183, col. 2077.

possibly be tempered by a leaven of rural staidness. To the townsmen Mr. Walpole attributed a peculiar aptitude for making 'their opinions more distinctly understood and appreciated.' But that is the very purpose of parliamentary representation. Members of Parliament are appointed for that very object of giving utterance to the will of the nation. Therefore the commixture of townsfolk and their rural neighbours would be calculated, according to Mr. Walpole's own argument, to effectuate the main object of parliamentary elections.

Mr. Walpole appealed to ancient Constitutional usage —an argument which always deserves great consideration, though unfortunately it is very often applied erroneously in the House of Commons. The old rule, in the time of Edward I., when Parliaments became regularly established, and for centuries afterwards, was undoubtedly this: the burgesses voted by themselves in the choice of their representatives. The counties were deemed to have a separate representation, but the elections took place in the County Courts, which were usually held in or near boroughs, and were open to the burgesses. We have direct evidence that boroughs as well as counties were bound to send 'suitors,' or persons to do suit and service in the County Court. Consequently, it is absolutely beyond dispute that burgesses participated in county elections. But the conditions of society are now so much altered that these historical facts furnish no inference, one way or the other, with respect to modern practice. Town and country were formerly kept asunder by difficulties of travelling, which no longer exist. The intermixture of the two classes of voters which Mr. Walpole deprecates has taken place to a very large extent, and in a manner which at least is not one-sided. The Reform Act of 1832 confirmed the ancient principle of owners of freeholds in towns voting in counties; but, on the other hand, it allowed a large number of persons living far beyond the municipal limits to take part in the election of burgesses. The rated owners of 10*l.* houses in those towns are entitled to vote if they reside within seven miles of the boroughs (sec. 27). So also with respect to various ancient qualifications preserved by the Act, the persons qualified retain the electoral right if they reside within seven miles of the polling place (sec. 32). These sections have been modified by the Reform Act of 1867, which now extends the limit of distance with reference to the electors of London to twenty-five miles.* Such an alteration may be fairly justified by reference to modern habits of travelling. It is obvious that the twenty-five miles' limit with respect to London, and the seven miles' limit with respect to other towns, must include a large number of persons whose interests and associations are very closely connected with those of the rural population.

The law just mentioned is based on the beneficial principle, that the interests of the rural and urban populations are not antagonistic, but closely connected. The modern rule, at least, is not open to the objection of want of mutuality. If it allows the owners of town property to vote in counties, it allows a considerable proportion of the inhabitants of counties to vote in towns.

Mr. Disraeli, who spoke in support of Mr. Walpole's amendment, was pressed with the argument that in 1859 he had recommended a county occupation franchise (10*l.*) still lower than that proposed by Mr. Gladstone. He answered:—

> The proposition made on the part of the Government of Lord Derby with regard to the county franchise was not made on the sole condition which has been referred to in this discussion—namely, that the freeholders in boroughs should vote for the borough in which their property qualification was situated. The House was told over and over again that the proposition we made must be taken as a whole and as one; and avowedly

---

* 30 and 31 Vic. c. 102, s. 46.

the chief condition of our proposing that the qualification in counties should be 10*l.* was that there should be no lower franchise for the boroughs.*

That is, he supported Mr. Walpole's amendment for a reason not merely different from, but actually opposed to, that on which the Member for the University of Cambridge mainly relied. Mr. Walpole wanted the town and county qualifications to be widely different. Mr. Disraeli wanted them to be identical, and, because he could not succeed in that respect, supported a proposition for widening the difference between them. It was strange logic.

The view that the proposals of 1859 were to be taken 'as a whole, and as one,' is inconsistent with the principles which Mr. Disraeli has on many other occasions advocated. He has frequently insisted, as will be seen in these pages, that the suffrage qualification should be fixed not with reference to the probable numbers to be admitted, but the individual fitness of the persons admitted. On the present occasion, however, his reference to the unity of his plan of 1859 evidently implies that the balance of political power, or the number of persons enfranchised, was in his eyes all important.

Mr. Walpole's amendment was rejected (June 7, 1866) by a majority of fourteen. The numbers were—for the Government proposal of 14*l.* franchise, Ayes, 297; Noes, 283.†

The subsequent motions of Mr. Hunt, that the occupier's qualification in counties should depend on the *rateable* value of his tenement, and the corresponding motion of Lord Dunkellin respecting the qualification in boroughs, may be conveniently considered together. Clause 4 of the Reform Bill of 1866 gave the county franchise to 'the occupier as owner or tenant of pre-

* *Hansard*, vol. 183, col. 2116.   † *Ibid.* col. 2120.

mises of any tenure within the county of *a clear yearly value* of fourteen pounds or upwards.' Clause 5 gave the borough franchise to 'the occupier as owner or tenant of premises of any tenure within the borough, of *a clear yearly value* of seven pounds or upwards.' Mr. Hunt, a member for Northamptonshire, who subsequently became Secretary to the Treasury under Lord Derby's Government, moved (June 11, 1866) to add to clause 4 the words 'such clear yearly value being the rateable value of the premises as ascertained for the purpose of the poor rate.' Lord Dunkellin, member for Galway, who had voted against the Government on Lord Grosvenor's and Mr. Walpole's motions, but with the Government against Lord Stanley's motion, moved to leave out the words 'clear yearly' in clause 5, in order to substitute the word 'rateable.' It will be seen, therefore, that the two motions agreed in all respects, except that the one related to the county, the other to the borough franchise. Mr. Hunt's amendment was rejected by a majority of seven; that of Lord Dunkellin was carried by a majority of eleven, and led to the resignation of the Government.

In the discussions upon these motions ignorance respecting the law and history of the subject in question was displayed more conspicuously than in any other debate of the Session. Mr. Gladstone, in the introductory speech in March, had distinctly explained why the Government had chosen 'gross estimated rental' as the basis of value for the occupier's qualification. But it is quite clear from the debates of June, that many of his audience possessed in an eminent degree the faculty of not listening. He had strenuously insisted upon the importance of determining the value of qualifying tenements by reference to the rate-book. His opponents in June insisted upon the value of that reference to the rate-book, as if it were something to which Mr. Gladstone objected. The language which several of these speakers used is utterly irreconcilable with the idea that they had heard or heeded his original exposition of the Bill.

The subject is by no means difficult or abstruse for those who will take the slightest pains to understand it. Perhaps the most direct way of illustrating the matter in controversy will be to print the form of valuation lists given in the schedule to Mr. Villiers' Union Assessment Committee Act, 1862.*

Name of Occupier	Name of Owner	Description of Property	Name or Situation of Property	Estimated Extent	Gross Estimated Rental	Rateable Value

This is the form in which overseers are required to prepare valuation lists of all the rateable hereditaments in their several parishes. These lists are subject to certain processes of appeal, revision, and correction, and when finally settled by the Union Assessment Committees are the basis upon which the poor-rates are assessed.

Attention must be particularly directed to the last two columns, 'gross estimated rental' and 'rateable value.' Gross estimated rental is defined by Mr. Villiers' Act to be the 'rent at which the hereditaments might reasonably be expected to let from year to year, free from all usual tenants' rates and taxes, and tithe commutation rent charge, if any.'†

'Rateable value' is computed from 'gross estimated rental,' by making various deductions. Unfortunately, the practice with respect to these deductions has varied extremely in different places. A return was made to Parliament in August, 1866, showing 'the scale of

* 25 and 26 Vic. c. 103. † *Ibid.* c. 15.

deductions from the gross estimated rental in the assessment of the rateable value, acted upon by the several Union Assessment Committees.' From this paper it appears that the practice varies widely in different parts of the country. In some places 'rateable value' of houses is taken at 10 per cent. less than gross estimated rental, in other places at 15 per cent. less, in many others at 35 or 36 per cent. less. The usage seems to have been quite arbitrary, and the valuers to have been guided by no better principle than the 'rule of thumb.' *

Mr. Gladstone, when introducing the Franchise Bill, had explained why he preferred the last column but one of the valuation lists as a basis of the occupier's suffrage. That column represented closely, almost exactly, the real value of the occupier's tenements. Whereas the last column was variable, uncertain, and dependent upon local usage or personal caprice.

The explanation was utterly thrown away upon many of his auditors. Many of them spoke and voted upon both Mr. Hunt's and Lord Dunkellin's motions, evidently ignorant of the fundamental fact that the valuation on which Mr. Gladstone relied was to be found in the rate-books, side by side with that which would be substituted by these amendments. A considerable portion of the press favoured the same error. Some of the newspapers descanted vehemently on the advantages of making an officially compiled document the test of value, utterly unconscious or oblivious of the fact that this was common ground between themselves and Mr. Gladstone.

* Even so early as 1832, Parliament determined that rateable value was not a proper basis of the franchise. In committee on the Reform Bill of that year, Mr. Evelyn Denison proposed an amendment to the clause relating to the ten-pound householder, for the purpose of adopting such a basis. After much discussion the amendment was negatived. Lord John Russell said, 'the assessments were so irregular in different parishes, that it would not be possible to have recourse to them with effect.'—*Hansard*, vol. 9, col. 1237. February 3, 1832.

In his speech of March 12, 1866, when asking leave to bring in the Franchise Bill, he had said:—

The question of a rating franchise has always been one of the greatest interest to those who have been engaged in the preparation of our numerous, and I will add our too numerous, Reform Bills. The advantage of having an external standard to determine the claim for registration, not based simply upon a process which, as often as the question is raised, each man must conduct anew for himself, but dependent upon the evidence of a public authority, though guarded by an appeal (it being the business of that public authority to fix the value of a holding for certain parochial purposes, which are not political) —the value of a franchise of that kind, considered narrowly and closely from such a point of view, is obvious. . . . . Now rating is good, if we consider it as the adoption of a public independent standard—a standard supposed to be impartially chosen for local taxation. But in everything in which the rating is good, the gross estimated rental is good also, whereas it escapes many sources of error and of inequality which are inherent in rating.*

The Franchise Bill accordingly provided that 'the gross estimated rental for the time being of any premises, as ascertained for the purposes of the poor-rate, shall, until the contrary is proved, be deemed the clear yearly value of such premises.' In other words, the sixth column of the valuation list was to be taken as evidence of the value of the qualifying tenements.

Mr. Hunt's and Lord Dunkellin's propositions were, in effect, to substitute the seventh column of the valuation lists, the one with respect to the county, the other, with respect to the borough franchise.

Mr. Hunt's speech (June 11, 1866), in moving his amendment, showed that he had misapprehended the purport of the Government Bill. He said:—

As he understood the Bill, it was not a necessary condition of the franchise that a man should be on the rate-book at all, and therefore it would be quite possible for a man to vote as a rated occupier without his name appearing on the rate-book.†

* *Hansard*, vol. 182, col. 50.   † *Ibid.* vol. 184, col. 178.

This remark shows conclusively that the speaker had not read the Bill which he criticised and affected to amend. The very provision which he says is not to be found in it is expressed in the most distinct and explicit manner. By section 9 :—

Every house or other set of premises occupied by a different person as owner or tenant shall be entered separately in the rate-book, whether the owner is or is not assessed to, or has or has not compounded for, the rate payable in respect of such premises.

This section refers to the practice in various towns where landlords of several houses pay a lump sum or composition for the whole of them, in lieu of the separate rate of each tenement. In such instances the lump sum only, and not the rates of the several tenements, was entered in the rate-book. Consequently the tenants whose rates were thus paid vicariously did not appear as ratepayers, and as a general rule were not put down by the overseers in their annual lists of persons claiming votes. Mr. Gladstone had distinctly explained at the beginning of the Session the manner in which a large number of persons were thus excluded from the franchise, and the mode in which the defect was to be cured. The remedy was simply this, that all tenements without exception were henceforth to be entered in the rate-book. Mr. Hunt's stricture shows that he had not read this clause.

It is not quite clear whether he imagined that the reference to the rate-book as evidence of the value of tenements for electoral purposes was a peculiarity of his own scheme. At all events, it is certain that he used language which must have given the unlearned portion of his hearers—a considerable number—that impression. Thus after showing that in Scotland and Ireland the valuation book was accepted as proof of the occupiers' qualification, he adds :—

The extension to England of the principle thus found to operate beneficially in Ireland and Scotland might seem a small matter to hon. members anxious to extend the franchise wider; but, though the Committee might not be anxious to go alone to as low a figure as some hon. members desired, he would doubtless obtain their concurrence in saying that all those to whom the franchise was ultimately to be given ought to enjoy the greatest facilities for being placed on the register. In this country, owing to the want of connection between the rate-book and the register, county voters had the greatest difficulty in securing their right to vote.*

Any person not informed to the contrary would suppose from this, that Mr. Gladstone's Bill did not establish a ' connection between the rate-book and the register.' The question—why do you not do a particular act?—implies to most minds an assertion that you have not done that act.

Mr. Hunt, however, principally relied on the circumstance that ' if the amendment which he proposed was carried, the effect would be to raise the county franchise to a higher standard than if the clause passed without amendment,' and he adduced statistics to show that what he deemed an excessive number of votes would be introduced by a 14*l.* rental franchise in counties.

Mr. Gladstone answered that this proposition to raise the county franchise was an indirect attempt to reverse the previous decision on Mr. Walpole's amendment. He also stated that the Government had at one time been disposed to base the occupation franchise on rating:—

Before we were fully informed we had thought of a rating franchise : but upon a careful and accurate examination of the whole case we found that every advantage of a rating franchise was to be had by another operation, while at the same time the great disadvantages incident to a rating franchise might be completely avoided.†

* *Hansard*, vol. 183, col. 179.   † *Ibid.* vol. 184, col. 190.

The argument thus far did not touch the question of the abstract merits of rental and rateable value as tests of the voters' qualifications. In a few weighty sentences, the Chancellor of the Exchequer gave an exhaustive answer to this question:—

We take the column of 'gross estimated rental,' because by it we can test the tenant's ability to pay. What, on the other hand, does the 'rateable value' column mean? It indicates simply the value of the building to the landlord, and with that we have nothing to do for the purpose of enfranchisement.* The true test we have to deal with is the capacity of the man to pay the rent, and if he finds it worth his while to pay that rent, it does not matter to us whether he expends 1, 10, 20, or even 50 per cent. in order to keep the building in habitable condition.

In the course of the discussion, the Solicitor-General adverted to the speech of Mr. Disraeli in 1859—noticed in a previous page of this book†—in which the opinion was expressed, that the difficulty of making rating a basis of suffrage was insurmountable. Mr. Disraeli replied:—

I certainly said that I found the difficulty as to the rating proposition to be insurmountable, but that was in 1859. But there have been great changes in the law in reference to this subject since then. There have been two union rating assessments since then, and the whole tendency of our legislation in recent years has been towards effecting an equalisation of rating.‡

Equalisation of rating! As a specimen of this equalisation, the following extract from the electoral

---

* By 6 & 7 Will. 4, c. 96, the poor-rate is to be 'made upon an estimate of the net annual value of the several hereditaments rated thereunto; that is to say, of the rent at which the same might reasonably be expected to let from year to year, free of all usual tenants' rates and taxes, and tithe commutation rent-charge (if any), and deducting therefrom the probable annual average cost of the repairs, insurances, and other expenses (if any) necessary to maintain them in a state to command such rent.'

† *Ante*, p. 0.   ‡ *Hansard*, vol. 184, col. 197.

returns of the same Session may be read with profit. In the returns for Exeter it is said:—

> In three parishes a deduction of or about 33½ per cent. is made from the gross estimated rental in estimating the rateable value of houses at and under 10*l*. In two parishes a deduction of from 25 to 33½ per cent., in two parishes from 20 to 33½ per cent., in one parish from 20 to 50 per cent., in one parish from 15 to 50 per cent.*

So then, in the city of Exeter alone, the difference between rental and rateable value in different streets varied from fifteen to *fifty per cent.*! The deduction depends on no fixed rule. In some parishes it is described vaguely to be '*about*' 33½ per cent. To refer the suffrage to such a variable test would be like making the standard yard of elastic tape.

It would be easy to multiply extracts from the speeches on this occasion, which show that many honourable members had a fixed idea that the Government did *not* make the rate-book the primary evidence of value. Thus Col. Loyd Lindsay says:—

> A great advantage in adopting the assessment as the real value would be, that the rate-book would also form the register. Nothing could then be easier than to give instructions to those whose duty it was to make up the register to transfer the names of the ratepayers from the rate-book to the register.†

The very provisions thus desiderated were to be found in the Bill. But many members of Parliament had an immovable belief to the contrary, and it never occurred to them to read the Bill for themselves.

The hallucinations respecting the actual effect of the Ministerial measure are of some historical importance, because they serve to explain the conduct of the House of Commons, with reference to Mr. Hunt's and Lord Dunkellin's amendments. The former was rejected

---

* Electoral Returns, 1865-6, p. 123.   † *Hansard*, vol. 184, p. 384.

by a majority of 7 (Ayes, 273 ; Noes, 280).* The latter, which raised precisely the same point with respect to the borough franchise, was carried by a majority of 11. The House thus directly reversed its former decision. Lord Dunkellin's motion was to substitute 'rateable' for 'clear yearly,' in the clause defining the value of the tenements, entitling the occupiers to vote in boroughs. This proposal was certainly made in the perfectly sincere belief that it would tend to improve the system of representation. But it is equally certain that in the debate upon it (June 18) the mistake already noticed respecting the actual provisions of the Bill is committed by several speakers. They erroneously assume that the rate-book is not made evidence of value by the Government Bill. Thus, Mr. Stephen Cave, who seconded the amendment, says (speaking of election expenses):—

These, he believed, would be much lessened by making the rate-book the basis of the list of voters. In that way a self-acting registration would be secured, and there would be fewer squabbles before the Revising Barrister. When the franchise was an incident of the rate-book it was more likely to be correctly fixed than when rental valuations were given in for the express purpose of acquiring it.†

Mr. Gladstone was accused of treating his opponents with impatience; but the persistent disregard of his reiterated explanations would have taxed to the utmost any human powers of endurance. Over and over again he had shown that the very thing which his opponents wanted had been already provided by the Franchise Bill.‡

---

* *Hansard*, vol. 184, col. 405. † *Ibid.* col. 584.

‡ The clause in question is so simple that no legal acumen is required to ascertain its meaning. The words are :—' For the purpose of this Act, gross estimated rental for the time being of any premises, AS ASCERTAINED FOR THE PURPOSE OF THE POOR RATE, shall, until the contrary is proved, be deemed to be the clear yearly value of such premises.'

Another clause provided that overseers should make out lists of all occu-

They did not controvert this statement—they simply refused to listen to it.

As the debate proceeded, indeed, some of the Opposition speakers, who were better informed, correctly treated the question as one of choice between two columns of the rate-book; but to the very last, there were other speakers utterly ignorant of the real issue, and they represented a considerable number (quite sufficient to turn the scale in a closely contested division), who voted under a full impression that they were rescuing the rate-book from unmerited neglect. How firmly rooted this conviction was may be seen from some observations of Sir Robert Peel, made toward the close of the debate, after several speeches in which the true issue had been distinctly explained:—

> It has been stated two or three times over, and it cannot be stated too often, that the rate-books are drawn up without any question of political bias—that they are perfectly fair towards the occupier, and that the occupier's interest is not to exaggerate the value of his holding; for the result would be that he would subject himself to additional taxation.

As if there were any difference between the sixth and seventh columns of the rate-book in this respect!

Again he says:—

> Looking at the importance in my view of the rating qualification in boroughs, and believing that there is risk of manipulation of the register which should be guarded against by every means, and that the amendment of my noble friend is more likely to propose safeguards than the proposal of the Government—without further occupying the time of the Com-

piers entitled to vote as occupiers under that Bill, in the same way that overseers are now required by the Registration Acts to make out lists of 10*l.* occupiers.

The Registration Act of 1843 (6 & 7 Vict. c. 18) required overseers in every borough to make out annually lists of persons entitled to vote as 10*l.* occupiers; and for this purpose to refer to the Tax Assessments (sec. 12). Electors are also entitled to inspect the rate-books for the purposes of claims and objections (sec. 16).

mittee or going into any figures, I must say that I shall be glad to see the amendment adopted.*

Of course it was hopeless to argue with speakers who reasoned in such a manner as this.

Lord Robert Montagu, who figures in these debates, asserted, that according to the ancient constitution of Parliament—

The ruling inhabitants in each borough, the mayor and aldermen, who had jurisdiction and a common seal, were those who sent members to Parliament.†

And he cites a passage from Dr. Brady's History of Boroughs in support of this preposterous assertion. Lord Robert Montagu was evidently ignorant of the fact that the authority of Brady is utterly worthless—that he was a grossly inaccurate, dishonest writer, who, in the corrupt times of the later Stuarts, compiled his so-called 'History' to serve the interests of a Court then bent on the destruction of municipal liberties, and that his errors have been repeatedly exposed, in terms of the gravest reprehension, by modern constitutional authorities of the highest repute.

But this display of ignorance respecting the character of Dr. Brady is trivial, compared with the following astounding specimen of Lord Robert Montagu's historical lore. In a debate on the Reform Bill of 1860 he said:—

Next was the theory that representation ought to depend on the possession of property, that land ought to be represented; because that no stability or permanence can be expected unless the electors have something at stake. . . . . It was the principle under which our liberties have taken root and grown up. This was proved by an old Act of the 8th Henry VI. c. 7, declaring 'what sort of men shall be chosen knights of the Parliament.' . . . . It was a little after this, in 1264, that burgesses of towns first had seats in Parliament. At this time the House of Commons consisted of knights only.‡

* *Hansard*, vol. 184, col. 605.   † *Ibid.* col. 594.   ‡ *Ibid.* vol. 157, col. 2194.

It is to be regretted that the conventional schoolboy was not present to inform Lord Robert Montagu that Henry VI. reigned not before 1264, but more than one hundred and fifty years after that date, that burgesses sat in Parliament during the reigns of the seven preceding kings, namely Henry III., Edward I., Edward II., Edward III., Richard II., Henry IV., and Henry V.; and that the parliamentary franchise of boroughs had been established and minutely regulated by innumerable precedents, statutes, and proceedings in Parliament, before the Act of Henry VI., respecting forty shilling freeholders in counties (to which he refers) was passed.*

Lord Dunkellin's amendment was carried (June 18, 1866) by a majority of 11, the numbers being—for the clause proposed by the Ministers, 304; against it, 315. At the conclusion of the debate Mr. Gladstone had announced that he could not 'enter into any engagement that we will accept an adverse vote, or regard it otherwise than incompatible with the progress of the Bill.' Accordingly he stated in the House of Commons on the following day, that in consequence of the vote at which the House had arrived, the Ministers had found 'it their duty to make a communication to her Majesty;' and a few days afterwards the resignation of the Government was more explicitly announced in both Houses of Parliament.

* In 1867, the office of Vice-President of the Committee of Council for Education was conferred upon Lord Robert Montagu by the Conservative Government.

CHAPTER V.

ACCESSION OF THE CONSERVATIVE MINISTRY IN 1866.

The causes of Lord Russell's resignation, page 80.—*Mr. Bright's position and opinions,* 83.—*Influence of Lord Grosvenor and Mr. Lowe,* 85.—*The Conservative ministry of* 1866, 86.

On the 26th of June, 1866, Earl Russell, in the House of Lords, and Mr. Gladstone, in the House of Commons, announced that the Ministry had tendered their resignations to her Majesty; that the Queen at first declined to receive the tender; but subsequently, upon hearing the personal explanations of the Prime Minister, acquiesced in the resolution of the Cabinet.

The recession of Earl Russell and his colleagues from office was not the fall of a Ministry, but a reasonable refusal to continue an unequal combat with the ignorance of that not inconsiderable number of members of the House of Commons who did not understand the Reform Bill, and the strategy of another less numerous but more active knot of politicians zealous for nothing but a Parliamentary victory.

These are strong words; but it will not be difficult to justify them. In the first place, with respect to the imputation of ignorance to one portion of the House of Commons, the final vote on the Reform Bill was, on the part of several members, as we have seen, a gross blunder and obstinate misunderstanding respecting a plain matter of fact. Moreover, the House had stultified itself by coming to two contrary conclusions. On Mr. Hunt's motion, it was resolved to prefer rental to rateable value as a basis of the county occupation franchise. On Lord Dunkellin's motion, with reference to boroughs, the conclusion had been just the other way. If the Government had accepted these resolutions, and proceeded with the Bill, the absurd result would have followed that the occupation franchise in counties and boroughs would, without the slightest reason, have been regulated by two different systems of valuation. But this statement does not exhaust the list of anomalies to which the last vote of the House of Commons led. In explaining (June 26, 1866) the reasons of his resignation and refusal to proceed with the Bill, Mr. Gladstone said :—

When we came to examine the motion and to consider whether it were possible for us to adopt it, we were struck by those difficulties; in the first place the difficulties, I may say impossibility, of choosing any form or figure of enfranchisement founded on mere relation to rateable value, which would express faithfully and exactly without material deviation on one side or the other the scale of enfranchisement, which we had contemplated and submitted to the House. . . . . We found the following to be the result. In sixteen boroughs there would have been enfranchised, by adopting a franchise founded upon rateable value of above 6l., a number at least equal to the number which we propose to enfranchise. In thirty-nine boroughs we should have required to take not merely those above 6l., but of 6l. and upwards. In one hundred and twelve boroughs we must have gone to 5l. and upwards. In twenty-one boroughs we must have gone to 4l. and upwards. In five boroughs it required us to take in even those rated under 4l., in order to give a number not less than that which would be obtained by a 7l. rental. . . . . We felt very acutely the difficulties in which we should be involved from the establishment of different rates of franchise in the same borough, owing to the differences of rating which frequently prevail in different parts of the same town.*

In other words, the last vote of the House of Commons had forced upon the Government this alternative—either to accept a franchise fantastically irregular, or to correct the irregularities by a grotesquely complicated

* *Hansard*, vol. 184, col. 686.

law, varying not only in different towns, but in different parts of the same town.

It is obvious, then, that Reform in 1866 was rendered impossible by the amendment of June 18, considered alone and apart from collateral circumstances. The result cannot, however, be properly regarded in this aspect. The resolution was one of a series supported by a large party who were ready to avail themselves of any and every opportunity of obstructing the Bill— who were ready to vote for any conceivable motion, even if it had been written in an unknown tongue, provided that it was understood to be hostile to the Government. The Chancellor of the Exchequer briefly and dispassionately recapitulated the series of attacks to which the Ministry had been subject:—Lord Grosvenor's motion in April, which, if it had been passed, would have compelled the Government to produce the Seats Bill before the House had given any vote or indication upon the Franchise Bill; Sir Rainald Knightley's instruction in May to incorporate provisions respecting bribery and corruption; Captain Hayter's amendment, in June, directly censuring the principle of the Seats Bill; Lord Stanley's proposal (June 7) to postpone the suffrage question to that of distribution of seats; Mr. Walpole's motion (June 7) to raise the county tenants' franchise from 14*l.* to 20*l.*; Mr. Hunt's amendment in favour of a rating franchise for counties (June 11) ; and lastly, Lord Dunkellin's amendment. The motion of Lord Stanley was described in the following terms:—

On June 7, the noble lord the member for King's Lynn made a motion for the purpose of postponing the clauses of enfranchisement to the clauses affecting the redistribution of seats. Sir, that motion was made without any public notice whatever. But it came within the knowledge of the Government at a subsequent period, that, through channels I am not able to point out, information that either that motion, or some

* *Hansard*, vol. 184, col. 690.

such motion, would be made on that day and at that hour, had been conveyed to certain gentlemen on this side of the House whose views appeared likely to be favourable to the motion.*

That is, the intended surprise on the Government was studiously concealed from those who were likely to resist it, but was stealthily communicated to sympathisers in the opposite camp. We have seen what was the fate of this chivalrous enterprise, in which a large number of the gentlemen of England permitted themselves to be associated. It failed, but the degree of support given to it and similar stratagems showed that the House of Commons in 1866 was not prepared to discuss the Reform Bill on its own merits.

The failure of the Bill was indeed due chiefly to personal antipathies. Among the most effective opponents was the section represented by Lord Grosvenor, who expressed his indignation at the Government for deserting the old traditions of the Whig party, in favour of a more democratic policy—though how that could be it were difficult to understand, seeing that in the measure of 1866 the occupiers' franchise, both in towns and counties, was set at a higher figure than in the Bill of Lord Palmerston's Government in 1860. The Government was so repeatedly accused of being unduly influenced by Mr. Bright, and he himself was so incessantly charged with designs to 'Americanise' our institutions, that though no particle of evidence was adduced in favour of either of those statements, the mere reiteration of them was accepted by many in lieu of proof. Mr. Bright declared in the House of Commons (May 13, 1866) that he had not been consulted by the Government respecting the Bill, and that it was not a Bill which, if he had been consulted, he should have 'consented to present to the House.'* He also read in the House an extract from his speech† at a public meeting

* *Hansard*, vol. 182, col. 224.
† In a speech at Rochdale, Jan. 28, 1859, reported in the *Times* of the

at Rochdale in 1859, in which he had expressed a distinct and decided opinion against manhood suffrage, and even unrestricted household suffrage, because there were thousands of persons living in small tenements who were 'in a condition of dependence.' A speech addressed to a great popular assembly at Rochdale in 1859 could hardly have been manufactured for the purpose of influencing a debate in the House of Commons in 1866. Mr. Bright repeatedly directed attention to his avowed objections to indiscriminate extension of the suffrage, and challenged his opponents to produce proofs that he had ever advocated the extreme democratic doctrines which they imputed to him. The challenge was never accepted. It was considered sufficient to reiterate almost frenzied warnings against the republican designs of the hon. member for Birmingham. In 1866 a Conservative speech on the Reform question was considered incomplete without an allusion to the arch-conspirator against the British Constitution. In 1867 the principal clause of his Reform Bill was adopted almost verbatim by the Tory Ministry.

following day, Mr. Bright explained and recommended a Bill by which he proposed to amend the representation. The following is an extract from this speech:—'But the question may be asked—Why keep up the condition as to the six months, or why take only those who, during that or some other period, shall pay their rates? I put it to every man, whatever may be his theoretical notions, whether he believes it would be beneficial throughout the boroughs of the kingdom, for the constituency, as a whole, to include some scores in a very small borough—some hundreds in others—and a few thousands perhaps in the largest—of a class of which unhappily there are so many among us; I mean the excessively poor, some of them intemperate, some profligate, some, it may be, only unfortunate, some naturally incapable, but all of them in a condition of dependence, such as gives us no reasonable expectation that they would be able to resist the many temptations which richer and unscrupulous men would offer them at elections, in order to induce them to give their votes in a manner not consistent with their opinions and their consciences (if they have any in the matter), and inconsistent also, it may be, with the interest of the representation of the town or city in which they resided.'—*Times*, Jan. 29, 1859.

The points of resemblance and difference between Mr. Bright's Bill of 1859, and Mr. Disraeli's Reform Bill of 1867, will be considered in a subsequent chapter.

This mode of resisting the Reform Bill of 1866 was successful with the considerable section of the community which prefer declamation to proof. Again, the Trojan Horse undoubtedly did much mischief to the Bill. *Fuimus Troes, fuit Ilium* had been the burden of Mr. Lowe's prophetic song throughout the session, and he so frequently reproduced Virgil's mythical and rather absurd story * of the fall of Troy, and so skilfully applied it to modern political circumstances, that he infected others with his own terrors. He made men believe that the Reform Bill, like the fabled wooden monster, was an instrument of destruction, which Mr. Gladstone, like another Sinon, plotted to bring within the sacred citadel of the British Constitution. Mr. Lowe played the part of Laocoön, but with better success and a better fate. The gods did not send sea serpents to destroy him: he was merely condemned to assist, the next year, in amending the Conservative Reform Bill.

To Lord Russell's announcement in the House of Lords (June 26, 1866) of his resignation, Lord Derby made a reply, in which he treated the conduct of the retiring Government as 'injudicious and dictatorial.' He said:—

It would have been perfectly competent to the noble Earl and his colleagues, when rating was carried against rental, to say that as that proposition would raise the franchise above what they intended, they would reduce the figure from 7*l.* to 5*l.*; that would have been the fair, the reasonable, and obvious course of the Government. But, instead of this, when rating had been carried by a majority of 11, including 44 of their own supporters—thus proving the annihilation of the majority of 70 which they had at the beginning of the Session, and which they had frittered away—up jumps the Chancellor of the Exchequer and declares that he regards the principle of rental as an essential part of the Bill, and the substitution for it of a principle of rating as a vote of want of confidence in her Majesty's Ministers; and that whatever may be the inconvenience to the country, and notwithstanding the state of

* The historical value of this myth may be ascertained by reference to the first volume of Grote's History of Greece.

foreign affairs — notwithstanding all these things which he urged so forcibly against a change of Ministry—the Government intend, because the House of Commons had exercised its judgment, to throw the country into every confusion to which it will be subjected, and to offer to the Crown the resignation of their offices—I hope with the sincere intention that the Queen should be advised to act upon that resignation, and that it should not be a merely fictitious resignation.*

With regard to Lord Derby's insinuation of a 'fictitious resignation,' it is sufficient to remark that her Majesty, when the resignation was first proffered, declined to accept it, and did not consent to do so until Lord Russell and Mr. Gladstone had proceeded to Windsor, and personally explained the necessity of their retirement from office. The majority of 70, which they were supposed to have 'frittered away,' never existed, except on paper: it was merely a newspaper computation with reference to the members returned at the general election of 1865, who adopted the conveniently vague political principle of adhesion to Lord Palmerston. The suggestion that after the vote respecting rating had been carried, the Government might have met the difficulty by proposing a 5l. rating franchise in boroughs, is made upon a misapprehension of the real nature of the difficulty. As Mr. Gladstone demonstrated, the rating was so variable a basis, that no one figure could have been adopted, without absurdly anomalous results.

On the 6th of July new parliamentary writs were directed to be issued on account of the vacation of their seats by several members of the new Government. Mr. Disraeli became Chancellor of the Exchequer, Mr. Walpole, Secretary of State for the Home Department, Lord Stanley, Foreign Secretary, General Peel, Secretary for War, and Lord Cranborne, Secretary for India. Among the members of the Upper House who became

* *Hansard*, vol. 184, col. 665.

members of the Cabinet were Lord Chelmsford, Lord Chancellor, and the Earl of Carnarvon, Colonial Secretary. On the 9th of July the Earl of Derby announced to the House of Lords his accession to the office of First Minister of the Crown.

By retiring at this juncture Lord Russell and his colleagues took, as subsequent events have proved, the most effectual means of promoting the cause of Reform. A Ministry, of which Mr. Disraeli and Lord Stanley were chief members, would be ready to make almost any concessions which enabled them to retain office. In an answer dated to an invitation from the 'Working Men's Association,' which he declined, Mr. Gladstone said:—

I shall not be supposed to indicate a disposition to recede from the ground on which we have stood during the contest. I look upon the recent resignation of Lord Russell's Government of their offices as one more onward step towards the accomplishment of this object; and in the hour of defeat I have the presentiment of victory.

The Reform Act of 1867, extorted from the fears of the Tory Government, is a conclusive proof of the accuracy of this prophecy.

But at the time when it was uttered, the change of Ministry was not regarded with equal complacency by Reformers and the working classes. Large public meetings were held all over the country, east, west, north, and south, in which the conduct of the Tories was denounced in very strong terms. The people were angry, not merely at the defeat of the Bill, but principally at the craft and chicanery employed for the purpose. It was the conviction that they had been baffled by secret manœuvres which rendered them chiefly indignant. The new Government and its supporters in the press affected to consider these meetings unimportant, and systematically under-estimated the number of persons attending them. The fact was, however, not to be denied that in every great town of England meetings open to all comers publicly condemned the arts by which the Reform Bill of 1866 had been obstructed. The assemblies which attracted the greatest share of public attention were those convened by the Reform League, of which Mr. Beales, a barrister, is president. The proceedings of this association had, beyond all question, a considerable influence upon the conduct of the Conservative Ministry in the following year, and by forcing the subject of Reform upon their attention promoted in a material degree the enactment of a statute to amend the Representation.

During the remainder of the Session 1866, the discussion upon Reform was not renewed in Parliament. In his speech in the House of Lords (July 9, 1866), announcing his accession to office, Lord Derby stated his desire to see the question settled, but declined to make any pledge to bring in a Bill with reference to it in the next Session. He said:—

I reserve to myself the most entire liberty, and after what has passed, it is not, I think, an unreasonable reservation, as to whether the present Government should or not undertake in a future Session to bring in a measure for the amendment of the representation of the people. Of this I am quite sure, that if there is no reasonable prospect of passing a sound and satisfactory measure, it is of infinite disadvantage to the country that Session after Session should be lost, and that measures of useful legislation should be put a stop to by continual contests over Reform Bills, which after occupying the whole Session, fail in passing and only leave the Session barren of practical results.*

Parliament was prorogued Aug. 10, 1866. The Royal Speech referred to various questions of domestic and foreign policy, but did not touch the subject of the Representation of the People.

* *Hansard*, vol. 184, col. 740.

CHAPTER VI.

THE REFORM RESOLUTIONS PROPOSED BY THE GOVERNMENT IN 1867.

Reform resolutions proposed by Mr. Disraeli, February, 1867, page 91.—His error as to the electoral rights of freemen, 92.—The resolutions opposed by Mr. Lowe and Mr. Bright, 95.

THE ROYAL SPEECH on the opening of Parliament, February 5, 1867, contained the following passage:—

Your attention will again be called to the state of the representation of the people in Parliament, and I trust that your deliberations, conducted in a spirit of moderation and mutual forbearance, may lead to the adoption of measures, which, without unduly disturbing the balance of political power, shall freely extend the elective franchise.

At the time when the Queen's advisers put this passage into the Royal Speech, they were very much enamoured of the 'balance of political power.' The nature of that balance has never been explained, nor its existence demonstrated. Supposing that it existed and was worth preserving, it would seem rather absurd to warn Parliament against 'unduly disturbing' it. Any disturbance of a just balance is undue.

The idle, pompous phrase would not be worth notice now, except that it affords an indication of the principles of Reform which the Ministry entertained. Their view evidently was, that the extension of the suffrage was to be determined not with reference simply to the fitness of the persons to be enfranchised, but upon considerations of their number and the ratio which it would bear to that of the existing constituencies. The same idea was elaborated in one of the resolutions proposed by the Chancellor of the Exchequer, on the 11th of February:—

3. That, while it is desirable that a more direct representation should be given to the labouring class, it is contrary to the constitution of this realm to give to any one class or interest a predominating power over the rest of the community.

This idea of 'balancing' classes, or of establishing 'fair proportions' among the electors, was not new. In a debate the previous year (April 27), Mr. Disraeli stated that the number of artisans who were electors was increasing, and that in ten years 'that increase would make the working classes one-third of the whole borough constituency.' He added, 'One-third of the borough constituency seems to me rather a fair proportion.'*

If this philosophical theory of representation were applied in practice, it would lead to some rather curious results. It is not stated upon what principle any given proportion is determined to be 'fair;' but supposing that preliminary objection removed, and a fair proportion of the 'working' or any other class enfranchised, this difficulty arises. If subsequently other members of the class equally fit to exercise the suffrage applied for it, the answer would be that a sufficient number of their fellows had the privilege already: that they must wait for vacancies in the electoral body. It would be highly satisfactory to A at one end of the kingdom to be debarred from the enjoyment of a right, because B at the other end possessed it. Conversely, supposing that by various social causes any 'class' †

---

* *Hansard*, vol. 183, col. 101.

† The difficulty of effecting the requisite classification must not be overlooked. Various conflicting systems would have their advocates. One party would recommend the division of men into the upper, middle, and lower classes; another, into the agricultural, manufacturing, and commercial

of voters became too large, it would be necessary to curtail the 'class' by new legislation. Evidently, the 'balance' of political power would require much watching, and the management of it would be very troublesome in practice. It is, however, but justice to Mr. Disraeli to acknowledge that, at a later period, he abandoned this visionary theory, and adopted the more reasonable view that a citizen fit to be enfranchised ought to be enfranchised, simply because he *is* fit, without reference to the number of persons similarly qualified.*

On the 13th of February, the Chancellor of the Exchequer directed the attention of the House of Commons to Thirteen Resolutions, which he proposed as a basis of an amendment of the representation. Having procured the passage of the Queen's Speech relative to the subject to be read at the table, he proceeded *ore rotundo* to dwell upon the necessity of laying aside party passions and strifes on this occasion. He thought it 'expedient that Parliamentary Reform should no longer be a question which should decide the fate of Ministries,'

---

classes. If either of these arrangements were adopted, those who preferred the other might complain of injustice. The allotment of equal shares of power to each of three classes, the upper, middle, and lower, might, and probably would, be equivalent to a very unequal distinction among the other three—the agricultural, manufacturing, and commercial.

There are many other difficulties in the way of the theory of class-representation. To practical people it will be a sufficient objection that it has never been adopted in England. The Corn Law agitation would have given one of the fairest chances of trying it. But it is not true that in that struggle the agricultural classes were arrayed against the rest. It was ascertained that the six greatest landowners in this country were in favour of Free Trade.

* In his speech on the introduction of the Reform Bill, March 18, 1867, the Chancellor of the Exchequer said, 'I do not think it is our business to act the part of electioneering agents, and to make estimates, always of a most speculative character, of the number of persons who will vote under the plan we propose. That is not our business as Ministers in Parliament. We are to see who, under the laws of this country, are to have the opportunity of acquiring a vote.'—*Hansard*, vol. 186, col. 18. And again (March 26, 1867), 'We never considered the numbers, but we looked to the principle. We looked to the means by which we might unite competency and fitness with variety of character, in order to form the constituency of the country.'

—a doctrine which he had not espoused in the previous year, but which was highly convenient to the present possessors of power. In like manner, an astute batsman might stipulate that he should not be 'out' if the ball took his wicket.

He then proceeded at great length to demonstrate the necessity of a Reform—a work of supererogation, seeing that everybody, except, perhaps, Mr. Lowe and two or three other members, were agreed upon *that* point at least. In this unnecessary demonstration the Chancellor of the Exchequer began with a blunder in a matter of history and law. He asserted that the rights of freemen were abolished by the Reform Act of 1832— a statement which is not correct. He said:—

> The memorable words of Sir Robert Peel on this subject are familiar to this House. He warned the Government of the day, that in putting an end to the rights of freemen as they then existed, and terminating all those other means by which the householder in many boroughs registered his vote and exercised it, they were embarking in a course which eventually must involve them in great danger and inconvenience. . . . The rights of the existing generation were in another place not only vindicated, but saved, by no less a person than Lord Lyndhurst.*

Mr. Disraeli, in the passage just quoted, states in effect, that the Reform Act of 1832 extinguished the electoral rights of freemen, with the exception of a reservation in favour of the existing generation. This, however, is not correct. The earlier Reform Bill of 1831 did indeed provide for such an extinction, but in 1832 the Whigs reluctantly yielded to the suggestions of their opponents on this point, and modified their measure so as to keep alive the privileges of large classes of freemen, not merely those of the existing generation, but also of their successors. And accordingly, the statute as actually passed preserves the electoral rights of

---

* *Hansard*, vol. 185, col. 217.

freemen admitted since the 1st of March 1831, 'in respect of birth or servitude.'* So effectually has this provision operated that in some boroughs the number of freemen entitled to vote is larger at the present time than it was in 1832. For instance, in Coventry the number was then 2,756, and at the date of the electoral returns for 1866, was 3,911; in Exeter, the number increased between the two dates from 586 to ⊦98; in Ipswich, from 344 to 360; in Newcastle-upon-Tyne, from 1,619 to 1,842; in York, from 2,342 to 2,571. In many other places, the number of freemen and other 'ancient-right' voters is very considerable.†

But upon this unsubstantial foundation—the supposed destruction of the rights of freemen by the Reform Act of 1832, Mr. Disraeli, in his speech of February 11, 1867, based the claim of the working classes to the possession of the franchise. The greater part of his speech was, however, devoted to a prolix argument in favour of passing preliminary resolutions before the introduction of a Reform Bill:—

> The position of the House of Commons with regard to this question of a Parliamentary Reform Bill is different from that which exists between the House generally, and all other great questions which are introduced and initiated in this House by a body of men, who are in the possession of office, or who are candidates for office. . . . We presume to recommend to the House that before we introduce a Bill, we may be permitted, upon its main principles and upon other points of great and paramount importance, to ask the opinion of the House, and see whether they will sanction the course which we recommend. ‡

This notable project for evading the responsibilities

* 2 Will. IV. c. 45, s. 32. As a matter of some historical interest it may be noted that in 1831 Lord Derby, then Mr. Stanley, supported in a speech (Aug. 30) the extinction of the rights of freemen proposed in the earlier Reform Bill.—*Hansard*, vol. 6, col. 901.
† Electoral Returns, 1865-6.—Return A.
‡ *Hansard*, vol. 185, col. 220.

of his position was, however, speedily rejected, not merely by the Liberals, but also by his own party. Mr. Gladstone, who immediately followed him in the debate, pointed out that the Chancellor of the Exchequer proposed to deal with the subject in a manner altogether novel; and objected that, by his announcement, 'he leaves us to imply that, together with the increase of the responsibility of the House of Commons, there was a diminution of the responsibility of the Government.'*
He continued:—

I understand the right hon. gentleman that he cannot fix the amount of the reduction in his first Resolution, because that may depend upon the points to be disposed of by subsequent Resolutions. But does not the right hon. gentleman see that many members would refuse—would justly refuse—to commit themselves to an abstract principle of reduction unless they knew what form the reduction would take? †

The parliamentary campaign did not begin hopefully. The Ministry soon learned that their project of settling the first principles of the Bill by a tentative process was disliked on both sides of the House. The Thirteen Resolutions were so vague that almost any conceivable scheme of Reform might be based upon them. The first Resolution affirmed that the number of electors 'ought to be increased.' The second, that the increase might be best effected by 'reducing the value of the qualifying tenement in counties and boroughs, and by adding other franchises.' The third has already been quoted. The fourth recommended the 'principle of rating'—whatever that may be. The fifth declared that 'the principle of plurality of votes' would facilitate the settlement of the borough franchise. Then followed several resolutions respecting the distribution of seats, registration, voting papers, expenses of elections, and a boundary commission.

* *Hansard*, vol. 185, col. 245. † *Ibid.* col. 247.

It is obvious that if Parliament had accepted these vague resolutions, it would have committed a folly like that of a man who signs a blank cheque, or accepts a bill of exchange before the amount and dates are inserted. At a subsequent stage of the debate (February 25, 1867) Mr. Lowe happily observed:—

> The resolutions of the Government have no more to do with the plan of the Government than Squire Thornhill's three famous postulates had to do with the argument he had with Moses Primrose, when, in order to controvert the right of the clergy to tithes, he laid down the principles that a whole is greater than its part—that whatever is, is—and that three angles of a triangle are equal to two right angles.*

But the proposed method of procedure was open to another objection of still greater importance. It threatened to abrogate, irregularly and incidentally, the existing relations between Parliament and the Ministers of the Crown. Mr. Bright argued this objection very forcibly:—

> I undertake to say, that there has been no proposal made to this House during the four and twenty years I have been here which has tended so much to Americanise the House of Commons—the chief legislative assembly of this country—as the proposal which the Government has made to-night. What takes place at Washington? Mr. Seward, Mr. Stanton, and other eminent men, heads of departments under the President, do not make their appearance in the House of Representatives or even in the Senate. These two assemblies discuss any measures they like, they pass any measures they like, and it is not necessary that they should consult the President or his Ministers. †

This remark is perfectly accurate, and it comes with peculiar appropriateness from a member of Parliament who had been frequently accused of attempts to assimilate our institutions to those of America. Legislation without the co-operation of the executive Government,

* *Hansard*, vol. 185, col. 953. † *Ibid.* col. 967.

is, it may be conceded, possible. Such a system is maintained in the United States. In our country the doctrine of ministerial responsibility, as it is now understood, is comparatively modern. In very ancient times—under the earlier Plantagenets—laws were made upon the petitions of the House of Commons, with respect to which the advisers of the Crown took no part until the time came for answering them. Under the Tudor sovereigns and the Stuarts the idea that Ministers should resign because they could not carry measures through Parliament would have been deemed monstrous. In Queen Anne's time it was considered nothing extraordinary that the Cabinet should be composed of Whigs and Tories, in fierce opposition to each other. The existing system was not thoroughly established until the time of Mr. Pitt. It cannot therefore be said that legislation, independently of the executive Government, is impracticable. But is the country prepared to revert to that system? Whatever may be thought of its comparative merits, this at least is obvious: that it would require extensive and fundamental changes in the functions of Ministers and the tenure of their offices, and that such changes could not be safely effected without elaborate legislation. The revolution—for it would be a revolution now—is not one that could be properly accomplished by a merely incidental operation. The advisers of the Crown, by their patronage and presence in the Houses of Parliament, exercise a constant and potent influence upon the course of legislation. Under the suggested system it would be necessary either to abrogate that influence or to place it under constitutional control; for otherwise the most flagitious abuses of the authority of ministers might be practised with impunity. If they are to retain their parliamentary influence they must accept the corresponding responsibility to Parliament. *Qui sentit commodum sentire debet et onus.*

CHAPTER VII.

THE FIRST PROJECT OF A REFORM BILL IN 1867.

The Resolutions abandoned, 97.—*Another scheme selected at a meeting of the Conservative party,* 97.—*The scheme submitted to the House of Commons, but speedily relinquished,* 99.—*Resignation of three Secretaries of State,* 100.—*Their explanations of their reasons for retiring,* 103.

THE method of procedure by Resolutions as the basis of a Reform Bill was speedily discarded. On the night (February 25) appointed for the consideration of those resolutions in committee, the Chancellor of the Exchequer proposed another scheme for the amendment of the representation. This measure was more definite than its predecessor, but had even a shorter life; and is now interesting only on account of the circumstances which led to its introduction and abandonment. At a very numerous meeting of the Conservative party at Lord Derby's house in the earlier part of the same day the Premier addressed his supporters at considerable length and expounded the ministerial policy in regard to the Thirteen Resolutions then before the House of Commons. He then submitted to the meeting whether it would be advisable to base the new franchise on household suffrage accompanied by a plurality of votes, or on a reduction of the existing franchise in accordance with the plan which at a later hour of the same day was proposed by the Chancellor of the Exchequer to the House of Commons. After due consideration the second course was approved and adopted.*

Thus, by another deplorable innovation in politics,

---

* *Daily Telegraph*, Feb. 26, 1867, p. 6.

the scheme submitted to Parliament was brought forward, not upon the responsibility of the Ministry, but as the result of an arrangement between the Cabinet and a large section of the very body which was to decide upon the measure. Such a procedure, if it became general, would tend, in no small degree, to diminish the dignity and independence of the House of Commons and to increase unduly the power of the Executive. A favoured number of the representatives of the people are offered their choice of two particular measures. After they have selected one of them, it is offered to the remainder of the House with all the authority, not of a Ministry alone, but of a Ministry and a political party pledged to co-operate with each other.

Of the scheme introduced by Mr. Disraeli in this questionable manner, a very brief account will be sufficient. He proposed to confer the franchise upon graduates, certain classes of fundholders, and depositors in the savings' banks, and some others. The persons so entitled were to have double votes in boroughs, if they were also qualified as occupiers. The occupiers' qualification was to be reduced to 6*l*. rateable value in boroughs and 20*l*. rateable value in counties. Thirty seats were to be taken from existing constituencies and the vacancies were to be supplied by allotting fifteen new seats to counties, fourteen to boroughs, and one to the University of London. There was also a provision for taking votes by voting papers.* This scheme was not embodied in a Bill; but the following day the Chancellor of the Exchequer promised that a Reform Bill should be introduced in about a week's time.

The history of this still-born project, as subsequently narrated by Lord Derby to the House of Lords, is very curious, and furnishes an unusually direct illustration of a very trite remark on the small amount of wisdom exercised in the government of mankind. When Lord

* *Hansard*, vol. 185, col. 937.

Derby's supporters met at his house on the afternoon of February 25, it was, to use a colloquial expression, a mere toss-up whether household suffrage or the 6*l.* rating suffrage would be recommended to Parliament. The project actually adopted was a kind of burlesque of Mr. Gladstone's plan of 1866, with the substitution of rateable value for rental, and the selection of it was determined by the accidental preponderance of opinion in the Conservative meeting at Lord Derby's house. The Cabinet could not make up their minds which to choose, and so they gave the refusal of both to their own followers.—*Utrum horum mavis accipe.* But the selection made in this peculiar manner did not prove felicitous. The project which Mr. Disraeli was instructed by his followers to introduce into the House of Commons had a very short life indeed. The history of the unfortunate measure was narrated by the Earl of Derby in the House of Lords (March 4) with a candour which affords a marked contrast to the reticence and subtlety of his principal colleagues.

He commenced by admitting 'that the Resolutions were somewhat vaguely and indistinctly drawn,' and stated that when the House of Commons showed a disinclination to accept them it became the duty of the Cabinet to consider what Bill should be submitted to Parliament:—

> Two schemes were under the consideration of the Cabinet, varying from each other in that very essential particular—the amount of the extension of the franchise. One of these schemes was more extensive than the other . . . Both of these schemes were anxiously considered by my colleagues and myself; and though one very distinguished member of the Cabinet entertained strong objections to the course which we were endeavouring to pursue, yet he felt that in order to secure the great object of perfect unanimity in the Cabinet it was his duty to waive any objections he might personally entertain. . . . Two of my most valuable and distinguished colleagues, occupying most important posts in the Government, had, upon a recon-

sideration of the figures which had been presented to them, come to the conclusion that our proposed arrangements, especially in regard to small boroughs, would produce such an injurious effect that they were compelled to withdraw their adhesion to the proposal. I need hardly say that withdrawal relieved the other colleague of whom I have spoken from any obligation under which he might have felt himself placed. I and my other colleagues were now placed in the painful position of having to consider whether we should present to Parliament that which we believe to be the more desirable and the more extensive measure of Reform, when such proceeding would lead to our ranks being diminished by the loss of no fewer than three Secretaries of State. . . . Under these feelings I and the majority of the Cabinet consented to submit to the House of Commons a measure which I admit we felt was not perfectly satisfactory. . . . It became very shortly obvious that on neither side of the House did that proposition meet with a satisfactory reception. . . . We had therefore during the course of the past week to consider—and to consider most anxiously—whether we should adhere to our second proposition or recur to that which commanded the support of the great majority of the Cabinet, and at the cost of a sacrifice of three most esteemed colleagues, to present to Parliament that measure which in the first instance the majority of the Cabinet considered the most desirable one. . . . That measure will be in a very short time laid before the other House of Parliament. . . . I cannot express the regret I feel at parting with three of the most important and most valued of my colleagues.*

Stripped of the verbiage—which, however, is as respectable and proper in a 'ministerial explanation' as mistakes of grammar in a Royal Speech—Lord Derby's statement amounted to this: We offered to the House of Commons certain Resolutions; they were rejected. Then a Bill, which we ourselves thought unsatisfactory, was proposed, because a better one was disliked by our colleagues. The House of Commons again rejected our proposals; so we are going to introduce the more satisfactory Bill and throw the refractory colleagues overboard. We are very sorry to lose them—cannot sufficiently express our regret or our sense of their merits.

* *Hansard*, vol. 185, col. 1283.

The ship of Reform laboured heavily in the stormy seas of politics, and the captain and his crew gallantly sacrificed three Jonahs to their own safety. These were the Earl of Carnarvon, Secretary for the Colonies, General Peel, Secretary of State for War, and Viscount Cranbourne, Secretary for India. Following Lord Derby in the debate of March 4, Lord Carnarvon gave his version of the transactions which led to his retirement from the Cabinet. The more extensive measure contemplated by the Government appeared to him likely to 'effect an enormous transfer of political power and alter the character of five-sixths of the boroughs of this country.' He refused to sanction these innovations. With respect to the compromise of a 6*l*. rating introduced by the Chancellor of the Exchequer in the House of Commons—'if it was a measure distasteful to my noble friend, and, as I think he said, to the majority of the House of Commons, it was equally distasteful to me.'*

Earl Granville complained that the Government had not come to an agreement upon the subject of Reform and prepared a Bill during the recess. He observed that—

From the statement of the noble earl at the head of the Government and the noble earl who has just spoken, it appears that during the eight or nine months which elapsed from the time when they made up their minds that it was right to deal with the question to the period, when they placed those Resolutions before the House of Commons, the Ministers not only did not make up their minds on any practical measure, but did not even come to any decision among themselves as to the principles on which it was desirable to deal with the subject.†

Lord Grey also complained that 'we shall have no less than six weeks of the session wasted before any step whatever is taken.' Lord Derby repelled these charges, but his answer virtually admitted their accuracy. He said:—

With regard to the principles of the Bill and its main pro-

* *Hansard*, vol. 185, col, 1201.   † *Ibid.* col. 1202.

visions, Her Majesty's Government were perfectly agreed in the month of November last; and the only question then remaining for discussion among them was as to the extent to which the franchise should be extended.

Except the extension of the franchise the Bill had long been complete. *Except* that it had no head, the child was a very fine baby.

In the House of Commons the next day General Peel and Lord Cranbourne explained with great candour the reasons of their secession. In the previous session they had been among the most honest and uncompromising opponents of Reform. It is very remarkable, and in no small degree characteristic of the English lower classes, that the straightforward soldier-like opposition of General Peel raised him in their estimation. He was a thorough Tory and was not ashamed to avow his principles, and they liked him for his fearless candour. In the public meetings held about this time among working men the ingenuity of the slippery Conservative leaders in the House of Commons was described in language extremely unparliamentary, but the three members of the Cabinet who were most adverse to the extension of the suffrage were frequently mentioned with honour, simply on account of those qualities which Englishmen value most highly—truthfulness and courage.

General Peel stated (March 5, 1867) that when the Conservative Government was formed no pledge was given to bring in a Reform Bill, and that he would not have joined the Government if such a pledge had been required; but that at a later date he became convinced of the necessity of such a measure. He objected to the 'fatal fifth resolution,'[*] as he termed it, because he considered it inconsistent with the fourth, which stipulated

---

[*] 'That the principle of plurality of votes, if adopted by Parliament, would facilitate the settlement of the borough franchise on an extensive basis.'

that no class should have a predominant influence, and also because it would 'swamp the old constituencies, especially in small boroughs.' And with regard to the compensation derived from plurality of votes, he had 'no very great faith either in securities or pledges.' He added:—

It was not until Monday morning week or very late on Sunday night that I heard for the first time that two of my colleagues, in whom I placed the greatest confidence, and with whom I had acted with the greatest cordiality, had, without any communication with me or any reference to me, come to the same conclusion as I had done.

General Peel treated the ministerial measure as one of household suffrage, and so did Lord Cranbourne who followed him in the debate. With reference to the history of the Cabinet discussions Lord Cranbourne gave some curious particulars:—

After the speech of my right hon. friend the Chancellor of the Exchequer on February 11, it became evident—at least it was the belief of many of my colleagues—that the original view of the application of the fifth Resolution was untenable; and proposals, which to me—I only say to me—were new, were then entertained by the Government. . . . It was on February 16, that I first heard of the proposition which I believe has now received the formal sanction of her Majesty's Government. I then stated at once that it was a proposition which to my mind was inadmissible. I believed at the time that it was abandoned; but on the following Tuesday, the 19th I think, the proposition was revived, and revived with the statement of certain statistics. . . . After we separated on Saturday the 23rd I naturally gave myself up to the investigation of those figures. The position was one of extreme difficulty. The materials which I had were in my opinion exceedingly scanty. The time which I had for decision was forty-eight hours. On the Sunday evening I came to the conclusion that although the figures on the whole had a fair seeming, and although it appeared, when stated in block, that upon them the proposed reduction of the franchise might be safely adopted, yet it appeared to me that with respect to a very large number of boroughs they would scarcely operate practically, otherwise than as a household suffrage.'*

The statements of the three seceding Secretaries of State give an adequate idea of the amount of consideration and study bestowed upon the Reform Bill which was now about to be introduced. At a date some weeks after the meeting of Parliament the Government had not decided upon the nature of the measure which it would produce. Of the more extensive scheme ultimately selected Lord Cranbourne was first informed on February 16. In consequence of objections entertained by him and two of his colleagues, another and widely different measure was proposed to the House of Commons on February 25. This measure was instantly condemned. The Ministry thereupon withdrew this mere makeshift, and determined to adopt another Reform Bill at the expense of losing three of their principal colleagues. It is needless to add that the country and the House of Commons became impatient of the irresolution of the Government and its obvious disposition to trifle with the great subject committed to its charge. The Conservative leaders were in the position of a stage manager who, when the audience are assembled and the time for raising the curtain had arrived, has not resolved what piece he will put upon the stage.

The ultimate intention of the Ministry was announced on the day when General Peel and Lord Cranbourne explained the causes of their resignation, and the announcement was made in terms which forcibly recall the French proverb: *Qui s'excuse s'accuse:*—

It is our business now, said the Chancellor of the Exchequer, to bring forward as soon as we possibly can the measure of Parliamentary reform which, after such difficulties

* *Hansard*, vol. 185, col. 1340.

and such sacrifices, it will be my duty to introduce to the House. Sir, the House need not fear that there will be ANY EVASION, ANY EQUIVOCATION, ANY VACILLATION, or ANY HESITATION in that measure.*

Presumably the latter assurance was given because it was considered necessary.

* *Hansard,* vol. 185, col. 1345.

CHAPTER VIII.

THE REFORM BILL PRESENTED, MARCH 1867.

A Bill to amend the Representation introduced, 106.—*Mr. Disraeli's erroneous statistics,* 107.—*Extension of the borough franchise less under this Bill than under that of* 1866, 108.—*The Bill of* 1867 *would have increased the voting power of the wealthier classes,* 118.—*The irregular operation of the Bill,* 120.—*Mr. Gladstone's strictures on the scheme,* 124.—*The compound householders fined for their votes,* 126.—*Resolution of the Liberal party not to oppose the second reading,* 133.

ON March 18, 1867, the Chancellor of the Exchequer asked leave to introduce a Bill to amend the laws relating to the representation of the people in Parliament.

Omitting the parts of his speech which are merely rhetorical, the effect of it was as follows:—

He referred to the final vote on the Reform Bill of the previous year. The House, in his opinion, decided 'that the being rated to the poor and the paying of rates constituted a fair assurance that the man who fulfilled those conditions was one likely to be characterised by regularity of life and general trustworthiness of conduct.' Accepting that decision, he proposed 'that we should establish the franchise in the boroughs on this principle: *that any man who has occupied a house for two years and been rated to the relief of the poor and pays his rates*—every householder under these conditions should enjoy the borough franchise. By that means the 237,000 persons who are now rated and pay their rates would of course be at once qualified.'* He explained that there remain 486,000 who do not pay their rates personally because there are various local and general Acts of

---

* *Hansard,* vol. 186, col. 13.

Parliament under which the landlord compounds for his tenants' rates in various places. There are 58 boroughs in which this system wholly, and 98 in which it partially, prevails. With regard to the compound householders who are under this system, he proposed—that every facility shall be given them—that they shall be allowed to enter their names upon the rate book, to fulfil the constitutional condition to which I have adverted, and then they will, of course, succeed to the constitutional right which is connected with it.

The scheme also included the enfranchisement of every person paying 20s. direct taxes annually. If such person were also a qualified householder, in a borough he was to have a double vote. Other qualifications were those of possessors of 50l. in the funds or savings-banks, graduates, clergymen, and other professional classes.

In counties, the occupiers' qualification was fixed at 15l. rateable value, and the Chancellor of the Exchequer stated that an additional number of 171,000 householders would thus be qualified. It was not intended to confer the double vote in counties.

The numerical results of these changes were summarised as follows:—

'You would thus have more than 1,000,000 voters who could qualify themselves in the boroughs for the exercise of the franchise.'

With reference to counties, Mr. Disraeli said there would be 'an addition of upwards of 300,000 voters.'

In the redistribution of seats it was proposed to obtain thirty seats by disfranchisement and to allot them as follows: fourteen to boroughs, fifteen to counties, and one to the University of London.

This programme possesses Mr. Disraeli's most characteristic merit—brilliancy. His exposition conveyed or suggested a magnificent promise of the addition of 1,000,000 of voters to the borough constituencies and 300,000 to those of counties. The estimate demands scrutiny. The statistics are not merely interesting in themselves, but have also this value: that in examining them we compel ourselves to investigate thoroughly and intimately the new system of suffrage.

The returns which have been presented to Parliament establish the following propositions:—

1. *That the original Bill of* 1867 *would have added a smaller number of voters in boroughs than the Franchise Bill of* 1866.

2. *That the Bill of* 1867 *would have increased the voting power of the wealthier moiety of the borough population.*

1. In the speech just cited it is stated that there are in England and Wales 1,367,025 male householders, of whom 723,000 are now not qualified to vote; of these " there are 237,000 persons who are rated to the poor and pay poor rates."

These figures substantially agree with the return presented a few days afterwards on the motion of the Secretary to the Treasury,* showing the numbers of occupiers in boroughs, and the number whose rates are paid by their landlords. Various references to this return in the debates indicate that it contains the statistics to which Lord Cranbourne adverts in the speech announcing his resignation, and that it furnished the data for Mr. Disraeli's scheme of extending the suffrage. It is material therefore to compare the speech and the return with each other.

Apparently the figures underwent some slight revision after they had been furnished to the Government by the Poor Law officers. In Mr. Hunt's return the number of male occupiers whose rates are *not* paid by their landlords is stated at 245,910, which is rather in

* Moved for, returned, and ordered to be printed, March 15, 1867.— No. 136. (Mr. Hunt).

excess of the corresponding number given by Mr. Disraeli. The difference is not material.

The material point is this: that he has jumped to the conclusion that, because those persons are not compound householders, they would immediately be added to the electoral lists by his Bill. This statement is widely remote from the truth, and if he had applied to the skilful statisticians who gave him his figures they would doubtless have corrected it. From the gross number of occupiers under 10*l.*, not compound householders, we must make very large deductions, before we can arrive at the probable number of voters. In the first place, it is not correct to assume that every occupier whose landlord does not pay his rates pays them himself. The number of persons who are either exempted from rates on account of poverty or who make default with respect to them, though not very large, is considerable.

Again, many persons are disqualified by receiving parochial relief. This disqualification operates where either such persons or members of their families have had such bounty since the time of making out the list of voters. Unhappily a very large proportion of the population, about one-tenth of the whole, receives assistance under the poor-laws in the course of the year.*

Again, the occupiers to be enfranchised under the Bill

---

* There are no exact figures in any published Return, showing the number of persons who receive parochial relief during the year; but the Poor Law Report for 1866–7 shows that on a given day, viz., January 1, 1867, there were 903,000 persons in actual receipt of relief.

Taking these figures in round numbers at 1,000,000, it is the opinion of competent authorities that during the entire year an additional number of 1,000,000, making in the aggregate, 2,000,000, apply to the relieving officers for assistance.

The proportion of paupers to the whole population is therefore about 10 per cent., but the paupers are found generally, not among the 10*l.* householders, but among those below that class, and especially among those of a lower grade than the 7*l.* householders. It may be safely estimated that at least 15 per cent. of householders below the 7*l.* line will be disfranchised by receipt of parochial relief.

were required to occupy their tenements and pay rates for a period of two years. The corresponding period under the Reform Act of 1832 was one year.* The disqualification on account of non-residence would operate with greater frequency under the new Bill, both on account of the longer term of occupation required and also because the persons affected—those below the rank of 10*l.* householders—are a more migratory class.

From the gross number of occupiers, must also be subtracted about 15,000 freemen who are already on the register and are below the rank of 10*l.* householders.

Lastly, an allowance must be made in respect of the occupations of shops and other tenements without houses. The Bill enfranchised the occupier of a "*dwelling house*" only. The number of occupations which Mr. Disraeli cited included a considerable number of buildings held without dwellings.

It seems scarcely credible that on so serious an occasion as the ministerial explanation of a new Reform Bill these necessary elements of a correct estimate were entirely omitted. Mr. Disraeli contented himself with the off-hand statement that 'the 237,000 persons who are now rated and pay their rates would of course be at once qualified.' In the introductory speech with reference to the Reform Bill of the previous year Mr. Gladstone had made careful and elaborate deductions from the gross number of 7*l.* householders in computing the probable number of electors. He compared the numbers of 10*l.* *householders* and of 10*l. electors* (for which the data are given in the Electoral Statistics of 1866), and assumed that the same proportion would hold with reference to the 7*l.* householders. The consequent deduction was rather more than 30 per cent.† But a much larger de-

---

* 2 & 3 Will. IV. c. 45, § 87.

† The gross number of occupiers at rentals between 7*l.* and 10*l.* was between 207,000 and 208,000. This number was reduced by the rule-of-

duction is necessary with respect to the gross number of occupiers affected by Mr. Disraeli's Bill. At least 7 per cent. must be taken off for occupations of shops and other buildings without houses, and on account of the prolonged term of residence required under the Bill of March 1867. Also about 15 per cent. must be taken off in consideration of the circumstance that the persons disqualified by parochial relief are found principally among the tenants of houses below the annual value of 7*l*.* On the whole it will be a moderate esti-

three sum mentioned in the text to 156,000. A further reduction was made on account of freemen already on the register, and the final result was stated by Mr. Gladstone to be that ' 144,000 would be enfranchised by the reduction to a clear annual rental of 7*l*.' (*Hansard*, vol. 182, col. 53.) This computation was much less magnificent than Mr. Disraeli's, but has the advantage of being accurate.

* The following more detailed estimate of the numbers of householders who would have been enfranchised by the Bill as originally brought in, substantially agrees with the calculation in the text.

171 *Boroughs in which all or some of the Parishes are under Rating Acts.*

Total number of male occupiers under 10*l*. who are personally rated
  (Return 136, 1867 ; Mr. Hunt): Table I., 25,064 ; Table II., 106,467 ;
  Table III., 10,638 142,100
Deduct:—Occupiers now on the Register as freemen, &c., estimated . 10,000
                                                              ———
                                                              132,100

" Disqualified by insufficient residence, non-payment of
    rates, &c. (except in the parish of Liverpool, where
    the rates of tenements of 15*l*. rateable value and
    under are not paid in full,) 35 per cent. . . 46,100
" For male occupiers in Liverpool, say two-thirds of
    20,454 occupiers under 10*l*. 13,000
" For male occupiers in boroughs under 59 Geo. III.
    c. 12, and boroughs where the number of com-
    pound occupations under local Acts has not been
    ascertained 5,000
                                                              ———
                                                              64,100
Net number of male occupiers under 10*l*. personally rated who would
  register 68,000

29 *Boroughs not under Rating Acts.*

Number of male occupiers under 10*l*. ; (Return 136 ; Table IV.) 103,700
Deduct, freemen, &c. 3,000
                                                              ———
                                                              100,700
Deduct for occupiers of shops, &c., not being householders, for
  insufficient residence, receipt of relief, &c., 50 per cent. . 50,300
Net number who would register 50,400

Total number of male occupiers under 10*l*. in all boroughs who would
  register 118,400

mate to conclude that the net number of electors will be 50 per cent. less than the gross number of rated occupiers. Thus the number of ratepayers who would have been enfranchised by the Bill as it originally stood should have been stated at 118,500, instead of 237,000, the number stated by Mr. Disraeli.

At a later stage of the discussion Mr. Disraeli admitted the correctness of a reduction of 50 per cent. He said 'I admit that these 120,000 may be the most that are admitted to the exercise of the franchise by our proposal. . . . If we have to reduce the 240,000 by one-half, the same rule must of course apply to the 460,000 compound householders.' *

But on the earlier occasion, when he introduced the Bill, he replied in the following characteristic way to Mr. Gladstone's animadversion on his oversight:—

He said, ' You propose in your Bill to admit 237,000 persons who are now rated and pay their rates; but it won't admit half as many, for you do not make the deductions that are inevitable.' I never denied them. I gave returns showing them, and hon. gentlemen are quite competent to make them.†

The Chancellor of the Exchequer, ever ready with an answer, pleads that he was quite aware of the correction but deemed it superfluous. So Falstaff, with equal adroitness, extricates himself from a somewhat similar difficulty by exclaiming, ' By the Lord, I knew ye, as well as he that made ye!'

---

* March 26, 1867, *Hansard*, vol. 186, col. 661.

† *Hansard*, vol. 186, col. 90. Mr. Disraeli added, 'I suppose the chairmen of many assessment committees have seats in this House, and with a return before them are as capable of forming an opinion as any statist.'

This statement was perfectly correct. There are indeed, valuable members on both sides of the House, thoroughly versed in practical politics and parliamentary business, whose services to the country are not duly appreciated. Their presence in the House of Commons is an additional reason for regret that the chief conduct of intricate and important legistation should be left to fluent sciolists.

But the excuse will not avail. In the first place the Chancellor of the Exchequer did *not* give 'returns showing them' (the deductions). Mr. Hunt's return, which is that to which he refers, has not a word on the subject. Again, his own language precluded the idea that he was aware of these deductions. He said '237,000 now rated to the relief of the poor and paying their rates *would immediately be qualified to vote*:' a statement in no sense true, for it neglects the freemen already on the register, the owners of shops and other tenements without house, and the occupiers who are not ratepayers.

This number was a large item in a dazzling total of 'more than one million voters who could qualify themselves in the boroughs for the franchise.' But when we look at the details this magnificent project dwindles to very small dimensions. The large class of compound householders were almost entirely excluded by the bill. With respect to them the Chancellor of the Exchequer said:—

> In the case of the 486,000 who are compound householders, facilities would be afforded them, if they chose, of claiming their vote; that is to say, of inserting their names in the rate-book and paying their rates; and then they also as a matter of course will succeed to the enjoyment of the right.*

What are the promised facilities? The only provision in their favour is contained in clause 34, by which they might claim to be rated personally and become registered if they paid the *full rate* on their houses. This condition is more restrictive and onerous than the law of 1851 (Sir William Clay's Act) with respect to compound householders above the 10*l*. line. That Act enabled them to be registered if they paid the *reduced* rate or composition paid by their landlords.† Now we are not left to mere conjecture with respect to the extent of the

---

* *Hansard*, vol. 186, col. 14. † 14 & 15 Vict. c. 14, s. 3.

'facilities' proffered in 1851. Sir William Clay's Act has proved almost entirely a dead letter. The number of persons who have availed themselves of it during the last 16 years is merely a few scores. It is true that in some few parishes the overseers take upon themselves to put compound householders of the 10*l*. class upon the register; but the cases in which such householders voluntarily come forward to pay the rates in order to qualify themselves are so rare that for all practical purposes they may be entirely neglected. If compound householders would not spontaneously register themselves under the Act of 1851 which allowed them to pay the reduced rate, it is manifest that they would not register under the proposed Act, which required them to pay the full rate.

The practical operation of Sir William Clay's Act was accurately described by Mr. Gladstone, in his speech of May 9, 1867:—

> I should like to know whether at this moment there are 500 voters upon the register in the whole country, that have been enfranchised by an individual compliance with the Act of Sir William Clay. I do not believe there are 500. [An Hon. Member.—Not 100.] I am taking an outside number, and I challenge contradiction. . . . . As far as I can learn, of the number of householders who have come upon the register since the time of Sir William Clay's Act, by far the majority have been placed upon the register in utter disregard of the conditions of that Act. They never claim, they never pay, they never tender. They comply with no conditions at all. The parish officers, benevolent and philanthropic it may be, or strong political partisans, as I am afraid is often the case, by a vigorous exercise of benevolence, shoved them by the thousand upon the register. That is the way in which enfranchisement takes place for the most part under the Act of Sir William Clay.*

It is clear that the irregular and illegal operation†

---

* *Hansard*, vol. 187, col. 302.

† Of the capriciousness of these proceedings sufficient evidence is given in the Return No. 309 of 1867 (Mr. Gladstone) of the number of male compound householders and the number of them placed on the register. The return

here described could not be relied upon as a means of enfranchising compound householders under the Bill of 1867. That measure required that the person to be enfranchised should have 'been rated in respect of the premises,' and should pay the full rate for a certain period. The overseers, therefore, could not venture to put non-rated persons on the register. Consequently, only those compound householders who claimed to be rated or dis-compounded would have been enfranchised. The past experience of the effect of Sir William Clay's Act shows that their number would have been insignificant, and we may for the present calculation assume it to be virtually zero.

In the Bill of 1866 ample provision was made for compound householders both above and below the 10*l.* line. They were to be entered by the overseers in the lists of voters like other 10*l.* householders, and the condition of payment of rates was to be utterly abrogated. As far as any real relief was concerned these persons were utterly ignored by the Bill of 1867. It cannot be too broadly and positively affirmed that they were almost as effectually excluded from the franchise as if there had been a clause expressly prohibiting them from voting.

People are apt to talk of the 'compound householder' as if he were some rare and peculiar animal. There are 486,000 persons of this class; whereas in London and all the metropolitan boroughs together there are only 265,649 male occupiers of every class from the highest to the lowest. In other words, the class ignored by Mr. Disraeli's Bill was not much less than double the entire body of householders of this vast metropolis.

from Brighton shows that a large number of such persons have hitherto been registered there; but adds, that 'it is not the intention of the overseers of the present year to insert the names of compound householders on the list of voters except where claims have been made by such occupiers under the provisions of Sir William Clay's Act, and therefore this number will be largely reduced.'

Here is another way of showing the magnitude of this question. The total number of male occupiers in the boroughs of England and Wales is in round numbers 1,367,000. Consequently the class of compound householders is 35 per cent., or two-fifths the entire number of householders in the part of the kingdom to which the Bill relates. Of every 100 inhabitants it overlooked the claims of 35.

Before passing from this part of the subject it is desirable to advert to the invidious distinction made between compound householders of the 10*l*. rank claiming to vote under Sir William Clay's Act, and those below that rank claiming under the Bill of 1867. Why should the latter be required to pay the full rate and the former only the reduced rate or composition? The reduction is not insignificant. An allowance varying from 25 to 50 per cent. is made to landlords who undertake to pay their tenants' rates in the lump. It is clear now, that when the Government concocted their scheme they were ignorant of this as of other intricacies of the law with respect to rating and the franchise. When the Ministry were pressed with the discrepancy, the Solicitor-General, in the debate on the second reading, said that Sir William Clay's Act 'ought to be repealed.'* But the bill did not provide for such repeal and the suggestion was obviously an after-thought. Besides, it is impossible to require the tenants under existing tenancies to pay an increased rate without inflicting injustice somewhere. The increase must come out of their pocket or the landlords', and therefore one or other of the parties is subjected to a pecuniary burden contrary to the terms of the agreement between them.

The other items making up the 'million voters who could qualify themselves' are 35,000 by the educational franchise of graduates and professional men, 25,000

* *Hansard*, vol. 186, col. 548.

fundholders, 45,000 depositors in the savings-banks, and persons paying direct taxes, of whose number no information was given except that it ' would greatly exceed 200,000.'

It is obvious that a very large portion of these persons are qualified already as 10*l.* householders and that consequently the new qualifications add only to the number of *votes* where the double vote is conferred, and not to the number of *voters*. For example, the holders of property in the funds to the amount of 50*l.* and upwards almost universally live in houses of an annual value above 10*l*. So do the large majority of the depositors in savings-banks. There is a considerable number of professional men who live in lodgings, but on the whole the number of persons in the ' educational ' class who are not already qualified must be relatively small.

Probably the whole number of persons so enfranchised would have been under 24,000. Under the Bill of 1866 Mr. Gladstone estimated the number to be enfranchised as depositors in savings-banks, lodgers, copyholders and leaseholders, in towns, at 24,000; and this miscellaneous class is probably quite as numerous as that proposed to be qualified by the educational and pecuniary suffrages of 1867.

So then, what becomes of the ' million ' of new voters? The largest item of 486,000 must, as we have shown, be erased altogether. The 237,000 ratepaying householders are, by Mr. Disraeli's subsequent compelled admission, reduced to 120,000. Of the persons qualified by the possession of property in the savings-banks or the educational qualification, it would be a liberal estimate to suppose that 24,000 would be newly qualified. Consequently the addition to the borough franchise would be 144,000, or much less than the number of borough voters proposed to be enfranchised by Mr. Gladstone's Bill of 1866. That number considerably exceeded 200,000.

This conclusion establishes the first proposition above mentioned: *That the original Bill of* 1867 *would have added a smaller number of voters in boroughs than the franchise Bill of* 1866.

2. *The Bill of* 1867 *would have increased the voting power of the wealthier moiety of the borough population.*

This result would have been produced by the dual vote. It would have been accessible to nearly 300,000 of the wealthier class; persons paying rent at 20*l*. or upwards. The superior power given to them would have operated as a diminution of the power, not merely of the new voters, but also of the existing voters who are rated at rentals below 20*l*.

Mr. Macaulay's return made in 1861,* shows the number of persons charged with income or assessed taxes, and the number of such persons who are ratepayers at a rental of 20*l*. and upwards. The number was 230,863 in 1861, and has since greatly increased. It is on this second column that Mr. Disraeli relies; that is, he assumes that the persons paying 40*s*. direct taxes annually would be 20*l*. householders. Consequently the direct tax qualification would have have added substantially nothing to the number of *voters*, but it would have added greatly to the number of votes, for the persons in this class would have generally enjoyed the dual vote. This, as far as the rest of the electors were concerned, would have had a disfranchising effect, by reducing their votes to one-half their relative value. Clearly, it is the same thing whether we suppose each of them to have half a vote while the payer of direct taxes has one vote, or each of them to have one vote while he has two. It is the relative, not the absolute, number polled which decides an election. In the same way, at a game of cricket it would make no difference to the result whether each run were scored 1 or 10 or 1000.

---

* Return of persons charged to income tax or assessed taxes. No. 90, 1861.

The borough voters above and below the 20*l*. line were very nearly equal in number before the recent alteration of the suffrage. This appears as follows: and it can be easily shown that the Bill, instead of being democratic, would have considerably increased the relative influence of the superior class.

The total number of borough voters of all classes in England and
Wales is (Electoral Statistics, 1866, p. 8) 514,026
Male occupiers in boroughs; rentals of 20*l*. and upwards (Mr.
Macaulay's Return, 1861) 260,863
Difference 253,163

Since Mr. Macaulay's return of 1861 the number of persons assessed in a gross rental of 20*l*. has very largely increased. Mr. Disraeli stated in his speech, March 18, 1867, that the increase was probably 23 per cent. Now it is clear that not so large a proportion of this class as 23 per cent. would fail to register. We are, therefore, safe in assuming that the figure 260,863 represents this class. It is nearly equal to the remaining 253,163.

Hence, before the Bill, the borough voters were divided by the 20*l*. line into *two very nearly equal classes*.

Now let us see how the equilibrium would have been affected by the proposed changes. It has just been shown that it would have added about 144,000 to the borough register. Some of them, at least would be above the 20*l*. line; but, for the sake of simplicity, let it be assumed that they are all below it. This assumption is adverse to the proposition here sought to be established, and is therefore permissible for the purpose of the present argument. Adding this number to the 253,160, we have—

Borough *votes* below the 20*l*. line 397,163
The *votes* above that line would have been by the dual vote twice
260,863 521,726

These numbers are nearly in the proportion of 3 : 4. Thus the poorer class of voters would, under the Bill, have been outnumbered in the ratio of 4 : 3; whereas previously they were on an equality with the higher class. This is, however, an under-estimate of the increased power given to the upper classes. The effective addition to their number by the fundholders and educational franchises has been omitted for want of statistical information on those subjects.

This conclusion establishes the second proposition above mentioned—*That the original Bill of 1867 would have increased the voting power of the wealthier moiety of the borough population.*

There is another aspect of the ministerial scheme not a whit less important—the extreme irregularity in the effects of the Bill in different places. In those which are not under rating Acts it would have been almost equivalent to household suffrage. In places where the system of compounding for rates prevails, the large class of compound householders and tenants who pay their rates through their landlords would have been virtually excluded. The anomalies in this respect were absolutely ludicrous. For instance, in the great town of Brighton, as Mr. Gladstone showed in the course of the debate, the magnificent number of *fourteen* would have been added to the register; whereas in Sheffield, where the tenants pay their own rates, the whole body of inhabitant householders would have been enabled to become electors.

But even this statement does not express fully the absurdities of the projected arrangement. Of all the 200 boroughs of England and Wales there are only twenty-nine boroughs in which the practice of rating the tenants was exclusively adopted. There were considerably more than 100 boroughs *wholly* under the Small Tenements Act or some other rating Act. But besides these, there was an intermediate class of boroughs, in which rating Acts have been adopted in some parishes and not in others. In these it would happen that the people on one side of a street would have household suffrage, and those on the other side of the street would remain unenfranchised.

Nor was this all. The parishes have hitherto had the power, by resolutions in vestry, of adopting the Small Tenements Act; and they had also the power of rescinding such resolutions and recurring to the former system of personal rating. Consequently the composition of the constituencies would be in a constant state of fluctuation. It might vary almost incessantly, at the will of a predominant party among the ratepayers.

These absurdities were too much for the patience of even Mr. Disraeli's devoted adherents; and the House of Commons, as we shall see, subsequently got rid of them in a very trenchant fashion by abrogating the entire system of compounding for rates. Mr. Disraeli, as it will be shown, acquiesced in that method of extrication from his difficulties. He could not have foreseen them. No sane man would deliberately, and with his eyes open, suggest such a preposterous plan as that which has just been described. But when the anomalies were first pointed out, he and his official supporters affected to defend them. This was Mr. Disraeli's defence of the irregular operation of his Bill:—

Why, sir, I always thought that what we have been complaining of for years was the dreary monotony of the settlement of 1832, and the too identical character of the constituencies under that Act. Every time these discussions were brought on we were told over and over again that what the country languished for was the variety of franchise that they were deprived of by the Act of 1832; and that if that had been reintroduced in any of the schemes of later years, one of the great wants of the country would have been supplied.*

'Yes! True it is that our Bill operates very irregularly, but variety is charming!' So ran the apology; it

* March 26, 1867, *Hansard*, vol. 186, col. 659.

would scarcely be available, however, in the more ordinary concerns of life. Suppose, for example, that a sower went forth to sow, and cast great handfuls of grain on a few patches here and there, leaving the rest of the field unsown, he would be considered an indifferent husbandman. His master's wrath would not be appeased by the plea that when the crop grew up it would present an appearance of picturesque irregularity.

The argument which was most strenuously adduced for preferring the rate-paying condition to the standard of value, as a basis of the borough suffrage was this—that 'there is no principle in a figure.' The truth of this dogma depends on the definition of the word 'principle.' Either test—the payment of rates, or the possession of houses of a particular value—is artificial. The fact that a man provides for his taxes or any other pecuniary obligations with punctuality is some evidence that he is provident, trustworthy, and industrious, and therefore qualified for the exercise of the suffrage. But so also is the circumstance that he lives in a decent house. Both criteria are imperfect, and only in rough imperfect ways serve to eliminate the drunkard, the spendthrift, the sluggard, the vagrant, and the profligate. Such men *sometimes* live in very good houses, and pay their rates and taxes regularly. Therefore neither the test proposed in the Bill of 1866 nor that of 1867 can be said to involve a 'principle,' if by that word be meant a primary or fundamental truth susceptible of universal application.

It was said very frequently in discussions respecting the relative merits of the two systems, that if the franchise depended on the value of tenants' houses it would be constantly liable to alteration. If the 7*l.* householder might have a vote, why not the 6*l.*, 5*l.*, 4*l.*, householder? The suffrage, it was argued, would be lowered repeatedly, till at last the test became abolished altogether.

Those who supported this argument did not consider that artificial tests of figures are to be found in almost every branch of legislation. What was the test adopted in the very first Act of Parliament for restricting the suffrage—that of Henry VI., which gave the county vote to 40s. freeholders? That figure of 40s. remained unchanged for centuries. The qualification of the 10l. occupier under the Reform Act of 1832, served its purpose for an entire generation, and was at length altered, not because it involved a figure, but because it excluded a large number of persons whom Parliament and the country have declared worthy of the suffrage. The same contrivance of a numerical test is adopted with reference to a multitude of subjects. A young man attains his majority at 21. Why not according to the argument in question, at 20?—at 19?—at 18? until at last he comes of age the day of his birth. Cab fares in London are regulated by reference to a radius of 4 miles from Charing Cross; why not $3\frac{1}{2}$ miles? Surely there is no 'principle' in that figure 4. The qualification of jurymen, from the time of Edward I., that is, for a period of 600 years, had been defined by figures. Tithes have been paid to the English Church from the time of the Saxons. Why was that charge precisely one-tenth—neither more nor less? It has often been an object of popular odium: why has there never been an agitation to reduce it gradually until it became abolished altogether?

The Chancellor of the Exchequer could not find any principle in a figure. It is therefore very remarkable that his own Bill—even including the clause relating to the borough occupiers' qualification—is utterly 'unprincipled,' from beginning to end. Here are some of the figures. The enfranchised borough occupier was required to be resident and pay rates for a period of 2 years. The tenant voter in counties was to reside for 12 months

and occupy a tenement of the value of 15 pounds.
The graduate elector must reside for 12 months. The
savings-bank elector must have 50*l.* in the savings-
bank, the fundholder 50*l.* in the funds, the payer of
direct taxes must pay 20*s.* per annum. Polling places
were to be provided in every parish or township
containing 200 electors. All boroughs with two
members and a population of less than 7000 were to
be deprived of one member.* It will be seen that in
almost every part of his measure Mr. Disraeli recognised the necessity of drawing arbitrary lines. Only
with reference to property of tenant voters in boroughs
was it deemed necessary to be entirely unarithmetical.
The assertion that there is no principle in a figure had
however immense effect. It produced a great impression
upon that class, not unknown in the House of Commons,
whose type is to be found in 'Locksley Hall;' men
who

>Answer to the purpose, easy things to understand.

Immediately after Mr. Disraeli had concluded the exposition of his Bill (March 18, 1867) he was followed
by Mr. Gladstone in a speech which must be nearly unparalleled as a feat of skill in debate. This is a strong
eulogium, but it will be easy to justify it by very matter-
of-fact considerations. Criticism upon the ministerial
plan is comparatively easy now. We have the advantage
of innumerable discussions on the subject. We have
access to returns—especially those on which the Chancellor of the Exchequer relied and which were afterwards
presented on the motion of Mr. Hunt and others not
in the possession of the House when the Bill was introduced. Above all we can study the scheme deliberately,
and are not compelled to hurriedly follow a speaker as
he expounds more or less distinctly its several provi-

---

* *Hansard*, vol. 185, col. 950.

sions. Mr. Gladstone had none of these advantages. Without a moment's pause he commenced an elaborate and minute analysis of the Bill and of the statistics produced in favour of it, and his conclusions have not in one single instance been displaced by later researches. Doubtless, his former experience as Chancellor of the Exchequer had made him familiar with the arithmetic of rates, assessed taxes, and cognate subjects. The protracted defence of his own Reform Bill in the preceding year rendered him peculiarly well qualified to examine any subsequent measure with the same object. But with all these explanations, the power of rapid and accurate analysis shown in his speech of March 18 is almost marvellous. There may possibly have been half-a-dozen men in England equally well acquainted with the facts with which he dealt: it may be doubted whether, besides himself, there was another who combined that knowledge with the requisite faculty of exposition.

In the course of his speech Mr. Gladstone examined the different property qualifications proposed, and contended that three-fourths of the enormous number of voters whom Mr. Disraeli paraded in different regiments as 20s. direct taxes men, educational franchise men, and 50*l*. savings bank men, were 'little more than men in buckram.' After explanation of his methods of calculation he arrived at the following result:—

I will venture to say that of these 237,000, in point of fact not as many as 140,000, when you have made the necessary deductions, will be added to the Register.

The calculation which has been made in a preceding page of this chapter makes the number 118,500. This estimate has been made after careful examination of the returns, and differs but little from that which Mr. Gladstone made while Mr. Disraeli was speaking and without opportunity of consulting authorities on the subject.

But the most remarkable instance of acumen in this speech was the mode in which it at once hit the worst but by no means the most obvious blot in the ministerial scheme—the *fine* imposed on the compound householder for the possession of the suffrage. Referring to the proposal of the Chancellor of the Exchequer that facilities should be given to the compound householder to get himself registered, Mr. Gladstone said:—

> But what is the meaning of these facilities? I am afraid the meaning of them is this: perhaps it is that the compound householder is to be fined in the difference between the rate which the landlord is bound to pay under the landlord's assessment and that which constitutes the amount he would have to pay if individually rated.*

This discovery of a gross oversight was made, not by the framers of the measure, who had full opportunities of considering it, but by a debater whose only source of information was Mr. Disraeli's own speech. The charge of fining the compound householder for his vote was now suggested for the first time, and it made the ministerialists very angry. But the charge was so undeniably accurate that subsequently the Government was compelled to admit it, and endeavoured to get rid of it by a new provision in the Bill.

This question of a 'fine' has been much mystified by vehement discussion, but there is no difficulty in showing how it was imposed under the original Bill and what steps were taken at a subsequent stage to remove it.

Clause 34 provided that a non-rated occupier might, in order to get a vote, claim to be rated '*in the* same manner and subject to the same conditions' as the existing 10*l*. householders under former Acts; '*and all the provisions of the said Acts shall apply accordingly.*' But the new claimants were to pay the *full* rates, not the composition.

* *Hansard*, vol. 186, col. 33.

The effect of all this would have been as follows. Heretofore when a non-rated 10*l.* householder claimed to be put on the rate book the existing law required him to pay, not the full rate, but the composition or commuted rate. This appears by the Reform Act of 1832 and Sir William Clay's Act of 1851.* But the non-rated claimants, under Mr. Disraeli's Bill, were required to pay the *full* rate. Obviously, however, they could not, under their private contract with their landlord, recover from him more than he had bargained to pay on their account; namely, the composition or reduced sum. Therefore the loss of the difference fell upon the tenants themselves. Debaters might quarrel with the use of the word 'fine' to describe the transaction, but about the incidence of the loss there could be no controversy among persons acquainted with the law of the subject.

The infliction of this mulct or pecuniary loss on a tenant seeking to be registered was so manifestly unjust that the Government ultimately admitted the necessity of altering the provisions of their Bill in this respect, and accordingly a clause was inserted in committee which provides that the claiming tenant—

may deduct from any rent due or accruing due from him in respect of the said dwelling house or other tenement *any amount paid by him* on account of the rates to which he may be rendered liable by this Act.†

This clause, however, merely shifts or endeavours to shift the loss from the tenant to the landlord. The parish has agreed to deduct 25 or 50 per cent. from the rate paid by the landlord. Mr. Disraeli, however, steps in, and tells the parishes that they shall take the full rate—tells the landlord to pay a larger sum than he bargained for when he fixed the amount of the rent. He, the landlord, may very reasonably exclaim against

* 2 Will. IV. c. 95. s. 30. 14 & 15 Vict. c. 14. s. 3.
† 30 & 31 Vict. c. 102, s. 7.

this exaction. He may argue that whether the tenant get a vote or not is a matter of indifference to him, and that he ought not to be subject to an uncontemplated deduction from his rent because the tenant takes an interest in politics.

As a matter of fact, it is already clear that the burden will not be shifted to the landlords. They have a very simple means in their own hands of preventing a loss to themselves. The rent is raised to cover the amount of the increased rate. This seems a very harsh proceeding against the tenant, but from the landlords' point of view it is not utterly unjustifiable. He has a right to insist on the fulfilment of the original compact between him and his tenant. The amount due to him from the tenant is suddenly subject to a certain diminution for no fault of his, and he naturally seeks to recoup himself by raising the rent. It can hardly be said that the proceeding is unconscientious. The part in the transaction which is unconscientious is that taken by the Government, which violently interferes in an arrangement with which the three parties to it—the parish, the landlord, and the tenant—are contented, and disturbs vested interests to satisfy an artificial theory of representation.

All the principal defects in the original Bill were instantly exposed in the speech of Mr. Gladstone on the occasion of its introduction, March 18, 1867. He cited a number of instances, to show the unequal operation of the projected law. Among the most conspicuous examples, he contrasted the results in Leeds and Thetford. In the great borough, with a population of more than a quarter of a million, the extension of the franchise would have been insignificant. In Thetford, a mere village, the result would have been household suffrage. Leeds is wholly under the Small Tenements Act, and considerably more than half the houses in the borough are compounded for.* Mr. Gladstone asked whether it was possible that the enfranchisement of this large number of persons should depend on the will of a vestry. With respect to Thetford, on the other hand, where there is no rating Act in operation, he observed—

'In the borough of Thetford the Bill of the right hon. gentleman will go to establish very close upon the principle of universal suffrage. But it is no borough at all; it is like a great number of other boroughs which the right hon. gentleman finds of use in drawing fancy comparisons between the county and borough representation. It is a village, or rather an assembly of villages constituting a rural district. There is a population of 4,200, of whom 829, or one in five, are male occupiers. That proportion is close upon universal suffrage. *And the same proportion throughout England will give a constituency of nearly* FOUR MILLIONS—which I imagine will entirely close the mouth of Mr. Beales. This is the way the right hon. gentleman proposes to deal with the borough of Thetford. An immense proportion of the people there are the mere peasantry of the country—and by that I mean they are unskilled labourers. . . . Before I accede to a franchise which is close upon universal suffrage—equal to it or to manhood residential suffrage—in those rural districts where there is no Small Tenements Act in operation, I should like to ask myself, first of all, whether I am prepared to endure the application of the principle to all the county constituencies of the country. Nothing can be more preposterous than that you should say to a peasant, or common hodman or day-labourer, earning 1s. 6d. or 2s. a day in a town where there is no composition in force, 'You shall have your franchise for nothing and be put on the register without knowing it;' while in great communities such as the vast parishes and boroughs of London, and many other towns of the country, you absolutely fine in time or money, or both, the compound householder.'†

In order to see the extreme diversity in the operation of the Bill accordingly as it applied to towns under or *not* under rating Acts, one of the simplest ways is to compare its effects in half-a-dozen boroughs of either

---

* The total number of male occupiers is 44,315; of them 20,855 are compound occupiers at rentals under 6*l*. In some of the parishes, houses at rentals under 8*l*. 5*s*., are compounded for.—*Electoral Statistics*, p. 155.

† *Hansard*, vol. 186, col. 30.

class. Mr. Hunt's return, No. 136, of 1867, enables us to do this, for it shows the number of persons occupying at rentals under 10*l*., whose rates are not compounded. These persons were qualified under the Bill. The whole of them would not, of course, come on the register, but it is not necessary to make the deduction for the present purpose of comparing the *relative* effects in different classes of towns.

In the following tables the second column shows the number of ratepayers qualified under the Bill; the fourth column shows how many in a thousand of the population would be so qualified.

Six Boroughs under Rating Acts.

	Population in 1866.	Personally rated occupiers under 10*l*. rental.	Number of such persons in every thousand of the population.
Gateshead	38,495	173	4
Truro	11,652	38	3
Merthyr Tydvil	96,717	399	4
Hull	104,873	64	0·6
Brighton	97,750	14	1·4
Kidderminster	14,064	24	0·8

Six Boroughs NOT *under Rating Acts.*

	Population in 1866.	Personally rated occupiers under 10*l*. rental.	Number of such persons in every thousand of the population.
Oldham	107,729	11,844	110
Sheffield	216,020	28,334	131
Stoke-on-Trent	111,072	15,171	135
Thetford	4,276	642	140
Thrisk	5,366	684	125
York	48,128	4,884	100

Thus it will be seen that in towns under the rating Acts, and in which consequently the compound householders abound, the Bill would have had little or no effect. In Brighton, for example, it enfranchises only fourteen in 10,000 of occupiers under the 10*l*. line. In

Hull and Kidderminster the results would be still more insignificant. Whereas in places *not* under Rating Acts the enfranchising effect would be from 100 to 140 times as great. In York, 100 out of every 1000, and in other places still more.

It has been shown in a former page that in all the boroughs of England and Wales there would be 118,400 occupiers enfranchised. *Taking into account the deductions* for non-payment of rates and non-residence, &c., we have the following general results:—

	Occupiers enfranchised.	Population in 1866.	Ratio of new votes to population. per thousand.
171 boroughs under rating Acts, partially or wholly	68,000	8,376,350	8
20 boroughs *not* under rating Acts.	50,400	950,350	53

That is to say, the enfranchising effect is between *six and seven times* as great in the boroughs not under rating Acts as in the others.

Mr. Gladstone concluded his analysis of the measure by designating it—

a Bill which utterly excludes all principle of selection, which excludes a vast number of the most skilled and most instructed of our working men, and which, where it admits any of them, admits along with them the poorest, the least instructed, and the most dependent, members of the community.

We may well suppose that if the Government had foreseen the fantastic incongruities of their scheme they would not have offered it to Parliament. It is but justice to them to say that it does not seem to have been framed with any special design of favouring the Conservative interest. The anomalies of the Bill depend mainly on the adoption or non-adoption of the Small Tenements Act—a matter not connected with party politics. There is only one way of accounting for the capricious character of the new scheme of

Reform—sheer ignorance. The Ministry had concocted their Bill with extreme haste, and evidently without having taken the precaution of ascertaining the existing law of rating and its effect upon the suffrage. They attempted to fit round pegs into square holes without knowing the shape of either.

Such a formidable exposure of blunders as that contained in Mr. Gladstone's speech on the introduction of the Bill would have killed any parliamentary measure in ordinary circumstances. But the circumstances were not ordinary. The House of Commons was almost universally determined that a Reform Bill of *one kind or another* must be passed before the end of the session. That consideration reconciled Parliament to defects and errors which at any other time would have been deemed intolerable. A conviction that the credit of the representative assembly itself was at stake oppressed members of all parties without distinction. If two successive sessions were to be occupied in fruitless attempts to deal with the subject the inevitable inference throughout the country would be that the House of Commons elected in 1865 was an utterly incapable and incompetent assembly. The *esprit de corps* united it in a manner of which there has been no previous experience in modern times. The question *now* was not what was the best method of Reform, but how to avoid the humiliation and ridicule of repeated failures.

Hence the feeling on both sides of the House, that bad as the Bill was it behoved them to make the best of it. This feeling actuated a large meeting of Liberal members, held at Mr. Gladstone's house, March 21, 1867, to consider the course to be adopted by them with reference to the ministerial measure. Mr. Gladstone said—

Since the printing of the Government Bill, having applied

himself day and night to the plan, he had not the smallest doubt in his own mind that the wiser course of the two was to oppose the Bill on the second reading. But then he had to confront the necessity of maintaining the union of the party; and that union could not be had except by a disposition to give way in matters which did not involve a sacrifice of essential principle. While he would be too happy to recommend them to oppose the second reading, he did not think the general disposition of the meeting would bear him out in that course.

The leader of the Opposition therefore reluctantly advised that the second reading should not be opposed and added that, 'if the Ministers were content to abandon the dual voting and to equalise the privileges and facilities of the enfranchised in all cases, however the qualification arose, then the measure might be made acceptable. If they would not concede those points then he thought that the Liberals should not permit the measure to go into committee.' Mr. Bright at this meeting said that he should have preferred resistance to the second reading, but that he was not prepared to take any course which might cause a division among the Liberal party, and he therefore gave his adhesion to the recommendation that the second reading of the Bill should not be opposed.

CHAPTER IX.

THE SECOND READING OF THE REFORM BILL 1867.

Ten objections to the Bill enumerated by Mr. Gladstone, 134.—Examples of irregular operation of the proposed Franchise, 137.—Mr. Hardy's defence of the measure, 139.—Rights of compound householders to be repaid rates paid by them, 143.—Comparison of Mr. Bright's Bill and that of the Government, 145.—The Government abandon the dual vote and offer other concessions, 150.

AFTER two nights' debate in the House of Commons the motion for the second reading of the Reform Bill was adopted (March 26, 1867) without a division.

At the commencement of the discussion upon this motion, Mr. Gladstone enumerated *ten* principal defects in the Bill which required amendment. It is important with respect to the subsequent history of the measure to observe, that of the amendments thus suggested nine were ultimately adopted.

The objections to the Bill, enumerated by Mr. Gladstone were as follows:—

1. Omission of a lodger franchise.
2. Omission of provisions against traffic in votes of householders of the lowest class by corrupt payment of their rates.
3. Disqualifications of compound householders under the existing law.
4. Additional disqualifications of compound householders under the proposed law.
5. The franchise founded on direct taxation.
6. The dual vote.
7 The inadequate redistribution of seats.
8. The inadequate reduction of the franchise in counties.

9. Voting papers.
10. Collateral or special franchises.*

Every one of the suggestions contained in this list, except the second (which involved a proposal that occupiers of houses below some specified value should be excluded from the suffrage), has been carried out in the Reform Act now passed. (1) The omission of a lodger franchise has been supplied; the disqualifications of compound householders, both (3) under the former law and (4) under the scheme of the Government, have been abrogated by the summary method of abolishing composition of rates; (5) the franchise founded on direct taxation has been omitted from the Act; (6) the dual vote disappeared soon after the second reading; (7) the scheme for redistribution of seats was greatly extended in committee; (8) the county franchise, originally fixed at $15l.$ rateable value, was reduced to $12l.$; (9) the method of voting papers was rejected; and finally (10), all the clauses about the collateral or special franchises disappeared.

The criticism applied by Mr. Gladstone to the Bill on the motion for the second reading foreshadowed with curious exactness the changes which the measure subsequently underwent. The dual vote he disposed of in this fashion:—

At the head of the list stand those favoured children of fortune—those select human beings made of finer clay than the rest of their fellow subjects—who are to be endowed with dual votes. Upon that dual vote I shall not trouble the House, for I think that my doing so would be a waste of time. Next to those dual voters, before whose eyes the glittering falsity has dangled—although, I fear, they can have but little hope of grasping it—come the old $10l.$ householders of 1832.†

He then insisted strenuously on the invidious distinctions attempted to be established between this class

* *Hansard*, vol. 186, col. 475. † *Ibid.*, col. 477.

and the newly-enfranchised voters. Of the 10*l*. householders only one year's occupation was required as a part of their qualification; of the householders below that line two years' residence was to be demanded. The 'facilities' for getting registered, which Mr. Disraeli had promised to the compound householder, turned out upon examination to be new obstacles:—

The construction of law is, that if the 75 per cent., or the composition whatever it is, has been paid by the landlord the rate has then been paid in full, and, consequently, there remains nothing for the compound householder to pay. . . . But what is the real case with regard to a large portion of the compositions of the country? It is stated that the deduction made to the landlord amounts in many cases, not to 25 but to 50 per cent., and the deduction of 50 per cent. is made upon the principle that the composition money is intended to cover full and empty houses alike.* So that when the compound householder comes before the revising barrister to make his claim he has to pay 50 per cent. more, 50 per cent. having been already paid. He has to pay the full rate—according to the decision of the courts over again—and consequently he has to pay not only for his own house but also for the house inhabited or which may be inhabited by his neighbour and in which he possesses no interest whatever.

Mr. Gladstone then proceeded to analyse the return made on the motion of Mr. Hunt, and insisted that this document rendered the Government scheme with respect to the non-rated householders 'totally and absolutely hopeless.' But he went further, and showed that, unfavourable as this return was towards the Bill, it

---

* An instance of an arrangement of this kind receiving the express sanction of the legislature is the following. By a local Act, 10 & 11 Vict., c. xxx, for assessments in the township of Bilston, it is provided that the owner of small tenements under 6*l*. 10*s*. rateable value, may give notice 'of his intention to compound for the same by the payment of a reduced rate, whether such tenements be occupied or not; and such owner, until notice to determine such composition, shall be liable to pay one-half of such rate only.' See *The Queen* v. *Dodd*, 1 Law Rep. Q. B. p. 16.

represents the number to be enfranchised in several cases too favourably. For instance:—

Liverpool figures for a very respectable number of constituents. There are 16,347 persons who are represented by this return as being within the beneficent scope of the enfranchising provisions of the right hon. gentleman's Bill. But what is the fact? That in Liverpool there are scarcely any such persons. I will not say there are not a mere handful, but I will say that this 16,347 is a figure totally and absolutely delusive. . . . . With regard to houses under 15*l*. rental the rates are habitually paid by owners—I speak of the parish of Liverpool—not by direct provision of law, but by *arrangement between the owners and parish authorities*. There is not one of the occupiers of those houses who would not be in the position of a compound householder, and therefore prevented from getting the benefit of the proposed franchise. . . . There are many other towns in which a voluntary arrangement of that character exists, and in which the occupier would be ousted from the franchise.

Mr. Gladstone then proceeded to give some statistics illustrating the capricious and irregular operation of the Bill, which created 'an extravagant franchise, flooding some towns with thousands of voters, and only adding a few in other towns.' Some of these statistics may, for the sake of brevity, be represented in a tabular form. First, with respect to towns under the Small Tenements Act, comparing the number of householders under 10*l*. who would be qualified with the non-rated householders who would be excluded, we have these results:—

Towns under the Small Tenements Act.

	Qualified.	Excluded.
Abingdon	35	574
Calne	25	695
Carlisle	406	3,571
Chippenham	20	727
Christchurch	41	523
Devizes	55	487
Evesham	40	464
Gateshead	173	557

The total number qualified in boroughs under the

Small Tenements Act would be 25,064, while the number excluded would be 139,377.

The following figures were given with regard to boroughs partially under the same Act:—

Boroughs partly under the Small Tenements Act.

	Qualified.	Excluded.
Andover	40	623
Aylesbury	446	3,514
Barnstaple	151	1,047
Bridgewater	56	1,234
Frome	38	1,363
Hull	64	12,026
Kidderminster	24	2,343

The case of Hull was a very gross instance of the anomalies of the Bill. Mr. Gladstone asked—

Is it possible that anyone on the Treasury benches can get up in his place and recommend these clauses with respect to the compound householders, with all their anomalies?

Then, in contrast, he showed that in certain towns, not under the rating Acts, a vast increase of the number of voters would take place. For instance:—

Towns not under Rating Acts.

	At present qualified.	New qualifications.
Oldham	3,300	11,800
Rochdale	1,858	5,500
Sheffield	10,000	28,000
Stockport	1,695	7,257
Stoke-upon-Trent	3,410	15,000

Mr. Gladstone concluded thus:—

If the right hon. gentleman will accept that principle—if he will ask Parliament to determine the classes, numbers, and persons, be they many or few, to be enfranchised; if he will remove the artificial obstacles which now exist in the Bill; if he will strike out of the Bill the artificial distinctions which he proposes to introduce; if he will establish for the future the old constitutional principle which comes to us from the past, of the equality of all voters in the eye of the law—then, although we shall have a heavy task before us, we may hope to be able to go into committee on this Bill. The dual vote will then, of course, disappear. The fine of the compound householder will disappear, and the restraint already placed in their way will disappear. We shall then enfranchise those classes which are fit to exercise the franchise.*

The task of replying to this speech was undertaken by Mr. Gathorne Hardy, then Commissioner of the Poor Laws, who commenced his observations with a graceful and liberal acknowledgment of the mastery of his subject which Mr. Gladstone had exhibited. Mr. Hardy's reply deserves consideration because it is a fair and candid defence of the measure before the House. As a test also of the objections to the Bill, it is desirable to examine the best apology which could be made in its behalf.

After some general observations on the failure of former Reform Bills and the importance of settling a disquieting subject, the President of the Poor Law Board proceeded to deal with Mr. Gladstone's statistical arguments, as follows:—

He says—but I hardly know what I am to meet on this occasion. On one side I am told that I am a party to a revolutionary measure, and on the other hand I am told that the enfranchisement which we offer is entirely insufficient. We are told that the 7*l*. rental franchise of last year without the payment of rates would have brought in men of an entirely different quality from those we now seek to bring in, and that we should give up our Bill at once on that statement. But I venture to say that if any hon. member will take the trouble to look, he will find that the 7*l*. rental franchise would bring in men inferior in quality to those we seek to introduce by the personal payment of rates.†

In support of this assertion no evidence was produced. There are not any returns showing the 'quality' either of 7*l*. householders or of any other class. In boroughs not under the rating Acts the Government measure proposed to enfranchise the very lowest class of

* *Hansard*, vol. 186, col. 504. † *Hansard*, vol. 186, col. 507.

ratepayers, and therefore, obviously, many persons who are on the verge of pauperism. The 7*l.* line would certainly have excluded the greater part of this class.

Besides, Mr. Hardy entirely misconceives the argument to which he replies. Mr. Gladstone had never contended that the Bill proposed by the Ministry introduced *in the aggregate* too large a number of borough voters, but that in particular places its operation was extravagant. It cannot be too broadly stated that so far as *the totals* were concerned, the ministerial measure in its original form was less liberal to the artisan than that of 1866. The absolute number of new voters in boroughs would have been smaller. Moreover, the dual vote tended to diminish the relative power of the working classes; so that instead of being 'democratic' the Bill of 1867, in its inception, was designed to increase the political weight of the wealthier orders. The number of *votes* given to householders at rentals of 20*l.* and upwards would have been relatively greater than ever before. The Bill of 1867, before it was modified in committee, was, it must be emphatically asserted, essentially anti-democratic.

Mr. Hardy then proceeded to consider the obstacles imposed on the householders who sought to be registered:—

> The answer to the whole of this is, that we propose a certain franchise which is open to everybody occupying a house and paying his own rates. Every person who chooses to pay his own rates and does pay them, and who resides long enough, is entitled to be put on the register. The right hon. gentleman then says, 'Oh yes; but how is he to get on the register? Look at the burden which is imposed upon him; look at the difficulties under which he is placed.' If that is so, let the right hon. gentleman in committee propose that the claim shall be more readily received, and a means established by which he should be more easily put upon the register.*

* Hansard, vol. 186, col. 508.

This is virtually a surrender of the whole argument. Mr. Hardy says in effect, 'We have created the difficulty; you, the opposition, may suggest a way of obviating it.' How was the non-rated occupier to be 'more easily put upon the register?' Mr. Gladstone had provided a very simple plan for the purpose in the preceding year. But that plan depended essentially on the abrogation of the rule which required the borough voter to be rated. Now the Government insisted upon making this condition of greater importance than ever before.

With respect to the 'fine' imposed on the non-rated householder, the difference between the full rate and the commuted rate, Mr. Hardy said:—

> By the 7th section of the 13 & 14 Vict. c. 99, he will also see that any occupier paying any rate or rates in respect of any tenement where the owner is rated to the same, shall be entitled to deduct from his rent or to recover from the owner himself the amount so paid.
>
> *Sir Roundell Palmer.*—The provisions of that Act are not included in the 40th clause [of the new Reform Bill].
>
> *Mr. Gathorne Hardy.*—I can only say that they were meant to be, and that a man shall be entitled to recover from his landlord the amount he has paid. It is obvious justice requires that it should be so.*

If this reference to the Act 13 & 14 Vict. c. 99 (the Small Tenements Act of 1850), had been accurate, there would have been an end of the objection respecting a 'fine.' But the Act in question does not give the compound householder power to deduct from his rent a full rate paid by him. Section 7 provides that for the purpose of enjoying the *municipal*, not the electoral franchise, a compound householder may pay 'all money due on account of any rate or rates in respect of such tenement,' and deduct the amount from his rent. He may pay and deduct from his rent the amount 'due;' that is, the commuted or reduced rate.

The President of the Poor Law Board says it was

* *Hansard*, vol. 186, col. 512.

intended to incorporate that provision in the new Bill. But if it had been so incorporated the injustice of which Mr. Gladstone complained would not have been remedied in the slightest degree. The difficulty was inherent in the Government scheme, and could not be obviated by any contrivance of legislation. A new charge was imposed on the compound householder, the increase of his rates beyond the amount for which his landlord had bargained. That burden must be borne either by him or his landlord. A subsequent amendment of the Bill shifted or attempted to shift it to the landlord's shoulders; this was no cure for the injustice, but merely altered the incidence of it.

This very simple subject was mystified in the debates to a degree almost inconceivable. It was argued with some plausibility, that as the parish was not to have the benefit of the system of compounding it was only fair that the full rate should be paid. The relation between the two kinds of payment may be likened to wholesale and retail trade. The compounding landlord in fact *farmed* a certain public revenue, just as the *fermiers généraux* did in France before the Revolution of 1789. If the parishes were to lose the benefit of this system why, it was asked, should they not revert to the old system of full rating ? This point was thus put by the Solicitor General, Sir John Karslake, in this debate on the second reading:—

If, however, a person occupies a tenement the rates on which were paid by the landlord, and if for his own convenience, and for the purpose of exercising the privilege of voting, he desires to be rated, what reason is there why he should only pay the same composition as the landlord who had not the same advantage for the payment as the tenant? There was a reason for exempting the landlord in some degree; but there can be no reason why an occupier who desires to exercise the franchise should not pay the full amount of the rates to which the tenement he occupies is liable, just as other tenants are obliged to do.

It will be observed, in the first place, that the Solicitor-General directly contradicts the President of the Poor Law Board. Mr. Hardy says it is 'obvious justice' that the burden of the increased rate should fall on the landlord; Sir John Karslake is equally clear, that it ought to fall on the tenant. In the second place, it is observable that his argument is one which can be adduced on behalf of the parish only. As far as the parish is concerned, it may be admitted that the right to a full rate is complete, if the compounding system be abolished. But there are two other parties in the transaction—the landlord and the tenant, and the equities between *them* are totally ignored.

The Solicitor-General gave a strange exposition of the law of Landlord and Tenant. He said:—

> Is it not the case that from the year 1832 down to the present moment—at all events for years after the passing of that Act [the Reform Act of 1832]—persons who asked to be rated, in cases where the landlords had previously compounded for the rates, have had to pay, not the compounded but the full rate, and that there was *no provision for their being recouped by the landlord at all?* . . . From 1832 to 1851 they had been 'fined,' they had continued to pay the rate without power of recoupment from the landlord.*

Sir John Karslake thus asserts that from the time of the Reform Act to the passing of Sir William Clay's Act in 1851, compound householders paying their rates for the sake of being registered, could not recover the amount from their landlords. If the Solicitor-General had looked to the first general Act authorising composition of rates, that of 1819, he might have found in it the very provision which he says was not enacted until 1851.

Section 20 of the Statute (59 George III. c. 12) contains this provision:—

> Provided also, that every occupier who shall pay any such rate or rates, or upon whose goods or chattels the same or any part

---

* *Hansard*, vol. 186, col. 547

thereof shall be levied, shall and may deduct the amount of the sum which shall be so paid or levied out of the rent by him or them payable; and such payment shall be a sufficient discharge to every such occupier, for so much of the rent payable by him as he shall have paid, or as shall have been levied on his goods and chattels, of such rate, and for the costs of levying the same.

Thus it will be seen that the Legislature of 1819 did not commit the monstrous injustice which Sir John Karslake imputes to it. Moreover, it is well settled at common law, irrespectively of statutes, that a tenant voluntarily paying a tax for which the landlord is liable, may recover the amount from him.* A bargain having been made between the tenant and the landlord that the latter should pay the rates, it would have been preposterous to allow this obligation to be evaded. According to the Solicitor-General the landlord had merely to refrain from making the stipulated payment; the parish would then come down upon the unfortunate tenant for the rate; he would have no redress, and the landlord might cheat him with absolute impunity. The law of England contains many indefensible things, but nothing quite so gross as that.

What with Mr. Disraeli's erroneous statistics of the Bill, Mr. Hardy's misconception of its provisions, and Sir John Karslake's inaccurate view of the law proposed to be altered—is it surprising that the measure was a bad one? The truth was simply this: the compilers of the scheme had not taken the trouble to investigate the intricate system with which they were dealing. By 'muddling and meddling' they produced a result of intolerable confusion.

Mr. Bright, at the previous conference of Liberal members, had recommended that the Bill should be opposed in the second reading, but had surrendered his own opinion on that point for the sake of concord. In

* See *infra* note to Chap. x.

his speech on the motion for the second reading, he expressed a more uncompromising hostility to the Bill than Mr. Gladstone had done. He designated it as a measure 'in which, looking at the working-class question, there is nothing clear, nothing generous, nothing statesmanlike.' But he expressly guarded himself, as he had done upon several previous occasions, against the supposition that he recommended unrestricted household suffrage. He said:—

At this moment, in all or nearly all our boroughs, as many of us know sometimes to our sorrow, there is a small class, which it would be much better for themselves if they were not enfranchised, because they have no independence whatever; and it would be much better for the constituency also that they should be excluded, and there is no class so much interested in having that small class excluded as the intelligent and honest working-men. I call this class the *residuum* which there is in almost every constituency, of almost hopeless poverty and dependence.*

Mr. Bright then referred to the Bill † prepared by him in 1859, and added:—

In speaking of that Bill, I stated that there was a class which I thought it would not be any advantage to this class, or to the constituency, or the public, to admit to the franchise.

---

* *Hansard*, vol. 186, col. 637.

† The following is a copy of Clause xxv. of Mr. Bright's Bill of 1859:—

'In every city or borough which shall return a member or members to serve in Parliament, every male person, of full age and not subject to any legal incapacity, who for twelve months next previous to the last day of July in any year, shall have occupied within such city or borough, or within any place sharing in the election for such city or borough, as owner or occupier, any house, warehouse, counting-house, shop, or other building, in respect whereof he shall have been rated, during the time of such occupation, to all rates for the relief of the poor of the parish or township in which such premises are situate, and shall have paid, on or before the 12th day of July in each year, all the poor-rates which shall have become payable from him in respect of such premises, previously to the 5th day of January then next preceding, and who, during the time of such occupation, shall have resided within such city, or borough, or place respectively, or within seven statute miles thereof, or of any part thereof, shall be entitled to be registered, and to vote in the election of a member or members to serve in Parliament for such city or borough.'

L

The clause in Mr. Bright's Bill respecting occupiers who pay their own rates was identical in effect with the corresponding clause of the Ministerial Bill of 1867, excepting that he required only one year's occupation and included occupiers of other buildings besides dwelling houses.

With respect to non-rated occcupiers, the arrangement which he had proposed was that any compound householder, by paying the composition or reduced rate, should be entitled to be registered, and that he should be able to deduct the amount so paid from his rent. The Ministerial plan differed from this in requiring the occupier to pay the full rate.*

Then came a provision to which there is nothing analogous in the later Bill. Mr. Bright's proposition in 1859 was, that all compound householders of tenements rented at 4*l.* per annum, or rated at 3*l.*, should be placed on the Rate Book, and be entitled to be registered so long as the rates were duly paid.† It will be observed, that this plan is materially different from what would be ordinarily understood as a 4*l.* rental franchise. Mr. Bright proposed that *all* householders who chose to pay their own rates should be placed on the register; but of non-rated householders, those should be registered whose tenements were rented at 4*l.* or

* By Clause xxviii. of Mr. Bright's Bill, it was provided 'that in cases where, by any composition with the landlord, a less sum shall be payable than the full amount of rate. . . the occupier claiming to be rated shall not be bound to pay or tender more than the amount then payable under such composition. . . And any occupier so paying any rate in respect of any tenement where the landlord is rated to the same, shall be entitled to deduct and retain the amount so paid by him from the next payment of rent to be made by him to such landlord, or to recover the same, &c.'

† Clause xxix. provides that, 'where the landlord of any such premises as aforesaid, of the clear yearly value of not less than 4*l.*, and rated at not less than 3*l.* . . shall, on or before the 20th of July in any year, have paid all money due before the 5th day of January in such year on account of any rate or rates in respect of such premises, such occupier shall be entitled to have his name placed on the Rate Book in respect of such premises, and to be registered and to vote.'

rated at 3*l.* This plan is less 'democratic' than that which has now been adopted in the Reform Act of 1867, which abolishes composition *in toto,* and therefore renders all borough occupiers, without any limitation as to the value of their property, liable to be rated and registered.

Mr. Bright's objections to the Ministerial Bill were founded partly on the recent statistics, partly on the restrictive effect of the dual vote and two years' residence, and partly on the inadequacy of the scheme for the redistribution of seats. He concluded :—

It seems to me impossible to assist a Government which will not tell us frankly what it intends, what it stands by, and what it will get rid of—which is the most reticent Government that probably ever sat on these benches. If any gentlemen on this side were to treat you as you treated us last year, I should denounce them with the strongest language that I could use. I hate the ways and I scorn the purposes of faction ; and if I am driven now, or in any stage of the Bill, to oppose the Government, it is because the measure they have offered to us bears upon its face marks of deception and disappointment, and because I will be no party to any measure which shall cheat the great body of my countrymen of the possession of that power in this House on which they have set their hearts, and which, as I believe by the Constitution of this country, they may most justly claim.*

Mr. Roebuck took part in the debate. It is interesting to compare the sentiments expressed by him on this occasion with a speech which he made, about twelve months previously, to his constituents at Sheffield. On Monday, April 2, 1866, at a crowded meeting at the Temperance Hall in that town, the hon. member stated, in reference to Mr. Gladstone's Reform Bill, that ' the measure was an honest one. It proposed to do more than merely enlarge the franchise. It was to do away with the ratepaying clauses, to get rid of which he had been fighting for years.'†

* *Hansard,* vol. 186, col. 642.
† *Daily Telegraph,* April 4, 1866 (page 4, col. 6).

But further reflection tended to materially modify Mr. Roebuck's views. By March 25, 1867, he discovered that the ratepaying clauses, against which he 'had been fighting for years,' were supremely just and proper; that when a man was required to pay rates as a condition of the suffrage, he was 'simply called upon to bear his fair share of the burdens of the State.' The passage which contains this remarkable palinode is as follows:—

Why do compound householders exist? For the benefit of the State. In order that the landlord may have a *quid pro quo* for taking upon himself the duty of paying the rate, the rate is made less to him. But when a man, instead of having his rates paid by his landlord, becomes part of the State, and enjoys the right of voting, is he to turn round, and say he wishes to be in the position which he occupied before he possessed that privilege? No! We tell him, 'Now you are a voter you must do as other voters do.' That is but plain common-sense, and the invidious word 'fine' is, I think, not worthy of the right honourable gentleman. There is no fine in the case. A man is simply called upon to bear his fair share of the burdens of the State. I hope that the Government will not shrink in this matter. The virtue, the intelligence, and the sagacity of the country are anxiously looking for the settlement of this question.*

And so was Mr. Roebuck.

The debate on the second reading was concluded by the Chancellor of the Exchequer, in an oration of considerable length. The speeches of Mr. Disraeli are almost universally characterised by the fallacy which logicians term *ignoratio elenchi*. This unsound mode of argument occurs, according to Archbishop Whately, 'when the conclusion is not the one required, but irrelevant; which fallacy is commonly called *ignoratio elenchi*, because your argument is not the *elenchus* (i. e. the proof of the *contradictory*) of your opponent's assertion, which it should be; but proves, instead of that, some other proposition resembling it.' † For instance, in the course of the debate, Sir Roundell Palmer had

* *Hansard*, vol. 186, col. 543. † *Elements of Logic*, book iii. sect. 3.

given an elaborate exposition of the law of rates as it affected the suffrage, and had shown, by a frequent reference to authorities, that the Government had misconceived the legal obligations of compound householders. Of course it was possible that the learned Member for Richmond had mistaken the authorities cited, or drawn erroneous inferences from them. But, at all events, the argument was one which demanded direct refutation, if the Ministerial measure was to be carried by the force of reason, and not by appeals to prejudice and partisanship. Mr. Disraeli, however, considered it would be sufficient to convince his hearers that Sir Roundell Palmer's strictures were —not incorrect—but hypercritical. The Chancellor of the Exchequer condensed his reply into an anecdote. He amused the sympathetic portion of his audience with a somewhat pointless story of the mode in which an elaborate speech made in that House on a certain occasion by a lawyer was answered

by Sir James Graham, whose name is not often mentioned in this House, but is never by me to be mentioned without respect and affection; for he was one of the most considerable men we ever had in this House. He rose in his stately cynicism and exclaimed, 'Let us get out of the region of *Nisi Prius;*' and when we come here to offer the franchise to the people of England—notwithstanding the imputations of the hon. Member for Birmingham—in a spirit of sincerity and truth : when we offer to establish it on a principle that no one can controvert, and to apply it without limit—when I heard those observations of the hon. and learned gentleman the Member for Richmond, I recollected the observation of Sir James Graham, and say we must get out of the region of Nisi Prius ! *

This secondhand 'stately cynicism' was the sole and entire answer to an argumentative speech, in which, without invective, without any appeal except to the reasoning faculties of his hearers, Sir Roundell Palmer had demonstrated, or at least endeavoured to demon-

* *Hansard*, vol. 186, col. 657.

strate, that the Ministerial scheme involved fundamental errors respecting matters of law. Sir James Graham had refuted an opponent by an exclamation; why should not Mr. Disraeli do the like? This method of reply had the merit of extreme facility and brevity. The story had not much in it, but the Minister knew his audience. He knew that, to a great part of them, an exhortation to quit the region of Nisi Prius would appear a sufficient confutation of arguments which they would not endeavour to comprehend. Possibly this logic is less satisfactory to the larger audience out-of-doors. Possibly the ready acceptance which it obtains in the House of Commons may be deemed by reflecting observers an additional evidence of the need of reform in that assembly.

Mr. Disraeli's speech on the second reading was principally interesting for indications of those parts of the measure which he declared his intention to maintain, and those which he was already prepared to abandon. With respect to the dual vote, he acknowledged that it had been generally opposed; that 'from first to last no one had spoken a single word in its favour;' and that 'it would therefore have been worse than idle to persist against such opposition.' As to the condition of two years' residence, he admitted that there was, at first sight, something invidious 'in having one household qualification based on one year, and another for a longer term;' and added that, 'If you make any proposition in Committee with a view to remove this invidious character without destroying the fundamental condition, we shall, of course, be prepared to consider it.' Respecting the franchise founded on direct taxation, 'whether the House will abandon it or not is a subject for future consideration.' The proposal for a larger reduction of the county franchise was 'entirely for discussion in Committee.' The subject of voting-papers was one 'on which the opinion of the House ought to be taken.' Respecting the enfranchisement of lodgers, the Chancellor of the Exchequer said: 'The lodger franchise, if we get into Committee, will be discussed with candour and calmness.'

This large surrender tended to materially alter the character of the Ministerial scheme of Reform. The absolute abandonment of the dual vote, if there had been no other departure from the original plan, rendered the Bill substantially a new measure; for the dual suffrage, as was shown in a preceding page, would have given to the wealthier ranks such a large number of votes that the preponderance of their power over that of the working-classes would have been increased, instead of being diminished.

But with respect to the main objection to his Bill—the difficulty of the compound householder, and the irregular and capricious operation of the proposed borough franchise—Mr. Disraeli, at this time, gave no hope of concession. The arguments respecting the anomalous results he laughed away. Anomalies existed already, and afforded 'that varied representation of interests which India and our multifarious colonies, the settlements of two oceans and of two hemispheres, demanded.' The right hon. gentleman did not explain what relation colonies, oceans, and hemispheres have to the enfranchisement of compound householders in one-half of the town of Bristol, in the whole of Sheffield, but not in any part of Leeds. On this matter he observed:—

I say of these Local Rating Acts which have been so criticised—these Small Tenements Acts, which prevail, we are given to understand, with a power as secret and inscrutable as that of the Jesuits—that they can absolutely, though unintentionally, give us that variety which the country requires, and which I believe is an admirable quality.*

* *Hansard*, vol. 186, col. 650.

It is also worthy of particular observation that in this speech Mr. Disraeli distinctly refused that abrogation of the Small Tenements Acts which at a subsequent crisis he conceded. A few weeks later, the House was assured that by abolishing them it would promote the principles which he had all along maintained. On the present occasion he adopted very different language. Referring to Mr. Gladstone, he said:—

> The third menace of the right hon. gentleman was of this nature. He says the distinction between different classes of ratepayers must be abolished. Now, that is a very serious question, and one on which a decision ought not to be pronounced by the House in haste. I very much doubt the policy in a country like England, and with institutions such as here prevail, of attempting by artificial means to obtain anything like a similarity of suffrage, at a sacrifice of what I may venture to call the natural circumstances in which we are placed. It is most desirable not to deal, in a Bill like the present, with any privileges which happen previously to exist.*

The Chancellor of the Exchequer concluded his speech with these words:—

> We will not shrink from deferring to your suggestions so long as they are consistent with the main object of this Bill, which we have never concealed from you, and which is to preserve the representative character of the House of Commons. Act with us, I say, cordially and candidly—you will find on our side complete reciprocity of feeling. Pass the Bill, and then change the Ministry if you like.

As though he would say—Reform, not place, is the grand object of all our hopes and desires. It was for the sake of Reform, not place, that we struggled and fought last year, and used every wile and stratagem of parliamentary warfare, until we had overthrown our opponents. We are veteran Reformers, who have devoted our past lives to the exposure of defects in the Representative System. Have we not agitated, in and out of Parliament,

---

* *Hansard*, vol. 186, col. 649.

these many years to get it amended? Have we not, by pamphlets, speeches at public meetings, and every other legitimate method, laboured to make our countrymen understand the inequalities and injustice of the present state of the suffrage? Are we not ourselves profoundly versed in all its mysteries and intricacies? Do not our 'Resolutions,' and our Six-pound Franchise Bill, and this new scheme of a rating franchise, all show that we have thoroughly considered the subject, and have established in our own minds fixed, definite and thoroughly matured principles respecting it? Our zeal for Reform consumes us. To an ardent desire to amend the representation we are ready to sacrifice everything—place, honour, power, and patronage. We are ready—nay, eager—to become the martyrs of Reform. Our care is not for ourselves, but for our country. If by a self-sacrifice we can secure for our beloved country the blessings of Reform, we are ready to meet political death to-morrow!

CHAPTER X.

THE REFORM BILL OF 1867 IN COMMITTEE—BOROUGH SUFFRAGE.

Three classes of amendments of the proposed Borough Franchise, 156.—*The Ministerial Amendments affecting compound householders,* 158.—*Meeting of the Liberal Party; Mr. Coleridge's 'Instruction,'* 160.—*The 'tea-room' schism: part of the Instruction abandoned, and the rest accepted by the Government,* 162. — *Mr. Gladstone's Amendment to enfranchise non-rated tenants,* 165.—*The principle of 'personal payment' is not embodied in the Bill,* 169.—*Public meetings: addresses to Mr. Gladstone,* 173.

MORE than five weeks were occupied by the discussion of the borough franchise in Committee of the House of Commons. The discussion began on the 11th of April, and Clause 3 (relating to the occupation franchise for voters in boroughs) was passed on the 20th of May. As a prelude to this portion of the history of the Bill, it will be instructive to read Mr. Disraeli's own account of it, given in, after the close of the Session, at a public dinner at Edinburgh. In an elaborate retrospect of the Parliamentary campaign, he thus defended the enormous changes which the Government suffered to be made in their measure:—

As for attempting to do away with the compound householder when Parliament first met, we should have had all the vestries in London agitating; and Mr. Gladstone himself, quietly contemplating our difficulties, had announced that the laws under which the compound householder existed were the result of the civilisation of the age. But as things went on we got a little stronger, and our opinions were more understood. Months afterwards the Liberal party themselves proposed to do away with the compound householder. . . . . What was it our duty to do? It would have been most inconsistent in us to reject that. I say that the compound householder bowing down, giving up his peculiar position, and seeing that to exercise the franchise he would pay rates, was the very triumph of the principle of our Bill.*

It will be easy for us to test the accuracy of these statements by evidence which is irrefragable,—Mr. Disraeli's own speeches in Parliament. At Edinburgh he gave his audience to understand that the abolition of the compound householder was contemplated by him from the commencement of the Session, but that he abstained from postponing it at that time to avoid unnecessary agitation; that after a while the Liberals were driven, by stress of circumstances, to adopt the views which he had all along secretly entertained.

In these pages the reader will have the materials for forming his own opinion upon this point. Before Mr. Hodgkinson's amendment was announced, the Chancellor of the Exchequer had declared his objections to that very change which it proposed. On the second reading of the Bill, March 26, as we have seen, he insisted that the Small Tenements Acts operated advantageously, by producing a beneficial variety in the composition of constituencies, and commented on the injustice of procuring similarity of suffrage by a sacrifice of existing rights. The House, therefore, was led to believe, that at that period he was in favour of maintaining the Small Tenements Acts, and thought their operation positively beneficial. If, as appears from the subsequent statement at Edinburgh, Mr. Disraeli entertained in his own breast an altogether different policy, his statements to the House of Commons were of a class which it is not desirable to characterise in concise language.

Again, we shall find, in the course of these pages, that up to the eleventh hour, when Mr. Hodgkinson's amendment was suddenly interposed and accepted, the Chan-

* *Times*, October 30, 1867.

cellor of the Exchequer was offering expedient after
expedient—resolution after resolution—to facilitate the
difficulties of the compound householder. We are now
informed that at the very period when he was amusing
the House of Commons and the country with this 'century of inventions,' he had resolved upon a policy which
would render all his ingenuity and industry superfluous.
This, in effect, is the burden of his defence; and it was
addressed to sympathising auditors. Many persons
accept without scrutiny all statements offered on their
own side of a question. *Qui vult decipi decipiatur*.

The five weeks' discussion in Committee, respecting
the borough franchise, was intricate and confused. The
best way of presenting the results in an intelligible form
is to classify, broadly, the principal projects offered to
Parliament for the solution of the question. These
were:—

1. The Ministerial proposal to extend the borough
suffrage to occupiers who paid their rates 'personally.'
This plan was supplemented by various amendments,
intended to facilitate the registration of compound householders.

2. There were various plans to establish a 'hard and
fast line' respecting these tenants—that is, to make the
extension of the suffrage to them depend, in some way
or other, on the value of their tenements. Thus
Earl Grosvenor gave notice of amendments, 'limiting
the virtual extension of the franchise in boroughs to
owners and tenants occupying dwelling-houses within
the borough of the rateable value of 5l. and upwards, and fixing the personal payment of rates at the
same point.' Mr. Poulett Scrope, a highly-esteemed
member, who had devoted much attention to the
subject of rating, proposed 'that the occupiers of houses
under —— pounds' annual value be wholly exempted

from the payment of rates, and that those householders in parliamentary boroughs who occupy houses above that value shall alone be entitled to be registered as voters under this Bill; and such persons shall be so entitled, whether they are rated in person, or that the rates in respect of the houses occupied by them be levied from the owners under the Small Tenements or any other Act.' The two amendments just mentioned were placed on the Notice Book in March. At a somewhat later date, an 'instruction,' which stood in the name of Mr. Coleridge, recommended that 'in every parliamentary borough the occupiers of tenements below a given rateable value be relieved from liability to personal rating, with a view to fix a line for the borough franchise, at and above which all occupiers shall be entered upon the Rate Book.'

3. There was the solution ultimately accepted—the abolition of the system of compounding for rates.

All the schemes for making the borough franchise dependent on the value of the qualifying tenements failed, for various reasons. Among others was the influence of the Ministry, which fathered the 'rating principle,' and maintained it with parental affection. The parrot-cries about a 'hard and fast line,' and 'no principle in a figure,' were repeated so often that many members accepted them as incontrovertible truths. Lastly, the Radicals objected to the 'hard and fast line' as a formidable obstacle to household suffrage, which they desired. Upon this point they supported Mr. Disraeli rather than Mr. Gladstone. The latter recommended that a test of value should be adopted, as the only practicable method of drawing a distinction between qualified voters and occupiers whom it was desirable to exclude from the suffrage. The Chancellor of the Exchequer, of course, opposed any solution recommended by Mr. Gladstone. The Radicals calculated, and (as the event shows) correctly, that Mr. Disraeli, in his anxiety to retain power, would consent to have his Bill converted into an extremely democratic measure, and therefore dissented upon this point from the policy of the leader of the Opposition.

After the second reading, the Government, believing itself to be sufficiently strong, showed at first a disinclination to make concessions respecting the borough qualification. On the 2nd April, Mr. Gladstone asked in the House of Commons, 'Whether it is the intention of Her Majesty's Government to make any alteration in the arrangement or the provisions of the Bill for Amending the Representation of the People before inviting the House to discuss the clauses in Committee?' At that time the Chancellor of the Exchequer refused to suggest any such alterations. He said, 'I think the House in Committee will be able to find the best solution, and that we shall enter into that Committee with the most anxious desire, in co-operation with the House, to bring the subject of Parliamentary Reform to a speedy and satisfactory conclusion.' * But, two days later, the rumours of combined opposition by the Liberals to his scheme induced him to promise further modifications. On the 6th April he announced 'a series of clauses as to the modes by which the right of compound householders to claim the franchise should be established. He was in hopes that he should have been able to lay these clauses upon the table that evening; but he had not been able to do so, on account of the difficulty of the subject, and the great consideration which it required.'†

This statement should be compared with that made at the Edinburgh dinner in October. On the later occasion, the Chancellor of the Exchequer said that the abolition of the Small Tenements Act was contemplated by him from the commencement of the Session.

* *Hansard*, vol. 186, col. 903.   † *Ibid.* col. 1105.

On April 4, however, we find him offering a series of expedients which, retaining those Acts, sought to mitigate the difficulties in which Mr. Disraeli had involved himself by his ignorance of their effects.

The principal regulations now suggested by the Government with respect to rating were as follows:—The full rateable value and name of every occupier was to be entered in the rate-book; every occupier might send in his claim by post; the overseer in return was to state the amount of rate due; on payment of that amount, the overseer was to enter the occupier as liable to the rates. The occupier might 'deduct from any rent due or accruing due from him to the owner any sum which *the owner would have been liable to pay if the occupier had not paid the rates.*'

It will be observed that it was now proposed that the compound householder should be allowed to be registered on *payment* of the *full rate*, and should be permitted to deduct from his rent the commuted or *reduced* rate. That is, the difference was to come out of the tenant's pocket. In the Act as ultimately passed, the tenant is allowed to deduct the full rate from his rent, and thus an attempt is made to shift the burden to the landlord.

On Friday, April 5, a very large meeting of the Liberal party was held at Mr. Gladstone's house. The number of members of the House of Commons present is stated to have been 259. Mr. Gladstone said that 'he considered himself, in abandoning his opposition to the second reading, as having bound himself, and those whom he might influence, to take every possible means of working the Bill through the Committee, if they had a prospect which justified them in persevering in that course, and to keep that object in view in all good faith.' He deemed it 'necessary that they should go into Committee on the Reform Bill with power to alter the law of rating; and their special point should be that below a certain line the franchise should not be enjoyed, whilst above that line all occupiers should be admitted to vote. The power could be given only by an 'instruction' to the Committee.' He then suggested that Mr. Coleridge, the member for Exeter, should be requested to move the proposed Instruction.

Mr. Gladstone added:—

On Monday he had asked the Chancellor of the Exchequer whether he would be willing to make alterations in the Bill. The Chancellor of the Exchequer distinctly informed him that he intended to strike out the dual vote, but that for everything else they were to trust to the Government. That was on Monday. But it doubtless became known that it was their intention to press strongly for an enlargement of the franchise to be given by the Government Bill; and the consequence was that last night the right hon. gentleman told them that clauses would be prepared as additions to the present Bill which would facilitate the giving of the vote to compound householders.

The suggested 'instruction' was in the following terms:—

That it be an instruction to the Committee that they have power to alter the law of rating;

And to provide that in every parliamentary borough the occupiers of tenements below a given rateable value be relieved from liability to personal rating; with a view to fix a line for the borough franchise, at and above which all occupiers shall be entered on the rate-book, and shall have equal facilities for the enjoyment of such franchise as a residential occupation franchise.

Several members who attended the meeting objected to the latter clause of this instruction. Mr. Locke thought it would be better to give power to the Committee merely to alter the law of rating. 'The effect of the latter part of the resolution would be to lessen the number of persons who would be placed on the register.' Mr. Clay was of the same opinion. He was opposed to 'an Instruction which would be fatal to the Bill, whereas a good Bill might be made if they contented themselves with the first line only of the Instruction.'

Mr. Bright said:—

The Government Bill gave to a small number of boroughs household suffrage; but in by far the greater number of boroughs, it gave a suffrage which was scarcely extended at all. It was impossible to accept the Bill as it stood. Some thought the House might alter the Bill so as to give household suffrage, but he thought the House were not in favour of any such change. He wished they were. He would support it with a great deal of pleasure; but as they were not, he should be sorry that the Bill should come out of Committee as it goes in, and without some provision for a wide extension of the suffrage in many boroughs in which it will remain limited under the Government Bill. . . . . . It was just possible that a proposition might be made by the Government that would render it unnecessary and undesirable to take any steps before the Bill goes into Committee. But knowing what they knew, he gave his most cordial assent to the Instruction.*

The same evening, notice was given in the House of Commons that on the motion for going into Committee on the Reform Bill, Mr. Coleridge would move the Instruction above quoted.

This form was adopted because it was considered that the rules of the House did not permit the Committee to deal with the law of rating without previously receiving power for that purpose. The proposal was — not to relieve any houses from being rated—but to compel the collection of rates of houses below the 'line' from the landlords. For example, if the line had been fixed at 5l., the effect would have been to extend the system of the Small Tenements Act to houses of 5l. instead of 6l. rateable value, and to make the system compulsory instead of optional.

Many of the more advanced reformers believed that

* *Daily Telegraph*, April 6, 1867.

the Bill might be expanded into a measure of household suffrage in Committee. Three days after the consultation at Mr. Gladstone's house, a special meeting (April 8, 1867) of Liberal members was held in the 'tea-room' of the House of Commons, to consider the course which they should adopt with reference to the Bill. The members present were not satisfied with Mr. Coleridge's Instruction, and wanted to omit the latter part. They agreed to make an effort for this purpose, and a deputation of six members was appointed to submit to Mr. Gladstone the views of the meeting. In reply to the deputation, Mr. Gladstone reluctantly acquiesced in the proposal, provided that the Government accepted the former part of the resolution.*

In the House of Commons, the same evening, Mr. Locke inquired whether, if the latter part of the proposed Instruction were withdrawn, the Chancellor of the Exchequer would assent to the former part, which empowered the Committee to deal with the law of rating. Mr. Disraeli gave this assent; and immediately afterwards, upon Mr. Coleridge's motion, an 'Instruction to the Committee, that they have power to alter the law of rating,' was adopted without discussion.†

The anticipated debate upon the instruction proposed at Mr. Gladstone's thus suddenly collapsed, and the meditated assault upon the 'principle' of the Bill was rendered impracticable by the defection of a considerable number of Liberal members. Mr. Bernal Osborne complained that —

Enthusiastic reformers should have waited until Monday, knowing well on the Friday what was to be brought forward, and that they should have suddenly turned tail when they heard

* *Daily Telegraph*, April 9, 1867. The names of forty-five members present in the room at the time of the meeting are given; but it was subsequently stated that one or two of this number were there accidentally and did not associate themselves with the meeting.
† *Hansard*, vol. 186, col. 1273.

that a dissolution was in view. The position is a most peculiar one. We are now to go into Committee on a Bill the policy and principle of which have hardly been discussed by the House. The House will recollect that the second reading was shuffled through *pro formâ*, with the understanding that a discussion should take place upon the principle of the Bill before you, Sir, left the chair.

Mr. Lowe said very happily :—

This Bill has a double aspect, and that is the mischief of it. If looked at by the light of what it will immediately effect, it is not a large measure of enfranchisement, or one that even a timid man might fear. But if we look upon it in its potentiality, keeping in view that to which it may lead, it is a measure of the very largest nature.

Mr. Lowe described the Bill accurately, and his vaticinations respecting its possible growth were realised sooner than he could have expected. At the time when he spoke, it was *not* a very large measure. It added much fewer voters than the Bill of 1866. The new borough franchise, before it was moulded in Committee, was for all practical purposes a 6*l.* rating franchise in the fifty-eight boroughs wholly under the Small Tenements Act; because in those places the landlords of houses under 6*l.* rateable value were entered on the rate-books instead of the tenants. The same result would have been partially produced in ninety-eight other boroughs, of which portions were under that Act. But advanced reformers speculated upon converting the pending measure into one of household suffrage. By the abrogation of the Small Tenements and analogous Acts, to which Mr. Disraeli suddenly and unexpectedly assented in Committee, this object was subsequently accomplished. The illustration of Horace—

> Amphora cœpit
> Institui; currente rotâ, cur urceus exit?

was reversed. The measure, which at first was meant to

be no bigger than a pipkin, was moulded on the potter's wheel of politics into a mighty amphora.

The grounds upon which the Radical members refused to follow Mr. Gladstone's leading at this juncture were very distinctly stated by one of their number—Mr. Montague Chambers. He said :—

He should support the motion for going into committee. He was well satisfied at the result of the consultation which occurred before they met that evening. At the end of the proposed Instruction, there was something very equivocal to true reformers. *They thought it restrictive.* They had carried a point very useful as an Instruction, and he hoped when they went into Committee on it, they would carry a Reform Bill that would be suitable to the wants of the country.

The question for resolving the House into Committee upon the Bill was then put and affirmed without a division (April 8, 1867).*

Mr. Gladstone, however, did not relinquish the attempt to fix a limit of value for the qualification of borough voters. On the following day (April 9), he gave notice of various amendments.† By one of them it was intended to reduce the term of residence required of tenant voters in boroughs from two years to one year. Another amendment superseded the condition that borough voters should be rated, and substituted a provision that the qualifying 'premises must be of the yearly rateable value of 5*l.* or upwards.' The following day (April 10), he announced in the House that—

In order to prevent any confusion or misunderstanding which might arise as to the meaning of some of the amendments he proposed to move on the Reform Bill, which he found were not so clearly stated as he intended, he now proposed to insert in clause 3, lines 3 and 4 [the part of the Bill relating to two years' residence], the words, ' whether he in person or his landlord be rated to the relief of the poor.'

---

* *Hansard,* vol. 186, col. 1317.   † *Hansard,* vol. 186, col. 1338.

The previous day (April 9), Mr. Disraeli issued a circular to his followers which stated that Mr. Gladstone's 'amendments are Mr. Coleridge's relinquished Instructions in an amended form. The first of them relates to the vital question of residence; and if any one of them be adopted, it will be impossible for the Government to proceed with the Bill.'*

Anticipating slightly the course of events, it may be mentioned that not long afterwards the amendment relating to residence was adopted; Mr. Disraeli, however, discovered that this 'vital' change in his measure did not render it 'impossible for the Government to proceed with the Bill.'

On April 11, Mr. Gladstone moved his amendment giving the borough franchise to the tenant, 'whether he in person, or his landlord, be rated to the relief of the poor.' He observed that this motion did not affect the question of the *payment* of rates. The rule that the rates should be paid by somebody—either landlord or tenant—before the latter claimed the vote, Mr. Gladstone did not now attempt to abrogate. The House had become so firmly wedded to the idea that there was some magical value in the payment of rates that any attack upon that superstition would have been hopeless. What was now asked for was simply this—that the agreement of the parish with the landlord, by which his name was put on the rate-book instead of the tenant's, should not affect the title of the latter to the suffrage. Of course such a provision was quite compatible with the rule that the rates should be paid before the tenant claimed to be registered. It seemed a perfectly monstrous denial of justice to exclude a man, otherwise qualified, from the register, simply because of an agreement made behind his back between his landlord and the parish. Even allowing the payment of

---

* *Daily Telegraph*, August 11, 1867, page 2.

rates to be that wonderful security for a tenant's respectability which the Government affirmed, there could be no valid reason, so long as the payment was made, why the tenant should not have a vote. Mr. Disraeli said there must be a *personal payment*, but what was meant by 'personal payment' he never explained—a rather important omission, considering that it was the paramount principle of his measure. Certainly the phrase 'personal payment' does not occur anywhere in any one of the various editions of the Bill; nor is it in the Act of Parliament. Parliament went on for a whole session harping on this word 'personal' without defining its meaning or incorporating it in their great legislative performance; that is to say, the paramount principle of the Bill was something which everybody was supposed to understand, and which nobody thought it worth while to express. It could not be meant that the tenant was to pay the rate to the parish officers with his own hands—that he might not send it by a messenger or agent. Such a provision would be too fantastic to be sanctioned by the House of Commons even in its present tolerant mood. If, then, the tenant might employ an agent to make the payment, why might not that agent be his landlord?

Mr. Gladstone carefully and patiently resumed the task of making clear the ridiculous anomalies which resulted from the exclusion of compound householders in places which happened to be under Small Tenements Acts. Some of his figures have been given in a former page. The irregularities and inequalities which he cited are such that we may be quite certain that the Government had not contemplated them, for some of the results were so preposterous that no man in his senses would have deliberately contrived them. Mr. Gladstone said :—

You may go through the process of writing down something

on a piece of paper or parchment and calling it a law, but it can never attract the respect due to law when its operation would be partial, capricious, unfair to such an extent as this. And these inequalities are to be securities of the constitution, guarantees against democracy, are to be the firm, solid, well-built walls which are to stem the tide of agitation! This strange emanation of some ingenious mind, fanciful as if displayed upon the stage, but wholly alien from the spirit and history of British legislation, and for which there is nothing approaching to a precedent in the annals of the House, is to supply the new governing power of the nation. . . . I object altogether to making our political measures a means of interference with the social and economic arrangement of the people.*

The speakers who opposed Mr. Gladstone on this occasion scarcely attempted to answer his objections respecting the irregular operation of the Government Bill. The anomalies which it introduced were so directly demonstrated by reference to official documents that it was hopeless to contradict him on this point. The ministerial debaters treated the question superficially, and chiefly occupied themselves with objections to a 5*l*. household suffrage.

It is said (observed Mr. Gathorne Hardy), that there will be inequalities under the plan proposed by the Government. I will not go into the case of the 58 boroughs, where every compound householder is under 6*l*.; but I will take the case of the 98 boroughs. Suppose the compound householder claims to have his name immediately put on the rate-book, he will have to pay the occupier's rate in boroughs. As to inequalities, are there no inequalities connected with 5*l*. rating?

Mr. Hardy admitted the argument respecting the power which the Bill gave to vestries of altering the constituencies, but urged that the objection might be removed.

I am quite sure there must be discrepancies, however you may legislate, and I defy any man to frame a measure in which ingenious people, like the hon. and learned member for Richmond, and the right hon. gentleman the member for South

* *Hansard*, vol. 186, col. 1519.

Lancashire, will not be able to pick a hole, and show how difficulties will arise, especially if people are instructed how to make them. The vestries, it is said, may change all this, but I may remind the right hon. gentleman that, though he did not carry his instruction, part of it was adopted by the House. Let him then, in Committee, show some mode by which vestries shall be prevented from making the constant changes which are deprecated.*

It did not occur to Mr. Hardy that it was the duty of the Government which framed the Bill to foresee the objections to it. Mr. Gladstone—and not he merely but every reasonable person who was candid on the subject—considered it perfectly intolerable that vestries should be enabled by adoption or rejection of the Small Tenements Act, to vary the composition of constituencies from time to time. Surely, those who objected to intrust this vast political influence to parochial functionaries were doing something more than 'picking a hole.' But, says Mr. Hardy, let the objectors find a remedy for this evil. Obviously, that was the business of the Government which created the evil. Besides, how was a remedy possible? The Ministers insisted on payment of the *full* rate as a condition of the franchise, and thus all compound householders were to be excluded from the suffrage. As long as vestries retained the Small Tenements Act, that exclusion was inevitable; and up to the present stage of the discussion, the Government had declined to abolish the compounding system.

But the ministerial defence consisted principally in an exposition of the mystical beauties of the 'personal payment of rates.' Mr. Hardy continued:—

We say that the rate-book should be the register.† [Mr. *Glad-*

* *Hansard*, col. 1054.

† Here is another instance of the immovable belief among Conservatives, that Mr. Gladstone was opposed to making the rate-book the register. They could not or would not learn that his Bill of 1866 directly and effectually provided for this very object.

stone: Hear, hear!] The right hon. gentleman has certainly not provided for this in his amendments. He maintains that, though the landlord pays the rates, the tenant shall have the vote. We say, on the other hand, that, as the payment of rates induces an interest in local affairs, the man who so pays is more likely to be educated and take an interest in the concerns of his country.

Mr. Disraeli, in the same spirit, said, with reference to the persons whom he proposed to enfranchise:—

When they find that by the personal payment of rates, and by residence in a town for a certain time, they can secure for themselves the franchise, they will be disposed to look with extreme jealousy on those who do not conform to those conditions, and who do not lead those regular lives, being placed in the same condition. . . . . Athough we could not swerve with respect to the borough franchise from those principles which we regard as vital—namely, PERSONAL PAYMENT OF RATES AND RESIDENCE—still with regard to almost every other point which has been mentioned in our discussion, we are most anxious in Committee, after a fair deliberation, and after an interchange of opinions, to adopt that course which the House in its wisdom may think most expedient and desirable. . . . . Nor is it a novelty when we say that *personal payment of rates and residence* are the only conditions upon which we consent to the arrangement of the borough franchise.[*]

Such were the fervid—the almost impassioned eulogies lavished upon the principle of personal payment. What must have been the grief and amazement of the enthusiasts who fought and were almost ready to die for the blessed principle, when they discovered that they had forgotten to put it into the Bill. *It is not in the Reform Act; it never had a place in any edition of the Reform Bill.* There is not a syllable in the Bill about it. There is indeed, a condition in the Act that the tenant voter in boroughs shall have ' bonâ fide paid an equal amount in the pound to that payable by other ordinary occupiers in respect of all poor-rates.'[†] But it is perfectly well

---

[*] *Hansard*, vol. 186, col. 1685. [†] 30 and 31 Vic. c. 102, s. 3.

settled by judicial decisions * that such a payment made by the hands of the landlord is effectual for the purpose of entitling the tenant to vote. If Mr. Hardy or Mr. Disraeli, instead of reiterating their encomiums on the merits of personal payment, had sat down to pen a clause embodying that principle, they would have probably discovered the hopelessness of the task. By what form of language could they prohibit a tenant from registering who had paid his rates, but not paid them 'personally'? By requiring him to pay the money by his own hands? By prohibiting him from sending the money by post or by a messenger? That would be too absurd. Or would they tolerate payment by any other agent except his landlord? One might have imagined that the barest statement of these difficulties would have instantly revealed to the House of Commons that the vaunted principle was an impossible chimera. For a whole session, this personal payment was kept dangling before its eyes; it is a thing which has not—by the very nature of the case—cannot have, a real existence. The imaginary region in which their happy 'principle' was to be found is one of the most illus-

---

* That a payment of rates made on behalf of the tenant by the landlord will be a bonâ fide payment for electoral purposes was decided in 'Cook v. Luckett,' which was decided in the Court of Common Pleas in 1846 (1 Lutwyche's Registration Cases, p. 432). The question arose on the construction of the Act 6 Vic. c. 18, s. 75, which requires, as one condition of the borough occupiers' suffrage, that 'such person shall have bonâ fide paid' poor-rates for a specified period. Chief Justice Tindal said, 'The facts of the case show that the tenant was rated; that he held the premises under an express agreement with his landlord that the latter should pay all rates and taxes; that the landlord had called on him to pay, and he had paid all rent due in respect of the house. It appears to me that the tenant being rated, under the circumstances, the calling on the landlord to pay and the payment by him are equivalent to a bonâ fide calling on the tenant to pay and a bonâ fide payment by him.' The other members of the Court of Common Pleas concurred in this judgment.

Hence, when a house is let free of rates, or on the understanding that the landlord is to pay them, payment by him will be considered a bonâ fide payment by the tenant.

trious instances of a fool's paradise to be found in parliamentary history.

Mr. Gladstone's motion for inserting, in clause 3, the words, 'whether he in person or his landlord be rated to the relief of the poor,' was lost (April 12, 1867) by a majority of 21; the numbers being, Ayes, 289; Noes, 310.*

An analysis of the division list is somewhat interesting, for it shows what forces were at work to produce this result. There were on the Liberal side of the House two considerable sections which on certain occasions had refused to support Mr. Gladstone—the members who assembled in the 'tea-room,' and opposed the latter part of Mr. Coleridge's Instruction, and the 'Adullamites' of the preceding year, those Liberal members who in critical divisions had voted against the Bill of 1866. It should be observed that very few—not more than four or five of this Adullamite section—were included in the 'tea-room' opposition, which proceeded almost entirely from a different section of the Liberal members.

Upon examination of the division list of April 12, 1867, it will be found that the Adullamites, whose total number was about 50, were very equally divided; about 25 voted with, and the like number against, Mr. Gladstone. Of the 45 members present at the meeting in the 'tea-room' the great majority did not carry their opposition so far as to withdraw their support in the House of Commons. Of these 45 members, 35 voted with Ayes or minority, 8 with the Noes or majority, and 2 did not vote.

Thus it will be seen that the opposition in the 'tea-room' only partially contributed to the ministerial success. The Liberals who voted with the Government included about 25 Adullamites, and eight others who

* *Hansard*, vol. 186, col. 1609.

had objected to Mr. Coleridge's original instruction, besides a few other members of Radical opinions.

The general election of 1865 was supposed to have given a Liberal majority of about 70. On that hypothesis, the defection of half that number, or 35, would of course bring the two parties to an equality in a division. But on the present occasion, about 40 Liberal members voted with the Government in a division from which nearly 60 members were absent. The ministerial majority is therefore readily accounted for; it was due partly to the support of some five-and-twenty Adullamites, who were Liberals in name only, and of about a dozen Radicals, who believed that Mr. Disraeli's Bill might be converted into an extremely democratic measure.

A few days after the rejection of his motion, in reply to an inquiry on behalf of several members of the House of Commons, Mr. Gladstone announced by a letter, dated April 18, 1867, that he did not intend to proceed with the amendments to the Reform Bill of which he had given notice. He observed that—

> The country can hardly fail now to be aware that those gentlemen of Liberal opinions whose convictions allow them to act unitedly upon this question are not a majority, but a minority, of the House of Commons, and that they have not the power they were supposed to possess of limiting or directing the action of the Administration, or of shaping the provisions of the Reform Bill. Still, having regard to the support which my proposal with respect to personal rating received from so large a number of Liberal members, I am not less willing than heretofore to remain at the service of the party to which they belong.

Mr. Gladstone added that he should no longer 'assume the initiative in amending a measure which cannot, perhaps, be effectually amended, except by a reversal, either formal or virtual, of the vote of Friday, the 12th.'*

* *Times*, April 22, 1867.

The announcement contained in this letter appears to have been very generally misunderstood. Immediately after it was made, a large number of public meetings were held, at which votes of confidence in Mr. Gladstone were passed. It appears to have been commonly assumed that he had determined to relinquish all further efforts to amend the Bill and many of the resolutions adopted at these meetings, deplored the determination thus imputed to him. But Mr. Gladstone had not expressed any such intention. He had simply declared the abandonment of the amendments which stood in his name among the parliamentary notices. But he had at the same time distinctly pledged himself to co-operate with the Liberal party in their endeavours to remove or mitigate the grave defects of the Bill. And this pledge was unquestionably redeemed. During the remainder of the session, he was most actively and constantly engaged in the discussion upon the various clauses, and attended to the most minute details. The result was that the Bill was ultimately altered most materially by his hands. It has already been stated that of the ten particulars in which he stated that the measure absolutely required alteration, nine were ultimately adopted.

The supposed abandonment of his place, as leader of the Opposition, had, however, the effect of producing an unmistakable expression of the opinion of reformers throughout the country. Between the 22nd of April, when the letter was published, and the 7th of May, public meetings were held in the following towns, and in every one of these meetings, resolutions were passed expressive of confidence in Mr. Gladstone:—Ashton, Banbury, Bath, Batley, Birmingham, Borough Road, Boston, Bridport, Bristol, Carlisle, Christchurch, Colchester, Dalkeith, Dalry (Ayrshire), Dunfermline, Exeter, Greenock, Greenwich, Guildford, Hackney,

Hailsworth, Halstead, Hanley, Hawick, Hull, Kendal, Kelvedon, Lambeth, Liverpool, Llechryd, Luton, Maidstone, Malton, Merthyr Tydvil, Newbury, Newcastle-on-Tyne, Newton-le-Willows, Northampton, North Shields, Ramsbottom, Redditch, Sheffield, Shoreditch, St. Martin's Hall (London), Swansea, Tiverton, Wakefield, Walsall, Wolverhampton.* This list is not nearly complete; it includes only those instances in which the resolutions were forwarded to a single daily newspaper. From every part of the United Kingdom, from the extreme north of Scotland to Cornwall and Kent, in every considerable town of every county, open meetings were held for the express purpose of condemning the Bill, and encouraging Mr. Gladstone in his opposition to it. These resolutions are valuable as proofs of unanimity among reformers respecting the thing which the Ministry was pleased to term the vital principle of the Bill. The weight of this evidence is increased by the consideration that these meetings were not—could not have been—held in concert, and that the persons who organised them were in most instances entirely strangers to each other, and belonged to widely different sections of the community.

* *Daily Telegraph*, May 14 and 15, 1867, p. 3.

CHAPTER XI.

THE REFORM BILL OF 1867 IN COMMITTEE.—THE QUALIFICATIONS WITH RESPECT TO RESIDENCE AND PAYMENT OF RATES.

Amendment respecting residence of Borough Voters, 175.— Mr. Hibbert's Amendment to enfranchise compound householders on payment of reduced rates, 177.—Conference between the Secretary to the Treasury and Liberal members, 178. — The Government insist on the enfranchised compound householder paying full rates, 181.—And on personal payment, 187.

THE first important alteration of the Bill effected in Committee was the substitution of 'twelve months' for 'two years,' as the term of residence required with respect to the new tenant-voters in boroughs. Mr. Disraeli, in a letter quoted in a previous page, had declared the two-years' residence to be a vital point, and that, unless it was maintained, the Government could not proceed with the Bill.

In the Clause 3, defining the qualification of occupiers in boroughs, one of the conditions prescribed in the original Bill was as follows:—

2. Is on the last day of July in any year, and has during the whole of the preceding two years, been an inhabitant occupier, as owner or tenant, of any dwelling-house within the borough.

Mr. Ayrton moved (May 2, 1867) to leave out the words 'two years,' and to substitute 'twelve months' in this place. The supporters of this motion objected to the impolitic and invidious distinction which the Bill established between various classes of voters with respect to the term of residence. The Government resisted the proposed amendment. Sir John Pakington cited the Reform Bill of 1854, introduced by Lord Russell, in which a residence of two years and a half was required. An answer to this argument was briefly and satisfactorily given by Sir Roundell Palmer. The Reform Bill of 1854 had been dead and buried thirteen years. The public demand for extension of the suffrage had advanced greatly in the interval, and was not to be satisfied with the limitations and restrictions which the cautious statesmen of Lord Aberdeen's Ministry required. Another precedent, upon which Sir John Pakington relied greatly, was the term of residence required of *burgesses* in municipal corporations. To be entitled to be on the roll of burgesses, a man must be an occupier in the borough, and resident within seven miles, for a period of two years preceding the last day of August in each year.* But there is no analogy between the two cases. The list of persons duly qualified on the last day of August is immediately made up, and all the burgesses so enrolled are entitled to vote for town-councillors on the 1st of November, the day appointed for annual municipal elections.† But the parliamentary registration is not completed so expeditiously; the year's occupation required under the Reform Act of 1832 expires on the last day of July. The Revising Barrister settles the electoral lists in September or October. The existing Registration Acts enabled the persons on the lists so settled to vote at elections which took place after the last day of November.‡ Consequently, an occupation of one year and four months was the minimum required, and the period has now been increased to one year and five months; but in

---

* 5 & 6 Will. IV. c. 70, s. 9.   † *Ibid.* s. 30.

‡ 2 Will. IV. c. 45, s. 27; 6 & 7 Vic. c. 18, s. 49. This provision has, however, been altered by a section in the new Reform Act. By sec. 38, the register henceforth takes effect from the first of January in each year, so that the occupier under the present Act must be resident one year and five months at least, before he can vote.

practice the term is much longer, because of the comparative infrequency of parliamentary elections. It may be safely assumed that the term of residence before the parliamentary elector can exercise his right is, in general, much longer than the corresponding term of residence of municipal voters.

Mr. Ayrton's motion was carried (May 2, 1867) by a majority of 81, the numbers being, for the original provision, 197; for the amendment, 278.*

The following evening (May 3, 1867), the Chancellor of the Exchequer stated that he and his colleagues, though they regretted the decision on this subject, 'have not thought it inconsistent with their duty to defer to the opinion of the House.'

He, at the same time, announced certain verbal amendments, which he proposed to introduce in the clause defining the tenant's qualification in boroughs. The principal of these alterations was one intended to make it clear that the tenant-voter must pay the full rate. In the original Bill, the occupier was required to pay all poor-rates 'payable by him in respect of such premises.' The amendment rendered it necessary for him to pay 'an equal amount in the pound to that payable by other ordinary occupiers.'

The Chancellor of the Exchequer, at the same time, gave notice of his intention to propose a clause, abrogating the third section of Sir William Clay's Act (14 & 15 Vic. c. 14), by which the compound householder who takes the obligation of the rates upon himself, in order to get a vote, is allowed to pay the reduced or commuted rate.

Mr. Hibbert, Member for Oldham, had some time previously announced that he should move an amendment of an opposite tendency. He proposed that 'the occupier

* *Hansard*, vol. 186, col. 1907.

may claim to be rated, for the purpose of acquiring the franchise, in the same manner, and subject to the same conditions, in and subject to which an occupier may claim to be rated under the Act of the fourteenth and fifteenth Victoria' (Sir William Clay's Act). In other words, Mr. Hibbert wanted all enfranchised compound householders to pay the reduced rate. Mr. Disraeli, on the contrary, wanted them to pay the full rate.

On April 12, Mr. Bernal Osborne, member for Nottingham, read to the House a document, which contained a minute of a conference between Colonel Taylor, Secretary of the Treasury, and Mr. Dillwyn, as follows:—

At the request of certain members, Mr. Dillwyn has committed to writing, and at their request he has shown it to Colonel Taylor to know whether it is correct. After reading it over, Colonel Taylor has admitted it to be correct—the purport being that Colonel Taylor undertakes, as a gentleman and a man of honour, to press upon the Cabinet the desirability of adopting Mr. Hibbert's amendment; and, further, he gave an intimation *that Lord Derby and Mr. Disraeli were personally in favour of accepting it.**

Mr. Owen Stanley, Member for Beaumaris :—

I, in common with many other Members of this House, have seen and read this document; and I believe that its contents, or the purport of them as read by the honourable Member for Nottingham are substantially correct.

Mr. Dillwyn :—

I met the honourable and gallant member for Dublin county [Colonel Taylor], and I mentioned to him that the acceptance or non-acceptance by the Government of the proposition of the honourable Member for Oldham might influence my conduct with respect to other clauses of the Bill. . . . . I jotted down a minute of the conversation on some paper in the lobby. I showed this memorandum afterwards to the honourable and gallant Member for the county of Dublin, and he agreed that it correctly represented what had taken place; I also showed it to some honourable members among my friends.†

* *Hansard,* vol. 186, col. 1587.   † *Ibid.* vol. 186, col. 1590.

Colonel Taylor published a letter, giving his version of the transaction. The date of the letter is April 13, the day after the attention of the House of Commons was first drawn to the subject. He says that he had a conversation with Mr. Dillwyn, in which 'he expressed himself strongly in favour of the principle of Mr. Hibbert's amendment;' and in which Colonel Taylor stated, 'there could be little doubt the Chancellor of the Exchequer would bring the subject of the compound ratepayers before his colleagues, at the first convenient opportunity, and, as I believed, he was individually not indisposed to give the question a candid consideration.' Colonel Taylor also told Mr. Dillwyn, 'I had no objection to his repeating what I had said to any of his friends.' *

There is no substantial difference between this version and the others. On his own showing, it appears that the Government 'whip,' on the eve of a critical division, represented to a member of the Opposition, that Mr. Disraeli was probably inclined to support Mr. Hibbert's amendment ; and that this statement might be repeated to any of Mr. Dillwyn's friends. For what purpose? For no conceivable purpose, except to influence votes in the impending division.

The Chancellor of the Exchequer stated (April 12), that 'this negotiation was quite unknown to me'—a statement which is perfectly credible. A Parliamentary secretary to the Treasury is usually selected for tact, discretion, and astuteness, and would hardly manage his business so clumsily, as to compromise his chief by making him cognisant of negotiations with the Opposition. Nevertheless, it is beyond dispute that an official, who had peculiar means of ascertaining the sentiments of the Chancellor of the Exchequer, did, immediately before a formidable division, influence or attempt to

* *Times*, April, 1867.

influence votes of Liberals, by suggesting that his chief was favourable to a particular compromise; that Mr. Dillwyn, to whom the suggestion was made, voted in favour of the Government; and that, when the crisis was over, Mr. Disraeli announced that he was not favourable to the suggested compromise, but should support a directly contrary policy.

Mr. Lowe, in the discussion of May 6, thus described the transaction :—

> The honourable and gallant member, the authorised agent of communication between the Government and the House, represents to members, before a most important division, that the Chancellor of the Exchequer is favourable to the motion of the honourable member for bringing compound householders under 10*l.* within the clause of Sir William Clay's Act, and that he will no doubt bring the question before the Cabinet. After the division — after these reports have had whatever effect they may have had—the right honourable gentleman comes down, and says that the clause is a bad one; and, instead of consenting to bring other people under its efficacy, gives notice of a motion to repeal it altogether. . . . . This seems to me to require explanation.*

The story is an unpleasant one, but it was needful to tell it, for it is a material part of the Parliamentary history of 1867. It may be safely predicted that if the practice of privately soliciting members of the House of Commons for their votes, and of influencing them by auricular promises and suggestions, ever became general—Parliament would speedily lose its present independence and dignity.

The reasons which Mr. Disraeli now (May 6) assigned for refusing assent to Mr. Hibbert's amendment were as follows. The Chancellor of the Exchequer first of all acknowledged that Mr. Gladstone had converted him on the question of the incidence of the rate upon the compound householder:—

* *Hansard*, vol. 187, col. 12.

It would be disingenuous in me not to acknowledge that this point, at an earlier period of the Session, was placed before the House by the right honourable gentleman (Mr. Gladstone) and other honourable members with great powers of argument and illustration. I had entertained some doubts about it, but I am bound to say that subsequent researches, and the more enlarged information we now possess, justify the conclusion. Therefore, as I think it has been proved that the compound householder pays the full amount of rate, he has a right to deduct that amount from his landlord.

The acknowledgment came rather late in the day. After the second reading of the Bill, and an immense amount of discussion, Mr. Disraeli had at length discovered that the measure was in a most material point founded upon a misconception, and suffered himself to be set right by the leader of the Opposition. The Chancellor of the Exchequer continued:—

We propose, the moment the compounding householder claims the right of exercising the franchise and of paying the full rates, and deducting the full rate from the amount of his rent, to exonerate the landlord from the guarantee which he has given. It is impossible therefore to say that the landlord will be fined.*

If neither the landlord nor the tenant is fined, where does the excess of rate come from? The full rate is to be paid, instead of the commuted sum. Who pays the difference? The money does not come out of the clouds.

Again, the Chancellor of the Exchequer repeats the blunder respecting the liability of compounding landlords for rates paid by their tenants.

With regard to the 14 & 15 Vic. c. 14, s. 3 [Sir William Clay's Act], we propose to repeal that clause, of course saving all existing rights, and of course extending to compounders under the old Act the same privileges which compounders are to enjoy under the Bill. The compounders under the old Act

* *Hansard*, vol. 187, col. 18.

could not claim to be recouped from the landlord for the rates which they paid, and now they have the power of claiming to be paid the full amount.*

This statement is altogether erroneous. The Small Tenements Act, made the year before Sir William Clay's Act, provides, with respect to houses rated to the landlords, that where the occupier pays any rate he 'may (whether paying such rates voluntarily, or by compulsion) deduct the respective amount . . . from the rent.'† But, independently of any statute, the common law gives to a tenant who pays a tax for which the landlord is liable, the right to recover it.‡

The question whether the compound householder claiming a vote should pay the full or the reduced rate, was brought to a decision upon the motion of the Chancellor of the Exchequer (May 9, 1867), to insert, in the clause requiring the borough voter to be rated to the relief of the poor, the words 'as an ordinary occupier.' The clause so modified would be read as follows:—

Has during the time of such occupation been rated *as an ordinary occupier*, in respect of the premises so occupied by him within the borough, to all rates (if any) made for the relief of the poor in respect of such premises.

Mr. Hibbert opposed this alteration, which was directly contrary to his amendment, by which he sought to enable voters to come upon the register on the payment of the reduced rates.

---

* *Hansard*, vol. 187, col. 18 (May 6, 1867).

† 13 & 14 Vic. c. 99, s. 8.

‡ There have been many cases at common law to this effect. In Graham v. Tate (1 Maule & Selwyn's Reports, p. 609) a tenant had voluntarily paid to the collector a tax for which the landlord was liable. Afterwards the landlord distrained for the whole amount of rent without deducting this payment. The Court of King's Bench held that the tenant might recover the amount. Lord Ellenborough, C. J., said—he may 'bring an action for money had and received, if in the result the landlord has got money into his pocket which does not belong to him.'

He gave the following interesting statistics, respecting the non-rated occupiers under 10*l.* rental, in the 200 boroughs of England and Wales :—

	Compound Householders under 10*l.*
57 Boroughs wholly under the Small Tenements Act	139,327
99 Boroughs partly under that and other Rating Acts	249,472
15 Boroughs under Local Rating Acts	87,442
29 Boroughs not under any Acts for compounding rates	0
200	476,241

Mr. Hibbert's argument, respecting the probable effects of the Government measure in raising rents, has been already verified by experience. He said :—

> The landlord, not being recouped for the additional sum of money which he would have to pay, would be placed in a position very uncomfortable and inconvenient for him. Having been accustomed, for a long series of years, to receive the deduction, he would not easily or lightly submit to the change. What then would be the result? The landlord, feeling that he was called upon to pay money which he had not been accustomed to pay, would say to his tenant—'You came to me on certain terms. I have been quite willing to pay the composition rate on these terms; but if you apply for a vote, and make it necessary for me to pay this additional money, you must leave the house.' Or else the landlord would say to the tenant—'You have applied for a vote, and have put me to this additional expense, and therefore I shall require you to pay me additional rent.' *

The prediction has been exactly fulfilled. The Act of 1867 compels the tenant to pay the *full* rate, but allows him to deduct it from his rent where the landlord had agreed to pay the rates.† But the landlords, in many cases, reinstate themselves by raising the rents.

Mr. Hibbert insisted that 'the new compounders should come in on the same footing as the old ones,' and suggested the policy which was afterwards carried out by Mr. Hodgkinson's amendment. He said :—

---

* *Hansard*, vol. 187, col. 271. † 30 & 31 Vic. c. 102, s. 7, § 3.

Let the right honourable gentleman abolish the Local Tenements Act and the other compounding Acts, or put all the compounders on the same footing.

The answer which Mr. Disraeli made to this proposal to abolish compounding is remarkable. He said:—

Sir, we are told, when we have brought forward a scheme which we believe to be calculated to meet the difficulties of the case, so far as these rating Acts are concerned, that those difficulties can be obviated in a manner much more simple, by a clause that will at once supersede, rescind, and repeal all those Acts. *That is rash counsel.* It is difficult to carry a large and extensive measure of Parliamentary Reform. But that difficulty must be infinitely enhanced if we should attempt to carry a measure of Parliamentary Reform which should at the same time deal with all the rating Acts of England.

We shall see hereafter that the Chancellor of the Exchequer soon afterwards adopted this 'rash counsel' —not only adopted it, but declared that he had been in favour of it from the beginning of the Session.

Mr. Gladstone pointed out, in this debate, how completely the Government had come round to his view respecting the 'fine' on the compound householder:—

I contended, at the time, that the 34th clause* imposed a fine on the compound householder under 10*l*. My honourable and learned friend (Mr. Roebuck), in the guarded and mild language which he says he has learnt to adopt in these days of his ripe experience, described my observations as a series of pettifogging cavils. Another gentleman, an honourable friend of mine, whose lips have never been opened in this House except to utter words of mildness—I mean my honourable friend the Member for Derby (Mr. Bass)—said, as to the fine, it was 'all nonsense.' .... If we were to indulge in feelings of gratified egotism, my honourable and learned friend (Sir Roundell Palmer) and myself might have enjoyed something

---

* By the 34th clause, as it originally stood, the non-rated occupier might claim to be rated, in order to acquire the franchise, subject to the same conditions under which non-rated ten-pound householders might claim under the existing Acts. But the new claimant was required to pay the full rate.

like a mental banquet on the extraordinary fulness and breadth of the admissions which have been made,—that the 'pettifogging cavils' and 'nonsense' which we were supposed to have promulgated expressed, in the view of the Government, a truth of political economy, which is now to be adopted by them as the basis of their proposals.

The new scheme of the Government, it will be observed, had a retrospective operation. It provided not only that *new* tenant-voters should pay the full rate, but meditated the abolition of that clause of Sir William Clay's Act by which the old compound householders—those above the 10*l.* line—were allowed to be registered on payment of the reduced rate.

In the earlier part of this debate of May 9, Mr. Disraeli had, in reply to a question by Mr. Gladstone, stated that he thought there was

> Some obscurity of meaning in the first question of the right honourable gentleman. But if it should be his intention to ask whether the compound householder is by our Bill deprived of any advantage which he now possesses under the 14 & 15 Vict. c. 14, I answer that he certainly does not; and, of course, the moment he becomes personally rated he ceases to be a compound householder.*

Such an answer could not possibly have been made by any one versed in the subject with which Mr. Disraeli was dealing. Under Sir William Clay's Act, and the Reform Act of 1832, the non-rated occupier might claim to be rated for the purpose of the franchise, and was liable only for the reduced or commuted rate. Now it was proposed to take from him this privilege, and to rate him as an ordinary occupier. Mr. Bright observed:—

> The right honourable gentleman, in the audacious proposal which he makes to repeal this clause, is striking at the electoral rights which Parliament has guaranteed to not less than 94,000 occupiers above the 10*l.* value.

The only answer of the Chancellor of the Exchequer to this objection was that—

> My own impression, however, is that the 3rd clause of Sir William Clay's Act was interpolated in a manner that was highly disapproved by all persons of authority then in this House.*

But the House of Commons was by this time committed to the principle falsely described as 'personal payment of rates,' and consequently any reversal of that policy was for the present hopeless. Upon Mr. Disraeli's proposition to rate the borough voter as 'an ordinary occupier,' the Government obtained its largest majority hitherto—66. The numbers were—Ayes, 322; Noes, 256.†

The illusory nature of this principle of 'personal payment' was disclosed immediately afterwards, in the discussion of an amendment proposed by Mr. Denman (May 13), to insert, in the clause requiring the occupier to pay his rates, the words '*bonâ fide*' before 'paid,' and add 'or cause to be paid.'

The expression '*bonâ fide*' is an innocuous expletive, for between payment and *bonâ fide* payment there is no real distinction, though people who are caught by the mere sound of words may fancy that one exists. The insertion of the words 'or cause to be paid,' was proposed to enable the tenant to do that which it was already in his power to do. As far as the legal effect of the clause is concerned, the adoption or rejection of either of Mr. Denman's amendments was utterly immaterial. Mr. Hardy, on the part of the Government, graciously conceded '*bonâ fide*,' but refused 'cause to be paid.' The reasons which he assigned are instructive, because they show what differences of opinion existed at headquarters respecting the fundamental principle of the Bill. The President of the Poor Law Board said :—

* *Hansard*, vol. 187, col. 351.   † *Ibid.* vol. 187, col. 357.

The Government well insisted on the personal payment of rates. But the Bill had not the phrase 'personal payment of rates.' That was a description rather of the Government's intention. The Bill required that *a man should be responsible for* his rates. It was necessary, in order to come within the provisions of the Bill, that a man should have his name upon the Rate Book, and be personally responsible. Whether he paid the rate by his own hand, or by the hand of another, the receipt was made out in his name, and his liability ceased from that time.*

This exposition was ingenious rather than satisfactory. As an explanation of the fundamental principle, it came rather late in the day. The Chancellor of the Exchequer had reiterated the advantages of 'personal payment,' with the persistency of a musician who can play only one tune. In his introductory speech, he had insisted that the compound householder who wished to come upon the register must accept the duty of paying the rates instead of the landlord. In his latest speech—that on the introduction of the words 'as an ordinary occupier'—he had insisted half-a-dozen times on the necessity of 'personal payment.' For example, he 'wished the House, in considering this question, to be under no misapprehension, but to understand clearly that the borough franchise should be conferred upon an individual rated to the relief of the poor, and *personally paying his rates.*†

Now, at the eleventh hour, Mr. Gathorne Hardy informs the House that personal payment is only a 'description'—that it is not intended to be obligatory—that the tenant's rate may be paid 'with his own hand, or by the hand of another'—that all that was really required, was that the tenant should be personally *responsible.*

What, then, becomes of the fundamental principle? The landlord had hitherto paid the compound householder's

---

* *Hansard*, vol. 187, col. 443. † *Ibid.* vol. 187, col. 347.

rate, and he might continue to do so. How, then, could the payment be in any sense more personal than heretofore? How could it be considered a test of the tenant's qualification? The Government imposed no test, good, bad, or indifferent; for, so far as the act of payment was concerned, they left the law just as it was before.

But Mr. Hardy thought there was at least this shred of a principle left—the tenant was to be personally *liable*, though the landlord paid the rate. Even this poor little fragment of a security will be found, on examination, to be merely illusory. The Small Tenements Act of 1850 declares that, where the rates are assessed on the landlord, not only may they be recovered from him, and levied from his goods, but, 'further, the goods and chattels of the OCCUPIERS of such tenements shall be liable to be distrained and sold for the payment of such of the said rates as shall accrue due during their respective occupations, *in the same way as if such rates were assessed on such occupiers.*'* So that, when Mr. Gathorne Hardy claimed for the Government the merit of imposing a new liability upon occupiers, as a test of their fitness for the franchise, he must have entirely misapprehended the existing law on the subject. The liability exists already, for the Act of Parliament just cited declares that occupiers' goods shall be liable to seizure for the rates. And it subsequently provides that they may recoup themselves as against the landlords. Therefore, the Bill imposes no test whatever with reference to the rates—neither personal payment, upon the beauties of which Mr. Disraeli dilated; nor the new personal liability, upon which Mr. Hardy—receding from the ground previously occupied by the Government—now insisted. Like his colleagues on several previous occasions, he was ignorant of and misstated the law with which he was dealing. Mr. Disraeli wandered,

* 13 & 14 Vic. c. 99, s. 5.

during the whole Session, after that *ignis fatuus,* 'personal payment,' which certainly is not to be found in the Bill, and which merely served to lead the Government into a Serbonian bog. Next, Mr. Hardy attributes to the Bill another principle, that of personal liability, but that is not a distinctive feature of this measure, for the tenant was already legally liable to pay and to be distrained for the rates. Lastly, Sir John Karslake discovered late in the autumn that it was a matter of indifference whether the landlord or the tenant paid them. The 'principle' proved to be as fugacious as the ghost in *Hamlet.*

Bernado. 'Tis here!
Horatio. 'Tis here!
Marcellus.—'Tis gone.
      We do it wrong, being so majestical,
      To offer it the show of violence.

Under the present Reform Act, the occupier may pay his rates, either by his own hand or that of his landlord—as he might heretofore. Under the Reform Act he may deduct the sum so paid out of his rent—as he might heretofore. Under the Reform Act he is liable for the rates—as he was heretofore. When legal blunders involved in the conception and construction of the Bill were pointed out in the debates, Mr. Disraeli had a short and easy answer—' Let us get out of the region of Nisi Prius.' Others may be of opinion that it is desirable, before amending any law, to ascertain its nature. We expect the captain of a ship to know something of navigation, a surgeon to be acquainted with anatomy, an engine-driver to understand the uses of the levers, cranks, and valves placed under his control. Is it very unreasonable to ask that politicians who undertake to improve the Constitution of the country, should refrain from altering that most complicated mechanism, until they have examined its several parts and their relations to each other?

CHAPTER XII.

GENERAL ENFRANCHISEMENT OF HOUSEHOLDERS IN BOROUGHS.

Exclusion of compound householders from the suffrage, 190.—*Mr. Hodgkinson's method of enfranchising them,* 194.—*Accepted by the Government,* 196. —*Influence of public opinion in procuring this concession,* 199.—*Its extensive effect,* 200.—*Lord Cranbourne and Mr. Lowe oppose the democratic amendment,* 204.—*Mr. Disraeli tries to smodify it,* 207.—*The amendment has established household suffrage in boroughs,* 209.

AT length came the crisis of the Reform Bill—a change made suddenly, after a single debate, by which, without a division, and almost without opposition, the House of Commons added the whole body of compound householders to the list of persons who might claim to vote at borough elections, and thus converted the Bill into a measure of Household Suffrage. The change was startling, by its magnitude as well as its suddenness. Previously to this amendment, there can be no doubt that the compound householder remained almost entirely excluded from the electoral lists—not by reason of the ratepaying test, but because overseers were not required to put them on the electoral lists. The ratepaying test, as it was shown in a former page, is utterly nugatory. It was an elaborately-constructed barrier, which the persons it intended to exclude could simply avoid, by leaving their landlords to pay their rates as heretofore. The real effectual hindrance to the enfranchisement of compound householders was this—that names did not usually appear on the Rate Book, and consequently were not entered among the claimants of votes.

It is true that Mr. Disraeli's Bill permitted these persons to make the claim for themselves, and they might get registered if their poor-rates were duly paid. But it is found by experience that the great majority of qualified persons will not take the trouble to send in their claim. It may be said, of course, that where people are so indifferent that they will not take the trouble to ask for votes, they ought not to have them. But that observation might be applied to all classes of electors alike—freeholders in counties, 50$l.$ tenants under the Chandos clause, 10$l.$ occupiers in boroughs. Unless some public functionary puts these persons' names on the proper lists, they do not, as a general rule, get registered.

Statesmen must deal with observed facts, not with mere speculations upon the supposed duties of mankind. It is not enough to say that if the vote is not worth asking for, it is not worth having. If that principle were acted upon, it would operate as a disfranchisement of nine-tenths, probably, of the whole electoral body in counties and boroughs. Moreover, the neglect of qualified persons to seek for votes, is not always due to indifference; more frequently it arises from ignorance or uncertainty as to the mode in which, and the time when, the claim is to be made.

The mere palliatives which Mr. Disraeli had suggested with respect to the compound householder, scarcely touched this difficulty. He was to be allowed to send his claim by post, and other facilities were offered. Experience showed that they would be all but fruitless. The whole of Mr. Gladstone's argument respecting the extremely irregular operation of the Bill— the wholesale enfranchisement in some places and the inconsiderable effects in others—depended upon this hypothesis: that unless the names were officially put on the lists of claims they would rarely be registered.

Under the Reform Act of 1832, the 10*l*. occupier in a borough could not be registered unless he were rated to the relief of the poor. In cases where the landlord was liable for the rate, the tenant might claim to be rated, so as to complete his electoral qualification.* But he had to make a renewed claim with respect to each rate. Sir William Clay's Act of 1851 slightly mitigated this inconvenience by providing, that when such a person had once made the claim to be rated, he should not be required to renew it in regard to future rates, but should be entitled to vote, if in other respects duly qualified.† This Act, however, had not the effect anticipated. In some few places the overseers took upon themselves to place the 10*l*. compound householders on the electoral lists; but in most instances the tenants were left to take the initiative, and in those cases Sir William Clay's Act proved a dead letter. For example, the 'Electoral Returns, Boroughs and Counties, 1865-66,' state, that in the parish of S. Giles, Camberwell, '4,921 tenements, at and above 10*l*. rental, are rated to the owners instead of the occupiers. *There are at present only five of such occupiers* on the register,' that is, about one in a thousand availed himself of the Act. Again, in Rotherhithe, 'there are 1,426 houses of 10*l*. gross estimated rental, for which the landlords are assessed. Not more than six compound householders are placed on the parliamentary register.' In the parish of All Saints, Poplar, there are 4,052 houses for which the owners are rated; only twenty-three of the occupiers are registered. The vestry clerk adds: 'I am of opinion that if all the persons entitled under Sir William Clay's Act to be put on the register were to make their claim and attend to establish it, the numbers on the register would be increased three-fold, viz., from 1,450 to 4,350. But the usual reply I receive when I inform

* 2 & 3 Will. IV. s. 27, s. 30.   † 14 & 15 Vict. c. 14.

the claimants that they will have to attend the Revising barrister's court, is—' "Oh, I am not going to lose my time by going there. If you cannot put me on the register, I shall not trouble myself any further." ' *

But in some places, it has been observed, the parochial officers took the trouble of entering the 10*l*. compound householders on their lists; and this simple proceeding completely answered its purpose. For instance, in Southwark, in the parish of S. George the Martyr, the return states—

There are 4,293 compounded houses. It is the practice to send persons to all the houses rated to owners at 5*s*. per week rental or upwards, to ascertain the names of male occupiers, who have resided twelve months previously to July 21, in each year. Those names are placed on the list of voters, and vary from 1,500 to 2,000 upon lists of 3,600 to 4,200 names.

Again in the parish of S. Mary Magdalen, Bermondsey :—

When the rates are compounded for, the occupier's name appears on the rate-book, and the male occupants of such houses are annually placed on the register of voters, provided the landlords have complied with the requirements of the statutes for the registration of voters. The number of voters upon the year's register is 5,351. There are 4,388 male occupiers of compounded property rated at and above 10*l*., and it is estimated that about 4,000 are on the register. †

So in Clerkenwell, the compound householders are entered by the collectors on the register in almost every case; while in the adjacent Holborn Union 'no compound occupier has hitherto been placed on the register.'‡

In the case of S. George the Martyr just cited, the names of qualified occupiers have been ascertained by a house-to-house visitation, but in the majority of cases

* Electoral Returns, p. 233.   † *Ibid.* p. 210.   ‡ *Ibid.* p. 126.

the parishes have been unwilling to incur the necessary labour and expense.

Whatever differences of opinion may exist respecting the extension of the suffrage, no one can seriously dispute the expediency of establishing uniformity with respect to the registration of compound householders. No one will contend that it should be left to the caprice of parish officers to determine whether a constituency should or should not be quadrupled or quintupled by the enfranchisement of that class. Moreover, the question becomes still more important when it is considered with reference to occupiers below the 10$l.$ line, for the great majority of compound householders are below that line.

Mr. Gladstone's Bill of 1866 established the requisite uniformity in the most direct and simple way, by requiring the parochial officers to place the qualified householders on the electoral lists.

Mr. Disraeli's Bill contained nothing of the kind. He merely brought in some amendments when the Bill was in committee, allowing the non-rated occupier to send his claim by post. Past experience of Sir William Clay's Act showed that such palliatives were utterly futile.

Mr. Hodgkinson's amendment, now about to be considered, got rid of the difficulty by a very trenchant expedient—by *abolishing the system of compounding for rates in parliamentary boroughs.*

The debate upon this amendment was by far the most important and interesting of the session. On May 17, Mr. Hodgkinson, member for Newark, moved the insertion of the following words:—

Provided always, that except as hereinafter provided no person other than the occupier shall after the passing of this Act be rated to parochial rates in respect of premises occupied by him within the limits of a parliamentary borough, all Acts to the contrary now in force notwithstanding.*

The mover of this amendment stated that he dealt with compound householders in a very summary way, 'namely, by annihilating them altogether as compound householders, and reviving them in their original character of ordinary rate-payers.' He observed:—

It might be said that it would be impossible to carry out the rate collecting in large towns were it not for the compound system; but he took the liberty of doubting that, because he found that it was not in operation in many large towns; and he asked if Liverpool could do without it, could not Manchester? If Stockport could do without it why could not the neighbouring towns of Lancashire? If Oldham, why not Rochdale?†

Mr. Gladstone said:—

My hon. friend offers us this advantage. He offers us, at the expense of an economical and social inconvenience—at the expense at any rate of foregoing an economical and social advantage—he offers us, instead of an extension of the franchise, which we conceive to be limited, unequal, equivocal, and dangerous, as tending in many parts to corruption, an extension of the franchise which is liberal, which is perfectly equal. . . . I am sorry that in deference to what seems to me an unwise judgment of the House it is necessary to interfere

---

* It will be convenient to compare this clause with the corresponding section ultimately adopted. The words of the enactment are:—

'After the passing of this Act no owner of any dwelling-house or other tenement situate in a parish, either wholly or partly within a borough, shall be rated to the poor-rate instead of the occupier, except as hereinafter mentioned.'

The exception in the Act refers to compositions existing and rates made before it was passed. Existing compositions were to remain in force until the 29th of September then next.

It will be observed that the Act abolishes composition for *poor*-rates. Mr. Hodgkinson's amendment extended to all *parochial* rates, and therefore included the highway rate.

Again, the clause in its original form abolished compounding only with respect to tenements within the borough limits. The Act abolishes compounding *throughout* parishes which are partly within the borough limits, and therefore will sometimes operate in parts of parishes which lie outside the municipal boundary.

† *Hansard*, vol. 187, col. 710.

with the system of composition which exists throughout the country. But if the practical considerations are to prevail my duty is plainly to choose the lesser of two evils.*

To the amazement of the House and of the country, the Chancellor of the Exchequer accepted the amendment which revolutionised his Bill. With artistic *nonchalance* he commenced his speech as follows:—

The hon. gentleman (Mr. Hodgkinson) very accurately described the position of the question, when he said that the proposal which he brought forward was not at all opposed to the principles upon which the Bill of the Government is founded. There can be no question about that. On the contrary, it must be evident, that if the policy recommended by this clause should be brought into action it would enforce the policy which we recommend, give strength to the principles which we have been impressing upon the House as those which are the best foundations for the franchise, and give completeness to the measure which we have introduced.

The Chancellor of the Exchequer then drifted into one of his frequent dissertations on the payment of rates as a qualification for the franchise:—

I say there must be something in this principle, hitherto decided, which has received such signal corroboration. In the principle of payment of rates, in the public duty which the acquirement of the franchise will convey with it, and in the discipline which it will entail, there is something that carries to the common sense of the country and to the mind of Parliament a conviction that this is a sound principle, on which the borough franchise ought to be established.†

With our present knowledge of the actual provisions of the Reform Bill, these laudations of its supposed

---

* *Hansard*, vol. 187, col. 717.

Mr. Gladstone said shortly afterwards, with reference to the abolition of compounding: 'I have deprecated it all along and have assented to it as I would assent to cut off my leg rather than lose my life, on the principle of choosing the lesser evil.' This observation was addressed to a deputation of Metropolitan vestry clerks, appointed to confer with him and to draw his attention to the loss of parochial rates apprehended as a result of Mr. Hodgkinson's amendment.—*Daily Telegraph*, June 12, 1867.

† *Hansard*, vol. 187, col. 723.

principle appear very comical. The 'sound and true principle' here eulogised may be deserving of all the praise heaped upon it; but it certainly is *not* in the Bill. The landlord is free to pay the tenant's rates as heretofore, and therefore the 'public duty which the acquirement of the franchise will convey' and 'the discipline which it will entail' exist in imagination only.

But the most important part of the speech was the announcement contained in the following passage:—

> I need not say that as far as the spirit, not of the amendment, but of the proviso of the hon. gentleman is concerned, her Majesty's Government can have no opposition whatever to it. It is the policy of their own measure—a policy which, if they had been masters of the situation, they would have recommended long ago for the adoption of the House. *

When Mr. Disraeli stated that the abolition of the compound householder was the policy of his own measure, he made an assertion which must be understood in a forensic rather than a parliamentary sense. His hearers could hardly have forgotten that upon the introduction of the Reform Bill he replied to Mr. Gladstone's exposition of the anomalies produced by the disqualification of those tenants that the irregularities and absence of uniformity were advantageous. In one of the numerous debates on clause 3 (May 9, 1867) the Chancellor of the Exchequer explicitly condemned the abrogation of the rating Acts:—

> Sir, we are told, when we have brought forward a scheme which we believe to be calculated to meet the difficulties of the case, so far as these rating Acts are concerned, that those difficulties can be obviated in a manner much more simple by a clause that will at once supersede, rescind, and repeal all those Acts. *That is rash counsel.* It is difficult to carry a large and extensive measure of parliamentary reform. But that difficulty must be infinitely enhanced if we should attempt to carry a measure which should at the same time deal with all the rating Acts of England.†

---

* *Hansard*, vol. 187, col. 724.   † *Ibid.* vol. 187, col. 354.

Again, on the second reading, he said:—

> I very much doubt the policy, in a country like England and with institutions such as here prevail, of attempting by artificial means to obtain anything like a similarity of suffrage at a sacrifice of what I may venture to call the natural circumstances in which we are placed. It is most desirable not to deal in a Bill like the present with any privileges which happen previously to exist.*

In March it was most undesirable to deal with the existing privileges under the rating Acts. On the 9th of May the proposal to abrogate those Acts was 'rash counsel.' On the 17th of May that very course was the policy of the Government—a policy which they would have recommended long ago if they had been 'masters of the situation.'

But this change of language involved—as Mr. Disraeli subsequently explained in his speech at Edinburgh—no change of purpose. It was due simply to the necessity imposed upon him of 'educating his party.' The accuracy of that explanation can be tested by a reference to dates. Only four days before this avowal of the 17th of May, Mr. Disraeli had characterised the persons who wanted the impediments in the way of the compound householder removed as 'obsolete incendiaries' and 'spouters of stale sedition.' Surely, if he were at this time engaged in the business of educating his party, he would have denounced the policy for which he wished to prepare them in somewhat less emphatic terms.

On the 13th of May, that is, before the grand change took place, the Chancellor of the Exchequer insisted that no further alteration in the borough franchise ought to be permitted. He said:—

> I should have been very glad if, after the vote of the House on Thursday, it had been considered that a definite decision had been arrived at on the subject of the borough franchise.

* *Hansard*, vol. 186, col. 649.

I regret very much that these spouters of stale sedition should have come forward to take the course they have. It may be their function to appear at noisy meetings; but I regret very much that they should have come forward as obsolete incendiaries to pay their homage to one who, wherever he may sit, must always remain the pride and ornament of this House.*

Allusion is here made to certain deputations which paid 'homage' to Mr. Gladstone on the Saturday (May 11) following that particular Thursday on which Mr. Disraeli thought the borough franchise was comfortably ettled. The 'obsolete incendiaries' included seventeen members of Parliament—Mr. Bright, Mr. Hadfield, Mr. Gilpin, Professor Fawcett, Mr. Ayrton, Mr. Baines, Mr. Bazley, Mr. Stansfield, Mr. J. B. Smith, Mr. Watkin, Mr. Potter, Sir J. Gray, Mr. Cheetham, Mr. Edwards, Mr. Cowen, Mr. Candlish, and Mr. Barnes. Among the 'spouters of stale sedition' were the venerable champion of free trade, George Wilson, of Manchester, Sir John Bowring, Sir Henry Hoare, twenty-four clergymen, and a host of wealthy manufacturers, iron-masters, and mill-owners of the north of England. The deputation numbered in all about 360 persons. The purpose of their visit to Mr. Gladstone was to place in his hands a large number of addresses to and votes of confidence in him which had been passed at public meetings. The following extract from the speech of Mr. George Wilson is a perfectly fair specimen of the sedition 'spouted' on this occasion:—

They were not there to say that they wished to oppose the Reform Bill simply because it was brought in by the present Government; but they objected to it because it was not a Bill which they could possibly accept. They objected to the way in which it disqualified rather than qualified. It entirely destroyed the value of that which the Chancellor of the Exchequer stated that it possessed—that it was a Bill based on household suffrage.†

* *Hansard*, vol. 187, col. 403.   † *Daily Telegraph*, May 13, 1867.

What was sedition on Saturday became sound wisdom on the next Friday. The disqualifications of which Mr. George Wilson complained were now to be removed entirely, and the course proposed by Mr. Hodgkinson for that purpose was described by the Chancellor of the Exchequer as 'a policy which is one to carry out our original view—to affirm, establish, and render triumphant the principle on which we have proceeded.' To preclude the idea that any change had been produced in the resolutions of the Government by the public meetings held in opposition to their Bill, the right hon. gentleman thought it expedient to add:—

Whatever may be the influences that regulate the conduct of others, I can assure the House that her Majesty's Government in the course they are taking are not influenced by the terrors which have been depicted and the agitation with which we have been threatened.*

To show the enormous effect of the change produced by Mr. Hodgkinson's amendment, it must be observed that the effect of it is to place upon the electoral lists of boroughs all occupiers of tenements, of however humble condition, provided that they are not disqualified by the receipt of parochial relief, change of residence, and other disqualifications which legally affect all classes of electors.

The number of male compound householders in

* As corroboratory evidence of the sudden change of counsels with respect to Mr. Hodgkinson's amendment, it may be mentioned that on the morning of the day when it was to be brought forward (Friday, May 17) the Conservative members of the House received a communication from the Secretary of the Treasury earnestly requesting their attendance, as an amendment of great importance was about to be proposed. (See *Hansard*, vol. 187, col. 184.) This was obviously an intention to assist Government in opposing the amendment. If the Government at the time when this circular was issued intended to accept the amendment, it would have been superfluous to invoke the aid of their supporters. The troops were rallied, because it was resolved to give battle.

boroughs is 570,704. Of these, 94,111 are at or above the 10*l.* line, and 476,593 below it.* Of the former or superior class, it seems safe, for the following reason, to suppose that about 50 per cent. will come on the register. About 25 per cent. are registered already †; the additional 50 per cent. will render the total (75 per cent.) equal to the proportion of the personally rated 10*l.* householders who actually become qualified.

Of the 476,593 compound householders below the 10*l.* line, probably about 55 per cent. will be placed upon the electoral lists.

Hence it will be found that the total addition to the borough constituencies, by the effect of Mr. Hodgkinson's amendment, is:—

```
50 per cent. of 94,111     .   .   .    47,055
55 per cent. of 476,593    .   .   .   262,126
                                       -------
                                       309,181
```

It has been estimated in a former page that the net number of electors in boroughs introduced by the Bill, as originally introduced, was 118,400. Consequently the total increase due to the original Bill and to Mr. Hodgkinson's amendment is about 427,000, besides lodgers, of whom no exact estimate can be given. It thus appears that the effect of the momentous amendment was to extend the franchise *almost four times as much as was originally contemplated.* The character of the Bill was so materially altered that for all practical purposes it became a new measure.

The present actual number of borough electors in

---

* Mr. Hunt's Return, No. 136, of 1867.

† The total number of non-rated 10*l.* occupiers in boroughs is returned at 95,120, and of these 25,004 are electors (Return 305 of 1867, Mr. Gladstone). Thus it appears that about 26 per cent. of non-rated householders have been put on the register by the irregular action of overseers in a few boroughs and metropolitan parishes. In the return, it is stated that the overseers of Brighton intend to discontinue the practice of putting compound householders on the electoral lists.

England and Wales, after deducting double entries, is returned at 488,920.* It follows that the recent addition is not far short of the number already on the register. There are not any data for estimating the number of lodgers, but we may very safely conclude that, including them, the effect of the Act of 1867 is to nearly, if not quite, double the borough constituency.

As this point is very material in forming a judgment upon the character of the Act, it will be desirable to show, by a *totally different process*, that the numbers just given are substantially correct.

Mr. Gladstone, in 1866, computed the net number of electors (at rents between 10*l*. and 7*l*.) which would be introduced by his Bill at 156,000. But from this number we must deduct, for occupiers of separate shops and other buildings (not houses) who are not qualified under the Act of 1867, say 7 per cent., or about 11,000., and another deduction, of probably 10,000, must be made for freemen already on the register. Thus we get the net number of electors, at 7*l*. and under 10*l*., enfranchised by the present Act = 135,000.

With respect to the male occupiers under 7*l*., it will be approximately correct to assume, according to the principle explained in a former page,† that of the total number in boroughs (516,080) about one-half, or 258,000, will come on the register. We must also add, as in the former computation, 55 per cent. of the 94,111 compound householders above 10*l*. (= 47,055). Consequently, the number of persons enfranchised in boroughs under the Reform Act of 1867 may be estimated as follows:—

Householders under 10*l*. and not exceeding 7*l*.	135,000
Under 7*l*.	258,000
Compound householders above 10*l*.	47,055
Total	440,055

* Electoral Returns, 1865–66, p. 8.   † *Ante*, Chap. VIII.

By an entirely different process, the total addition to the borough franchise has been just computed at 436,000. Considering how widely the methods of calculation differ, the accordance of the final results is as close as could be reasonably expected.

In the first computation, the compound householders and the non-compounders are considered separately. We find first the number of non-compounders or personally rated occupiers enfranchised under the Bill in its original form; and add thereto the compounders enfranchised under Mr. Hodgkinson's amendment. In the second calculation the separation of the two classes is not observed. The occupiers under 10*l.* are reckoned together, whether personally rated or not. But with regard to compound householders above 10*l.*, the estimate is the same in both calculations.

Taking the increase of the borough constituency under the Act passed at 440,000, besides lodgers, and bearing in mind that before Mr. Hodgkinson's amendment the number enfranchised would have been about 118,000, it follows that by this alteration of the Bill the increase was made nearly four times as much as was originally contemplated.

The enormous concession made by the Chancellor of the Exchequer on the eventful 17th of May took his own followers by surprise. The Attorney-General recoiled from the abyss of household suffrage into which his leader was about to leap; in the course of the debate of that evening he said:—

> Any attempt to tie the Reform Bill to any Bill for settling rating and compounding—to make the one in any degree dependent upon the other—would be fatal to the Bill now before the Committee. . . . . He repeated, that to attempt to tie such a Bill to the clauses now before the House would be sure to defeat the Bill. Hon. and learned gentlemen opposite, who were perhaps more facile in drawing Bills than he could pretend to be, might present such a Bill in the course of the present

Session; but to him it appeared that it could not be satisfactorily done.*

Lord Cranbourne said that the right hon. gentleman had 'announced a change of startling magnitude,' and added:—

> It seems to me that it is not right that changes so enormous should be introduced in a Bill, transforming it entirely from the character which it wore when first introduced, without giving the House and the country, more than three hours at least to think over the alteration proposed.

On these grounds he moved that the chairman should report progress and the debate was accordingly adjourned. On the following Monday (May 20) the committee was again occupied with the borough franchise and Mr. Hodgkinson's amendment, was then adopted without amendment, after an eloquent but ineffectual protest by Mr. Lowe. He said that from first to last the House had 'been engaged in the most revolting details, endeavouring to adapt the proposals of the Government to a state of things as regards rating to which it was not possible to adapt it, but which it has at last destroyed to make a place for itself.'

The hon. gentleman assigned three causes for the willingness of the House to accept the proposed 'revolution in our Constitution': (1) weariness of the subject; (2) dread of a dissolution of Parliament; (3) a fear of offending the new voters who would probably get the franchise.

These were not exalted motives, but those to whom they were attributed listened without expressions of dissent. Except a small section which had long been openly in favour of household suffrage, there was no considerable party in Parliament which thoroughly approved of the changes now to be effected. The question of Reform had drifted into its present position, nobody knew how, and the House accepted the position simply because it was inevitable.

* *Hansard*, vol. 187, col. 735.

Nobody, said Mr. Lowe, could get up last year without making use of the strong vernacular expression 'swamping.' Who talks of swamping now? .... Last year my right hon. friend the member for South Lancashire, wished to enfranchise skilled labour, the *élite* of the working class. That has dropped out of our discussions. .... The question now is not, What is the opinion of the *élite* of the working class? but, What is the opinion of the unskilled labour class? For instance, in the borough which I represent, you will, I rather think, give us some Wiltshire labourers with 8*s.* a week wages. Will any gentleman favour me with a *précis* of the politics of these men?

Mr. Lowe forgot to mention that he himself had helped to render the present measure possible. His orations of 1866 had been a material obstacle to the enfranchisement of 'the *élite* of the working classes.' He had joined in an unnatural alliance with men who affected to defend the Constitution against the inroads of democracy, and who now sanctioned democratic schemes which the most sanguine Radicals would in 1866 have deemed utterly hopeless. The grief with which he contemplated this disaster must have been rendered more poignant by the reflection that he had contributed to it.

> So the struck eagle stretch'd upon the plain,
> No more through rolling clouds to soar again,
> View'd his own feather on the fatal dart,
> And wing'd the shaft that quiver'd in his heart.

In this remarkable speech of May 20, 1867, Mr. Lowe referred to an unavowed argument which secretly reconciled many Conservatives to household suffrage— the hope that the humble classes of voters would prove themselves amenable to good influences: by which they meant the influences of their own party. This was an argument which, for obvious reasons, could not be very explicitly stated in debate, but it had a considerable effect both inside and outside the walls of Parliament.

There is a feeling among hon. gentlemen opposite that something will be gained for party by their measure. They think that the middle classes have been uniformly hostile to them, and that something may be gained if they get to a lower class—that the one will counteract the other. I have faith in no such speculation. We have inaugurated a new era in English politics this session, and depend upon it the new fashion will henceforth be the rule and not the exception. This session we have not had what we before possessed—a party of attack and a party of resistance. We have instead two parties of competition, who, like Cleon and the sausage-seller in Aristophanes, are both bidding for the support of Demos. Do not suppose that this is the product of the Reform Bill, and that when you get a new Parliament this unwelcome symptom will disappear.

The statement that the House was divided into two parties competing for the favour of the populace may be questioned. Mr. Gladstone, in the earlier part of the session, had the moral courage to incur unpopularity by recommending that the lowest classes of householders in boroughs should be excluded from the franchise. This he proposed to do by the 'hard and fast line'—the only practicable method ever yet suggested for the purpose; and he did not desist from his enterprise until the combination of the 'tea-room' section with the party in power rendered his endeavours hopeless. Whatever doubt may exist as to the merits of this plan, it is a mere matter of fact that Mr. Gladstone, Mr. Bright, and the other members who wanted Mr. Coleridge's 'instruction' carried in its entirety, had distinctly dissociated themselves from the parties which were 'bidding for the support of Demos.'

Mr. Hodgkinson's amendment was adopted without a division, May 20, 1867, but not in the precise form in which it was to be embodied in the Act of Parliament. A few days subsequently the Chancellor of the Exchequer laid upon the table of the House certain clauses containing new arrangements respecting compounding; but these appeared to Mr. Hodgkinson so unsatisfactory that he gave notice (May 24) that he should move other clauses instead. The main difference between his plan and that of the Chancellor of the Exchequer was as follows. Subject to an exception with respect to existing compositions, the honourable member for Newark proposed to prohibit the compounding system in Parliamentary boroughs, absolutely and entirely. The Chancellor of the Exchequer, on the contrary, sought to make the continuance of the system optional. The third of the clauses prepared by him provided that by arrangement between the landlord and tenant the existing system of rating the former might be continued: if, however, the tenant were rated, he was to pay the full rate. It is obvious that these clauses aggravated one of the principal objections to the original Reform Bill—that it rendered the extension of the suffrage dependent on the will of local potentates. As the Bill stood at first, it was in the power of vestries, by adopting or rejecting the Small Tenements Acts, to enlarge or contract the right of suffrage. Now, a similar power was to be put into the hands of the landlords: they were to be enabled to dictate whether their compounding tenants should be enfranchised or not. If they chose to confer on them the right to vote, they might do so by insisting that the occupiers should henceforth pay full rates. On the other hand, the house owners who did not want their tenants to vote, had simply to declare their determination to continue the composition. The clause, indeed, spoke of an agreement between landlord and tenant on the subject, but in most cases the former is the master of the situation. The owner of cottage property would generally have the power of saying to the occupier—' Either you must let me pay the rates as formerly, or you must cease to be my tenant.'

The truth is, Mr. Disraeli suggested this modification of Mr. Hodgkinson's amendment as a means of neutralising its effect. Many of the most docile followers of the

Government beheld with consternation the concession of household suffrage, and probably even among the Ministers there were some who shared in their apprehensions. However, it was too late to retrace their steps. The Government had opened the gates of the constitution to Demos, and could not shut them again. Mr. Disraeli's attempt to render the suffrage a matter of arrangement between landlord and tenant failed; but the fact of the attempt is another test of the accuracy of his statement, that abolition of compounding was a triumph of his own principles. The incident is material to our history. Mr. Disraeli had already stated in the House of Commons that the abolition of compounding was a triumph of his own principles; and in his speech at Edinburgh, in the following autumn, he represented this great change in the electoral system as the result of his own strategy. It is difficult to reconcile these statements with the fact, that immediately after Mr. Hodgkinson's amendment was accepted he endeavoured to nullify it in the manner just described.

The form in which the abrogation of the Small Tenements Act, with respect to boroughs, was ultimately enacted, is as follows.

No owner of a dwelling in a parish, either wholly or partially within a borough, is to be henceforth rated to the poor-rate instead of the occupier. The name of the occupier and the full rate in the pound, are to be entered in the rate book. Existing compositions were retained up to Michaelmas 1857. There is a saving, also, with respect to rates made previously to the passing of the Act. The occupier of a tenement 'which has been let to him, free from rates,' may deduct from his rent the rates paid by him.

Thus was household suffrage established in boroughs. Every householder was to pay his own rates and have his name entered on the rate books, and thence in due course to be transferred to the electoral lists, subject of course to the usual disqualifications on account of nonresidence, nonpayment of rates, receipt of parochial relief, &c.

Mr. Disraeli laboured hard to show that the result was not household suffrage. In a debate (July 5) he said:—

> There are 4,500,000 inhabited houses in England—I do not pretend to speak with severe statistical accuracy, but I think I do not make much of a mistake. Not more than a moiety of these, even if the Bill passes, will be inhabited by persons qualified to exercise the franchise. Then if household suffrage be democracy what is all this about? Why, in one portion of your constituency, in the boroughs of England, which altogether are represented by 334 members, in the unjust manner I have often called attention to, there are altogether only 1,500,000 houses, and you are in fact extending that household suffrage which has existed since 1832 to a class which will probably increase your constituency by about 300,000 persons.*

At Edinburgh, in the autumn, he went further, and denied absolutely that the Reform Act established household suffrage. In his speech at a public dinner (October 29) the Chancellor of the Exchequer said:—

> We have not established household suffrage in England. There are I believe 4,000,000 houses in England, and under our ancient laws and under the Act of Lord Grey about 1,000,000 of those householders possess the franchise; under the Act of 1867 something more than 500,000 were added to that million. Well, I want to know, if there are 4,000,000 of householders and only 1,500,000 have the suffrage, how can household suffrage be established in England?†

But this was mere trifling with the question. In the passage just quoted, the statistics of counties and boroughs are blended together instead of being kept distinct, as they evidently ought to be. Nobody contends that household suffrage has been established in

* *Hansard*, vol. 188, col. 1113.   † *Times*, Oct. 30, 1867.

counties. The real question is, whether it has been enacted with respect to towns. Now the total number of male occupiers in the boroughs of England and Wales is 1,367,025.* The number of persons already on the register is 483,920 (after deducting double entries),† and the additional number of voters introduced by the Reform Act of 1867 has been shown in a former page to be about 450,000. Hence, the total number of borough electors will be about 939,000, or very nearly 70 per cent. of the male occupiers. Of course the most ardent advocates of household suffrage never expected or desired that *all* male householders should be enfranchised. They never desired to give the suffrage to mere vagrants or paupers in the receipt of parochial relief. The disqualifications which arise from non-residence, neglect to register, and similar causes, must inevitably, under any conceivable system, prevent a considerable number of householders from becoming electors. These disqualifications exist with respect to all classes of voters, new and old. What Mr. Disraeli had to do was, to show that under the system which he espoused some special restrictions operated, which would render the borough suffrage under the Reform Act less extensive than household suffrage, in the sense in which that term is ordinarily used by politicians. This necessary link in his argument he wholly omitted. At the beginning of the session, he thought that 'personal payment of rates,' would operate as such a special restriction. It is now found that this vital principle, as it was considered, has no real existence, and consequently the system of household suffrage has been effectually established in boroughs.

* Return No. 120, of 1867 (Mr. Hankey).
† Electoral Returns, 1865-6, p. 8.

CHAPTER XIII.

THE COUNTY SUFFRAGE.

Reduction of the copyholders' and leaseholders' qualification, 211.—*Restrictions as to land in boroughs,* 212.—*Attempt to make the occupiers' qualification depend on residence,* 213.—*Estimate of number of new county voters,* 215.

THE Bill, as originally brought in, proposed to give the county suffrage to rated occupiers of 'premises of any tenure within the county of the rateable value of *fifteen pounds* and upwards,' and to persons qualified under what were termed the 'educational' and 'pecuniary franchise.' The latter two classes of qualifications had been abandoned before the Bill was considered in committee, and now the only proposal of the Government for the extension of the county suffrage was the clause enfranchising the occupiers of tenements of the rateable value of 15*l.* and upwards. This scheme was materially altered in committee by amendments proceeding from the Liberal side of the House. The first amendment which was adopted was that of Mr. Colville, member for South Derbyshire, by which it was proposed to make tenure of *copyhold* lands worth 5*l.* per annum a qualification for the county suffrage. This amendment was opposed by the Attorney-General on behalf of the Government, but was carried (May 20, 1867) by a majority of 44, the numbers being, Ayes, 201; Noes, 157.*

* *Hansard*, vol. 137, col. 848.

Three days afterwards (May 23) Mr. Hussey Vivian, member for Glamorganshire, proposed an amendment, giving the county suffrage to *leaseholders* under sixty years' leases of lands worth 5*l*. a year. The Chancellor of the Exchequer considered the decision with regard to copyholders to be conclusive as to this motion, and agreed to it, 'subject to this: that the 5*l*. qualification was to be enjoyed under similar conditions as the 10*l*. qualification under the Reform Bill of 1832.'* In reply to a further question on this point, Mr. Gathorne Hardy said, that it was to be understood, 'that the 5*l*. qualification would be enjoyed the same as the 10*l*. qualification, under the 24th and 25th sections of the Reform Act.'

The sections of the Act of 1832 here mentioned are to the following effect. Section 24 provides that no one shall vote for a county as *freeholder* of any house, &c., occupied by himself, where it is 'of such value as would, according to the provisions hereinafter contained,' confer on *him* 'the right of voting for any city,' &c. By section 25: no one is to vote for the county as *copyholder, lessee,* 'or as such *tenant* or *occupier* as aforesaid,' of any house, &c., 'of such value as would, according to the provisions hereinafter contained, confer *on him or any other person* the right of voting for any city,' &c.

Consequently, if any freeholder occupies his own freehold in a borough, and thereby becomes entitled to a borough vote, the property will not qualify him to vote for the county. But if somebody else occupies such freehold, the tenant may vote in the borough and the owner in the county. With respect to copyhold and leasehold qualifications the rule is different: if they confer a right to vote in the borough upon *any one*

---

* *Hansard,* vol. 187, col. 997.

they will not confer on the owner a right to vote for the county.

These provisions of the Reform Act of 1832 are apparently intended to be applied by the Act of 1837 to the new classes of voters. But the section which relates to this subject is very obscure and clumsily expressed.*

Several attempts were made during the discussions in committee to render the occupiers' qualification in counties dependent upon the occupation of a dwelling-house. The effect of such a condition would obviously be to restrict this suffrage very generally to residents. As the clause relating to county occupiers originally stood, it proposed to confer the franchise upon 'the occupier as owner or tenant of premises of any tenure within the county of the rateable value of fifteen pounds or upwards.'

Sir Edward Colebrooke moved (May 23) to substitute for 'premises of any tenure' the words 'a dwelling-house.' This amendment was rejected by a majority of 3, the numbers being, Ayes, 209; Noes, 212.† But on a subsequent day (May 24) the committee came to a conflicting decision, and by a majority of 10 resolved to insert in clause 4 the words 'with a house.'‡ The condition of residence was not, however, adopted ultimately.

---

* The section (the 59th) is as follows:—' This Act, so far as is consistent with the tenor thereof, shall be construed as one with the enactments for the time being in force relating to the representation of the people, and with the Registration Acts; and in construing the provisions of the 24th & 25th sections of the Act of the second year of King William the Fourth, chapter forty-five, the expressions, "the provisions hereinafter contained," and "as aforesaid," shall be deemed to refer to the provisions of this Act conferring rights to vote as well as to the provisions of the said Act.'

But in the Act of 1832 the ' expressions' here quoted from it relate only to houses of a *particular value*. Whereas in the present Act, rights to vote in boroughs are not conferred in respect of houses of any particular value. Consequently it is difficult to make the 'expressions' in question 'refer to the provisions of this Act conferring rights to vote.'

† *Hansard*, vol. 187, col. 1002.   ‡ *Ibid.* col. 1151.

Mr. Locke King moved (May 28) to substitute 10*l.* for 15*l.* as the limit of the value in the county occupiers' qualification. The Chancellor of the Exchequer offered on the part of the Government to fix the value at 12*l.* Mr. Gladstone recommended that this offer should be accepted. He said that he would vote with Mr. Locke King if he pressed his motion, but that the difference between it and the proposal of the Chancellor of the Exchequer was not sufficient to justify a division of the House. The form in which the occupation franchise of county voters finally received the sanction of Parliament is as follows. The suffrage is conferred upon persons who for twelve months have occupied, as owners or tenants, 'lands or tenements within the county of the rateable value of twelve pounds or upwards,' subject to a condition that such occupiers have been rated and duly paid poor rates.*

Clause 5, relating to the 'educational franchises,' clause 6, relating to 'pecuniary franchises,' and clause 7, relating to the dual vote, were abandoned by the Government and were negatived without a division (May 29). Clause 8, disfranchising the boroughs of Yarmouth, Lancaster, Reigate, and Totness, was carried by a large majority the following day. Royal commissions, appointed to inquire into the existence of corrupt practices at these places, had reported that such practices had prevailed for several years at the elections for each of them.

It will be interesting to compare the number of new county voters qualified under the original Bill and the number qualified by the effect of the amendments.

The principal data for the purpose of this calculation are to be found in the Electoral Returns, 1865-6, p. 286. The total numbers of several classes of county occupiers in England and Wales are given as follows:—

---

* 30 & 31 Vic. c. 102, s. 6 (corresponding to clause 4 in the original Bill).

Male occupiers at 12*l.* and under 50*l.*	. .	240,277
,, ,, at 15*l.* and under 50*l.*	. .	186,392
,, ,, at 50*l.* and upwards	. .	155,847
Electors registered as 50*l.* occupiers	. .	110,800

It thus appears that 75 per cent. of the male occupiers in counties actually come upon the register. We may suppose that the same proportions would hold with respect to the 12*l.* and 15*l.* classes. Hence, if the 15*l.* franchise originally proposed by the Government had been established, the number of electors thereby qualified would have been probably 139,894, or in round numbers 140,000.

Under the 12*l.* occupiers' franchise, we find similarly that the number of persons who will probably register is a little more than 170,000.

There are no data for ascertaining the number of persons who will register under the clauses relating to copyholders and leaseholders of lands worth 5*l.* per annum. In some districts the number of such persons is considerable. It will, perhaps, be not far from the truth to conclude that the total addition to the county register will be about 200,000. The total number of electors on the register for 1864–5 was 542,633. Hence it will be seen that the extension of the suffrage is much smaller in the counties than in the boroughs. It has been shown that the town constituencies are nearly doubled by the Reform Act.

CHAPTER XIV.

THE DISTRIBUTION OF SEATS.

Amendment to increase the number of partially disfranchised boroughs, 217.— Unsuccessful motion to give additional members to six large boroughs, 219.— Subsequent concession with respect to four of them, 224.— The schedules finally adopted, 225.— Statistics of their effects; preponderance of the power of small boroughs, 227.

THE progress of the Bill through committee was characterised by a continual enlargement of its scope. Every change which had hitherto been made tended to increase the number of voters. Mr. Ayrton's amendment reducing the term of residence required of borough voters, the lowering of the county franchise from 15*l*. to 12*l*. annual value, the lodger franchise, and above all, the abolition of rate-compounding in boroughs— all these amendments tended to a larger Reform than was originally contemplated. In the distribution of seats, also, most material alterations were effected by the Liberal party.

Of these amendments none had more immediate and direct effect in changing the balance of parliamentary power than the new provisions introduced with respect to the distribution of seats. The Government scheme was originally very limited. It was not intended to wholly disfranchise any towns except the four visited with this penalty for their venality. Twenty-three others were to lose one member each, and the vacated seats were to be transferred to other constituencies. The number was enlarged upon the motion of Mr. Laing, member for Wick, to thirty-eight. He moved (May 31) that—

No borough which had a less population than 10,000 at the census of 1861 shall return more than one member to Parliament.

The Chancellor of the Exchequer resisted this motion. He commented upon the proposals of Mr. Laing with respect to the allotment of the vacated seats, and concluded by expressing a hope that the committee would not 'enter into the sea of troubles they would find themselves in by the adoption of this motion.' It was, however, carried by a very large majority (127); the numbers being, for the amendment, 306, against it 179.

The number of boroughs affected by this decision was thirty-eight. Adding seven seats vacated by the total disfranchisement of Yarmouth, Reigate, Lancaster, and Totness, there were in all forty-five seats to be disposed of.

Mr. Sergeant Gaselee endeavoured to carry the process of redistribution still further. He moved (June 3)—

That every borough which has less population than 5,000 at the last census shall cease to return any member of Parliament.

Mr. Cardwell supported this proposition. He made the remarkable statement that the ten boroughs which it affected did not contain an aggregate population of 40,000—men, women, and children; whereas the number of householders who would be capable of being placed on the register under this Bill, in Liverpool alone, was 65,000.

The House was not, however, prepared to wholly disfranchise any small boroughs, and the amendment was rejected by a majority of 52.*

A fortnight after Mr. Laing's motion increasing the number of vacated seats had been carried, the Chancellor of the Exchequer explained the recommendations

* *Hansard*, vol. 187, col. 1523.

of the Government with respect to the enlarged scheme of redistribution which had become necessary. He proposed to add four members to the metropolitan representation, by creating a new borough of Chelsea and another of Hackney. Thirteen large unrepresented towns—Hartlepool, Darlington, Middlesborough, Burnley, S. Helen's, Barnsley, Dewsbury, Staleybridge, Wednesbury, Gravesend, Stockton, Keighley, and Luton—were to have one member each. Salford and Merthyr Tydvil were each to have an additional representative. Nineteen seats were thus disposed of. One member was to be given to the University of London in conjunction with that of Durham. The remaining twenty-five seats were alloted to counties.

In this scheme no provision was made for giving additional members to the six largest boroughs—Birmingham, Bristol, Leeds, Liverpool, Manchester, and Sheffield; nor for the increased representation of Scotland. The Chancellor of the Exchequer had already recognised the claims of the northern kingdom in this respect, and he now announced that they were to be satisfied by adding to the number of seats in the House of Commons. He said—

I am not at all prepared, if Scotland be not adequately represented, as I believe she is not, that the adequate representation should be secured by impairing the adequate representation of England. . . . . I think, under the circumstances, if the House of Commons is really of opinion that Scotland is not adequately represented, they ought to meet the difficulty and increase that representation. But that we should lay down the principle that the adequate representation of Scotland is to be obtained at the expense of the adequate representation of England or Ireland, is a proposition that I cannot at all support.*

But the grand defect of the Ministerial scheme was neglect of the just claims of such vast towns as Man-

* *Hansard*, vol. 187, col. 1784.

chester, Liverpool, Leeds, and Birmingham. The population of Liverpool in 1867 was very little less than 500,000. The computed number in 1866 was 482,409, and it is increased by several thousands every year. Liverpool with its 500,000 of inhabitants, Manchester with 380,000, and Birmingham with 333,000, had no more power in the House of Commons than Thetford, a mere village, with a population of 4,276. On what assignable principle of representation can these anomalies be justified? The country is not prepared for a system of equal electoral districts; but the very scheme of distribution offered by the Government was an admission that some relation ought to be observed between the numbers of the people and their representatives. Mr. Disraeli had argued in his speech of June 13 that the counties to which he proposed to allot 25 additional seats contained 4,000,000 of inhabitants, exclusive of those within boroughs. But the same argument might be advanced with still greater force on behalf of the six largest provincal towns in England. Their aggregate number of people is upwards of 1,500,000, and the total number of their representatives at the commencement of 1867 was twelve. Whereas the counties to which it was proposed to give increased power had already 45 members, besides those sitting for the boroughs within them. It does not need much arithmetical skill to perceive that if 4,000,000 of people were entitled to have the number of their representatives increased from 45 to 70, 1,500,000 of people were entitled to an increase upon the number (12) of their representatives.

Mr. Laing, member for Wick, brought this subject under the consideration of the House of Commons in an elaborate speech, June 17. He moved to insert words for the purpose of giving to each of the six great boroughs three members instead of two. He admitted that counties had a just claim to increased power, and showed very clearly that the consideration exhibited towards them by the ministerial scheme was withheld from the great boroughs.

Mr. Disraeli's reply was not an answer at all to this complaint. The tenor of his argument was this: comparing the rural population with that of towns, it will be found that the former have much the largest share of power in proportion to their numbers; the Government, therefore, propose to reduce the inequality to some extent by adding to the county representation. He added:—

> It is for this reason that it would be reasonable to increase the representation of large counties, without increasing the representation of large towns. We must take a broad and general view; we cannot decide the question by comparing one large town, such as Leeds or Birmingham, with some small borough. I might as well compare the population of some large county with that of some small county.*

Of course he might; of course he ought, and of course he did. For, in selecting certain counties which were to have additional members, he properly took those which at present have the smallest share of power with reference to their population. If one county, compared with another, had an inadequate share in the representation, it was reasonable that the inequality should be redressed. The injustice done to the great counties the Minister now proposed to deal with; but because it was to be dealt with, he contended that the equally grievous injustice to great boroughs was to be left unredressed. It does not seem to have occurred to the Chancellor of the Exchequer that both grievances ought to be remedied simultaneously.

The real obstacle to any thoroughly effective redistribution of seats is the over-representation of small boroughs. The experience of successive Ministries, ever

---

* *Hansard*, vol. 187, col. 1955.

since the great Reform of 1832, shows that an attack upon the privileges of these places is a perilous enterprise. But, unless some of them are disfranchised, how is it possible to obtain seats for new and important communities without increasing the already inconvenient number of members of the House of Commons? 'Sweet Auburn' and a number of other of the loveliest villages of the plain have collectively so much power that they are enabled to withstand the opinion of the rest of the community, and probably of every Ministry which in modern times has seriously approached the subject of Reform. In 1832 a great work of disfranchisement was accomplished; but we all know the loud outcry which the process occasioned, and that a popular agitation scarcely less violent than a revolution was required to induce the House of Commons to perform the surgical operation of cutting off its own dead limbs.

People appealed then, as they appeal now, to the wisdom of our ancestors as a proof that the representation of small boroughs is a constitutional benefit. The argument is founded on an entire misapprehension of the most ancient principles of representation. In the earliest Parliaments all cities and boroughs—great and small—were summoned to send representatives. Thence an inference is sometimes made that our ancestors did not consider it necessary to apportion the number of representatives to that of the people. Certainly, mathematical exactness was not observed; but a rough approximation to a uniform distribution of power was secured by the rule that *all* boroughs should be enfranchised. They were all considerable places, for until they had acquired importance, they did not obtain municipal privileges and separate jurisdiction. Moreover, Parliamentary majorities were of much less importance in the fourteenth century than now. Each town and each county were required to send agents or delegates to state what grant that town or that county was prepared to make to the Crown. We see this very clearly in the commissions for collecting subsidies in the reigns of Edward I. and Edward II.* The writ for each county speaks of the grant made by *that* county. Members of Parliament were not then representatives in the modern sense of the word, but agents appointed to declare the resolutions of those who employed them. Of course, so long as this theory of representation was maintained, the number of representatives was a matter of little moment. In 18 Edward I. the writs command the sheriffs to send for their counties *two or three* knights.† This discretion as to the number shows that the balance of political power was not regarded. It was not considered that any injustice was done by the election of as many members for the smallest town as for the City of London or the populous county of Norfolk.

When antiquity is cited in favour of the present power of obscure boroughs, the principles on which our ancestors proceeded are misunderstood. They were content with a very simple scheme, which probably was sufficiently uniform to answer its purpose without sensible inconvenience or injustice. The experience of later times was needed to disclose the necessity of a more accurate system. In modern times we frequently find that in a mere village, with a single, silent, grass-grown street, containing a few hundred of inhabitants, who never seem awake except at election time, when money passes freely and beer is abundant, the electors' choice is determined by the secret favours of emissaries from a London club, or the commands of a neighbouring duke or his

---

* For example, a writ of the 11th Edward I. to the 'knights, freemen, and whole community of Hampshire,' recites that they had lately by 'four knights sent on the part of the community of the same county,' granted a subsidy to the king. Similar writs were at the same time addressed to the other counties.—*Parliamentary Writs*, ed. by Palgrave, vol. i. p. 13.

† 1 *Parliamentary Writs*, p. 21.

still more formidable agent. Many such places possess as much influence in the national councils as the great Port of the Mersey with its enormous commerce, or the wealthy metropolis of the manufacturing districts. This is a monstrous wrong and fraud of political power to which long-continued usage may induce the country to submit patiently, but which no lapse of time can justify.

The period for completely rectifying this grievance has not yet come, but cannot be remote. The principle recently adopted in enlarging the representation of counties must ere long be extended to a redress of the balance between the large and small towns. The country does not demand absolute mathematical precision in the distribution of power, but disparities which still remain, are enormous, and especially the outrageous predominance of pocket and family influence in small boroughs must, so long as it continues, prevent the House of Commons from truly representing the nation.

Even the obviously just demands of the great towns of Liverpool, Manchester, Leeds, Sheffield, Birmingham, and Bristol failed, in the first instance, to obtain recognition. Mr. Laing's motion for giving a third member to each of these places was rejected (June 17) by a majority of 8.* But shortly afterwards the claims of four of these towns were more successful.

On the 1st of July, Mr. Horsfall, member for Liverpool, moved that boroughs having each a population ' of upwards of 250,000, shall respectively return three members to serve in Parliament.'

Statistical proofs of the existing anomalies of the representative system have been produced in abundance, but one contribution of this kind made by Mr. Goschen in the course of the debate, is so remarkable that it ought not to be omitted. He said :—

* Ayes, 239; Noes, 247. *Hansard*, vol. 187, col. 1909.

There were in England, including the metropolis, 4,250,000 living in towns with over 150,000 inhabitants. That was about half the borough population of England, and yet that 4,250,000 had only 34 out of the 334 borough representatives.*

In other words, half the borough population was represented by nine-tenths of the borough members, and the other half by the remaining tenth. This statement refers to the state of the constituencies before the late Reform; the extent to which the inequalities have been rectified by the recent statute will be presently explained.

In the debate upon Mr. Horsfall's motion for increasing the number of members for Liverpool, Manchester, and Birmingham, the Chancellor of the Exchequer announced a change in the counsels of the Government. He said:—

I think it would be most unwise of us to confer an increase of representatives on the great cities of Lancashire, and not to acknowledge the claim of the great city of rival industry— I mean Leeds. I shall therefore, on the part of the Government be prepared at the fitting time to make such changes in the schedule as would give an additional representative to each of these four constituencies. But I wish to be distinctly understood, that Her Majesty's Government are only prepared to give that increase of representation to those places by remodelling the schedules upon the table, and I must add that, if Manchester is to have three members, Salford must be content with one, while the additional seats for the other three cities must be withheld from those boroughs whose claims for increased representation we should otherwise have recommended to the House for favourable consideration.†

Shortly afterwards, the efforts to add Sheffield and Bristol to the list of triply-represented boroughs were unsuccessfully renewed. Mr. Hadfield, Member for Sheffield, and Mr. Berkeley, Member for Bristol, respectively moved (July 2) to add those places to the

* *Hansard*, vol. 188, col. 823.
† *Hansard*, vol. 188, col. 838. At a later date, however, the Government recurred to its earlier resolution to increase the representation of Salford.

list, but both motions were negatived by large majorities.

The schedules to the Reform Act, containing the lists of boroughs and counties affected by the redistribution of seats, were adopted (July 9) without division. The general results of the changes ultimately enacted are as follows. Twenty-five additional seats were given to English counties, or divisions of counties, viz.:—

Cheshire.
Derbyshire.
Devonshire.
Essex.
Kent (West).
Lancashire (North).
Lancashire (South).
Lincolnshire.
Norfolk.
Somersetshire.
Staffordshire.
Surrey (East).
Yorkshire (West Riding).

In each of these districts new divisions were established, and the number of representatives increased by two, except South Lancashire, to which only one additional seat was given.

Nineteen additional seats have been given to boroughs of England and Wales, viz., one seat to each of these six:—Birmingham, Leeds, Liverpool, Manchester, Salford, and Merthyr-Tydvil; and the rest to new boroughs, viz.:—

Chelsea (2).
Darlington (1).
Hackney (2).
Hartlepool (1).
Stockton (1).
Gravesend (1).
Burnley (1).
Staleybridge (1).
Wednesbury (1).
Middlesborough (1).
Dewsbury (1).

The nineteen seats given to boroughs, the twenty-five given to counties, and one assigned to the University of London, complete the number of forty-five seats rendered disposable by the partial or total disfranchisement of various boroughs, viz. those wholly disfranchised, which heretofore had altogether seven representatives, and thirty-eight others which will have henceforth only one member each, instead of two.

The following synopsis shows the distribution of seats with reference to population in the larger and smaller boroughs, and the counties of England and Wales. The total number of representatives of boroughs has been reduced to 308. The total number for counties is now 187.

The population of counties in England and Wales, exclusive of boroughs in 1861, was 11,427,655.* But this figures is now altered, by the enfranchisement of several towns, and the total disfranchisement of four others. The latter have about 64,000 inhabitants altogether. The population of all the places newly enfranchised under the recent Reform Act is given in the return just cited, and in the aggregate amounts to rather more than 225,000. Consequently, the county population, exclusive of the boroughs, may now be taken at 11,266,000.

In the following synopsis the boroughs are classed according to magnitude; the total population, in 1861, of all the boroughs in each class is given, and also the aggregate number of members by whom they are represented.

The population is stated only in round numbers, that is, only the number of thousands is given in each instance. As only comparative results are required, a more minute accuracy would have been superfluous.

---

* Return to House of Commons, No. 283, of 1864 (Mr. White).

Distribution of Seats under the Reform Act of 1867, with reference to the population.

	Population 1861.	Number of Representatives.
Counties exclusive of boroughs	11,266,000	187
19 Boroughs with population above 100,000	4,069,000	46
19 Boroughs with population between 100,000 and 50,000	1,385,000	36
51 Boroughs with population between 50,000 and 20,000	1,567,000	77
49 Boroughs with population between 20,000 and 10,000	692,000	81
68 Boroughs with population under 20,000	420,000	68

From this table we may obtain several instructive results. For instance, comparing all the towns with a population above 20,000, with all of which the population is below that line, we find that—

89 Boroughs with an aggregate population of 7,041,000 have 159 members.
168 „ „ „ „ 1,112,000 „ 149 „

The inhabitants of the larger boroughs are upwards of seven millions and a half. This vast population has little more power than the one million one hundred thousand of the smaller towns. It is clear that the latter get the lion's share of political influence.

Another way of regarding these figures is to consider the proportions of representatives to populations in the various classes. There are:—

	Inhabitants for each member.
In Counties	60,200
In Boroughs with population above 100,000 each	101,000
In Boroughs with population between 100,000 and 50,000	38,000
In Boroughs with population between 50,000 and 20,000	20,000
In Boroughs with population between 20,000 and 10,000	8,500
In Boroughs with population under 10,000	6,100

These are results presented, be it remembered, after the readjustment of political power effected by the Reform Act of 1867. A member for one of the largest boroughs represents, on the average, more than sixteen times as many persons as a representative of one of the smallest towns. If the counties have a right to complain of a grievance, these huge towns have a right to complain of one almost twice as great; for the ratio of their population to seats is nearly twice as great as in the counties.

Another very important deduction from these figures is obtained by comparing the boroughs of the highest class with the rest collectively.

	Population 1861.	Number of Representatives.
19 Boroughs with a population of more than 100,000 each	4,069,000	46
The Boroughs with a population less than 100,000 each	4,064,000	262

The nineteen great urban districts have an aggregate population considerably larger than all the rest together, and yet the latter have nearly six times as many representatives.

These facts ought to be borne in mind when complaints are made of the inadequate representation of counties. If they suffer, so do the great towns, in a much greater degree. It cannot be too emphatically or too positively stated that this kingdom is at present practically governed by the small boroughs. The only considerable argument for retaining their enormous power is that the powerful patrons who nominate their representatives have occasionally selected men of eminence. A few exceptional instances of happy selections do not compensate for the evil wrought by crowding that assembly with persons whom a legal fiction designates representatives of the people. The whole system of nomination boroughs is an abuse uncontemplated in the original constitution of Parliament; for the very name of the 'House of Commons' sufficiently proves that it was intended by our ancestors to be chosen freely and indifferently by all the commons of the realm, and by them alone.

CHAPTER XV.

DISTINCTION OF BOROUGH AND COUNTY FRANCHISES: BOUNDARIES.

Attempts to exclude owners of property in towns from the county franchise, 229.
—*Townsmen anciently voted in county elections,* 230.—*Restriction of this right by the Reform Act of* 1832, 232.—*Mr. Colville's motion to abrogate the restriction with respect to copyholders,* 233.—*Similar motion by Mr. Hussey Vivian with respect to leaseholders,* 234.—*The boundary commission,* 240.—*Comparison of the methods of rectifying boundaries adopted in the Reform Bills of* 1866 *and* 1867, 242.

OF late years, the right of owners of land situated within boroughs to participate in county elections has been the subject of much controversy, and the Conservative party has made frequent attempts to render the constituencies of shires exclusively rural. In the Reform Bill introduced by Mr. Disraeli in 1859, there was, as we have seen,[*] a provision that every elector, whose qualification was real property, should vote in the place in which it was situated. This provision, if it had been enacted, would have excluded from the county register a large number of freeholders of land in towns who had hitherto voted for knights of the shire. The same policy was adopted with respect to the Reform of 1867. The Government insisted, as we have stated, upon the insertion of a section (the 59th) incorporating those clauses of the Act of 1832 which prevent various kinds of interests in land situated within towns from conferring county qualifications.

The easiest way of understanding this somewhat com-

[*] *Ante,* Chapter i.

plicated subject is to consider it historically. The distinction between urban and rural electors, and the policy of our law upon the subject, will appear most clearly by reviewing the ancient practice in this respect. It is now well ascertained that at the original constitution of Parliament the distinction did not exist. It was, indeed, impracticable. The election of knights of the shire took place in the county courts — assemblies which were commonly held for this purpose in the open air, and which were freely accessible to all who chose to attend them. The primitive electoral machinery which existed in the time of the Plantagenets did not permit any scrutiny of votes, and the property qualification was a refinement unknown until a much later period. We have also positive proof that the same persons participated in the election of burgesses and knights of the shire. Evidence of this kind has been preserved in a curious way in ancient *indentures of return*, by which, according to a usage which continues to the present day, the names of the persons chosen were recorded. It was the practice in the fourteenth and fifteenth centuries, as it still is, that these indentures should be signed by a few of the electors, for the purpose of authenticating the returns. Now, we find in various cases that the returns, both of knights and burgesses, were signed by the same electors. Thus Prynne has given the indenture of return in 8 Henry IV., of the knights for the county and the burgesses for the borough of Cambridge. They are returned by *one and the same* indenture, in which twelve electors named testify that they have taken part in the election of John Howard and John Rocheford for the county, and Simon Bentibowe and Thomas Beverles for the borough. A like joint return is made for the county and borough of Huntingdon.*

---

* *Prynne. Brevia Parliamentaria,* page 252.

This is conclusive evidence that at the date of those records there was no rule prohibiting burgesses from choosing knights of the shire. These indentures were returned into Chancery. They were the most solemn authentic records of the elections, and the public officers who also signed them were liable to severe penalties if they returned any persons other than those who had been chosen freely and indifferently by the proper constituencies. It is manifest that these functionaries would not have openly and undisguisedly executed an instrument which recorded an illegal election.

About twenty-five years later a property qualification was, for the first time, established. A law of 8 Henry VI. restricts the county franchise to the class commonly known as the forty-shilling freeholders. Knights were henceforth to 'be chosen in every county of the realm of England by people dwelling and resident in the same counties, whereof every one of them shall have free land or tenement to the value of forty shillings by the year, at the least, above all charges.'* This statute remains in force to this day, and has never been construed as establishing any distinction between freeholds in boroughs and freeholds outside their boundaries. On the contrary, the practice ever since has undoubtedly allowed owners of both kinds of property to take part in the choice of knights of the shire.

The Reform Act of 1832, for the first time, drew such a distinction. It provided that if a freeholder occupied his own freehold in a town so as to be entitled to vote in the borough, he should not, in respect of that property, have a vote for the county. But he might let his land or tenement in the borough to somebody else, who thereby got a borough vote. In that case the freeholder might still vote for the county.

In the debate of June 24, 1867, the Attorney-General

* 8 Henry VI., cap. 7.

(Sir John Rolt) somewhat misstated the history of this subject. He said:—

The Government stood by the Act of 1832 loyally, and notwithstanding that they disapproved of the privilege which it conferred upon freeholders, and the introduction to that extent of the urban elements in counties, they accepted that provision and did not propose to alter it.*

This, however, was an erroneous and probably an inadvertent statement by a very able and learned lawyer. Mr. Gladstone, commenting upon it, observed:—

The Attorney-General has positively discovered that this plan of allowing freeholders in towns to vote for counties was an innovation introduced in 1832, and he has actually persuaded the hon. member for Norfolk, who likewise complained of the injustice inflicted in 1832. Why, it is the old principle of the constitution, and what the Act of 1832 did, was not to introduce the practice of freeholders in towns voting for counties, but to restrict that practice by disabling the voter from voting for the county where he occupied his freehold in the town.†

The Reform Act of 1832 went a step further with respect to the copyholders and leaseholders, upon whom, the county franchise was then conferred for the first time. It provided that they were not to have that franchise if their copyhold or leasehold property entitled them, or any one else, to vote for a borough. They could not, like the freeholder, let their lands in a a represented town and retain their vote for the county, while some one else voted in respect of the same property for the borough.

These preliminary remarks will serve to elucidate the discussion upon a motion by Mr. Colville, member for Derbyshire, for putting land in boroughs on the same footing as land outside them, with respect to the county suffrage. He moved (June 24, 1867) to insert the following proviso:—

* *Hansard*, vol. 188, col. 464. † *Ibid.*, vol. 188, col. 470.

Provided that so much of the Act of the second William the Fourth, chapter forty-five, as disqualifies the owner of any copyhold tenement situated within a city or borough (who would be otherwise qualified) from voting in the election of a member or members for the county during the time that the same tenement confers a right of voting for such city or borough on *any other person,* shall be and the same is hereby repealed.*

The words here marked by *italics* must be noticed. It was not suggested that the urban copyholder should have a double vote, one for the county and one for the borough. All that was asked was that, like the freeholder, if he did not occupy his own land in the borough he might vote in respect of it for the county. Mr. Henley fell into a mistake upon this point, as he afterwards candidly acknowledged. He said:—

He had always maintained that a person having a freehold in a borough not occupied by him, and out of which he did not vote for the borough, should have a county franchise. But the present proposal would give a man a vote for a borough in respect of the house in which he lived, and another for the county in respect of the same house.

Sir Roundell Palmer pointed out that Mr. Henley had misunderstood the tenor of the amendment, and remarked that—

He agreed with the right hon. gentleman that they ought not to give a man a vote for the county as well as for the borough in respect of the same qualification. The amendment however, would not interfere with the 24th clause of the Reform Act, which precluded persons from having two votes for one qualification, but would simply provide that a copyholder or leaseholder letting his property to a person who thereby gained a borough vote, should not be deprived of his vote for the county.†

The House had just agreed to a clause making copyhold lands worth 5*l.* a year, and lands of the like value held under sixty years' leases qualifications for the

* *Hansard,* vol. 188, col. 457.   † *Hansard,* vol. 188,

county suffrage. It was resolved that such interests were as valuable for electoral purposes as forty-shilling freeholds. Copyhold property differs from freeholds only in some incidents of tenure and technicalities of conveyancing, which do not materially affect their market value. As far as the use and dominion of the land are concerned, both stand on the same footing. Why, then, should there be any difference between them for electoral purposes? Why should the freeholder have a peculiar privilege with respect to exercise of the franchise?

But this is not the only, perhaps not the strongest, argument in favour of the motion for removing the special disabilities affecting copyholds, and of the subsequent motion of Mr. Hussey Vivian for removing similar disabilities with respect to leasehold property in boroughs. Unless such restrictions were removed, the Act about to be passed would have an extensive and probably uncontemplated effect of disfranchising a considerable number of persons enfranchised under the Act of 1832. This result was pointed out by the Marquess of Hartington, who observed,—

He could not agree with the Under-Secretary for the Colonies that this was not a question of disfranchisement, as under the provisions of the present Bill there were many copyholders in boroughs holding copyholds separately under the value of 10*l.*, but collectively above 10*l.*, now possessing votes for the counties, but who would lose their franchise as soon as their tenants obtained borough votes.*

Mr. Hussey Vivian made a similar observation with respect to the hardship which the Bill would inflict upon leaseholders.

A large number of persons, however, had under that qualification obtained votes for counties in respect of premises within boroughs. In many cases it happened that the owners

* *Hansard*, vol. 186, col. 404.

of long leases had upon their tenements houses under 10*l*., which singly conferred no vote for the borough, but being in the aggregate of a greater value than 10*l*. they conferred a county vote upon the owner of the lease. Under the present Bill the occupier of these houses became a borough voter, and therefore it disfranchised a large number of county voters. . . Under the sweeping provisions of that Bill, every rate-paying householder within a borough would be enfranchised, and consequently no owner of leasehold property within boroughs could continue to be a county voter.*

The provisoes which Mr. Colville and Mr. Hussey Vivian proposed to insert were rejected by majorities of 20 and 26 respectively. Consequently the Act as it now stands has a very considerable disfranchising effect. It was agreed on all sides that one of the fundamental principles of the new measure was to be a preservation of existing rights. But this principle has been violated. All owners of leaseholds in boroughs are now, as Mr. Hussey Vivian pointed out, excluded from the county franchise. Their number cannot be ascertained, but it must be considerable; for a large proportion of the small tenements in boroughs consists of dwellings erected on land held under building leases. In the majority of cases the long rows of workmen's houses which spring up year after year on the outskirts of large towns, stand on land which the landlord holds on a building lease, commonly for a term of ninety-nine years. These owners have a substantial interest in the property which they have created, but because it is a terminable interest, they are declared unfit for the suffrage.

The only plausible argument to these objections was that offered by the Chancellor of the Exchequer:—

With respect to those gentlemen who are perpetually counselling that there should be little or no difference between the population of counties and the population of towns, and who are really so exuberant in the expression of their sentiments in

* *Hansard*, vol. 188, col. 471.

that respect, I have never observed that there is the slightest
intention on their part to reciprocate the feeling which they
strive to inculcate. If it be true that a freehold in a town
should entitle a man to a county vote, why should not an occupation in a county to vote for a borough ? But nothing of that
kind is ever admitted.*

The conclusive answer to this argument is, that
nobody asks for any privilege with respect to land in
towns which is not already accorded with respect to
land in the country. Agricultural land commonly gives
two qualifications—one to the owner and one to the
tenant—and that is all that is demanded respecting property in towns. The owner of a farm is enfranchised
on account of the freehold or copyhold, and the farmer
on account of the occupation. The same rule applies
to long leaseholds not situated in towns, and not occupied by the leaseholder. He gets one county vote,
and his tenant gets another as a 12*l.* occupier. Why
is this principle inapplicable to land in boroughs? Why
should a leasehold house if just outside the town of
Birmingham qualify two persons, and if just inside it,
only one? The lessee, it is answered, ought not to vote
for the county. But where else can he vote? He
cannot do so in the borough, for law has annexed a condition of residence to the exercise of the burgess franchise; and therefore if the property is to confer upon
him a right of suffrage, it must be exercised in the
county.

The advocates of the policy of exclusion regard as
intruders all county electors qualified in respect of
lands in boroughs. This view, however, is not adopted
consistently and uniformly. A person resident in
London may have a vote for Warwickshire, although
he may be an utter stranger to that county. Surely
he is as much an intruder as the owner of property in

* *Hansard*, vol. 188, col. 467.

Birmingham. In a debate, July 1, Mr. Neate, member for Oxford, said,—

We have been told that in a neighbouring county there were 400 claimants at the registration who all gave as their address one of the great London clubs.*

Of course an unauthenticated statement of this kind cannot be accepted as reliable evidence; but it serves to point attention to a system which is allowed by law, and which notoriously prevails to a very great extent. It seems idle to talk of the borough landlord as an intruder in county elections, when persons resident at one end of the kingdom may vote in counties at the other end. Their qualification may be a rent-charge or other fugitive nominal interest in land which by no means implies an acquaintance with or concern for local affairs. Whereas, if the land be within a municipal boundary, the owner, though he may be intimately connected with the county, is regarded as an intruder if he takes part in the choice of its representatives.

The theory of non-intrusion in county representation rests upon an assumption, that owners of property in boroughs have no personal interest in the local concerns of counties. But this hypothesis is contrary to fact. Municipalities have never been so entirely separated from shires as to be altogether independent of them. For example, boroughs have to bear a proportionate share of the county expenditure for various purposes—as the prosecution, custody, and sustenance of criminals tried at the assizes, and the erection and maintenance of county gaols. The county justices, and the town councils, may agree to consolidate the county and borough police; and may enter into agreement for the establishment of district prisons.† There is no borough which does not contribute something to county expenditure.

* *Hansard*, vol. 188, col. 792.
† 5 & 6 Will. IV. c. 76, sec. 117; 12 & 13 Vict. c. 82; 3 & 4 Vict. c. 88; 5 & 6 Vict. c. 53.

A certain portion of the expenses of the county of Warwick are borne by Birmingham.* Can it be said then that this town has no business to interfere with Warwickshire? Obviously, upon questions arising in Parliament respecting the affairs of that county, Birmingham has a right to be heard; and if so, the borough has a legitimate interest in seeing that the county is fitly represented.

Necessary and unavoidable community of interests between counties and towns, was unquestionably the basis of the old law with respect to the election of knights of the shire. Mr. Disraeli observed, with reference to Mr. Colville's motion (June 24), that ' we shall never make the constitution of England a strictly logical one.' But why? The ancient system was perfectly logical, and had none of those anomalies which have subsequently become the subjects of frequent complaint. A man was entitled to vote only where he was resident. The ancient law prescribed, that ' the knights, the esquires, and others which shall be choosers of knights of the shires, be also resident within the same shires,"† and imposed severe penalties on any mayor or bailiff, who 'shall return other than those which be chosen by the citizens and burgesses of the cities and boroughs where such election be or shall be made.' ‡ But the old conditions, as to ' resiancy ' of electors, have been abrogated, and now the same person may vote in a dozen different counties; and thus, instead of a perfectly simple and uniform system, we have one full of anomalies and complications. To be consistent, those who espouse the theory of non-intrusion in county elections ought to advocate a return to the old law—ought to desire a revival of the ancient statutes which prevented residents in Middlesex and Yorkshire from voting in Cornwall. But that they do

---

* Reg. v. Bacchus. 6 *Jurist New Series*, 218.
† 1 Hen. V. c. 1. ‡ 23 Hen. VI. c. 14.

not desire. They want to localise the county suffrage, but only in a limited sense.

Half the confusion which arises in the discussion of this subject is produced by a misuse of the word 'qualification.' The occupation of a house, or the ownership of a freehold is not, strictly, the elector's qualification—but only a *test* of it—a rough and ready mode of ascertaining that he is probably a man qualified to vote discreetly and honestly. An elector is just as competent to form a sound judgment respecting the candidates for Warwickshire whether his property be situated just within or just without the municipal boundaries of Birmingham.

The present system of allowing owners of property in towns to participate in the election of knights of the shire has this very great advantage, that it tends to render county representatives less exclusive and narrow in their politics. If they are chosen all by one class, the agriculturists, the almost inevitable result is that their sympathies will be with that class exclusively. The most useful Member of Parliament is one who can take an intelligent interest in a wide range of topics, which affect the prosperity of the nation; and who, by connection and communication with people of various ranks and occupations, has acquired broad views of the wants and rights of the whole community. He ought to answer the description contained in the well-known line—

πολλῶν ἀνθρώπων ἴδεν ἄστεα καὶ νόον ἔγνω.

A large fusion of the urban element in the county representation has a beneficial effect in securing the return of representatives whose sentiments are, in the best sense of the term, liberal. And in the same way, it is willingly conceded an admixture of the rural element in the borough suffrage is equally advantageous. It is well that the representative of citizens should not

A bound within the narrow range of city politics—that he should be capable of taking thought and heed of the world outside the municipal boundary. The intermixture of different classes in borough elections was to a considerable extent provided for by the Reform Act of 1832. Under that Act, a resident within seven miles of a borough, if otherwise qualified, may vote for its members, and thus the constituency includes a considerable number of persons who live in the county. The same principle has been extended by the Reform Act of 1867, with respect to the city of London: citizens within a circle of fifty miles diameter are now qualified to participate in elections for the metropolitan city.

Of course this new rule does not operate as an extension of the area of the city for all electoral purposes. The rights of county voters within the extended area remain unaffected by it. Mr. Disraeli, it has been already shown, has a favourite theory, that all shire constituencies ought to be exclusively Bœotic, and it remains to be seen, whether the Reform Act of 1867 will not enable him to effectuate his design, by a subtraction of extensive suburban districts from the parliamentary areas of counties.

The boundaries assigned to new constituencies by the recent Act are expressly described as 'temporary.' In the schedule relating to new boroughs, the third column is entitled, 'temporary contents or boundaries,' and the schedule relating to division of counties describes the 'parts temporarily comprised in such division.' The corresponding sections of the Act (the 19th and 23rd) direct that the boundaries defined by these schedules shall remain 'until otherwise directed by Parliament.'

In the original Bill there was a clause providing that certain persons should be appointed a commission for the purpose of examining the limits of the *boroughs* constituted by the Act. The commission was to report, whether 'any enlargement of the boundaries of such boroughs is necessary, in order to include within the area thereof the population properly belonging to such boroughs respectively.' It was added, that 'such report shall be of no validity until it has been confirmed by Parliament.'

The Chancellor of the Exchequer drew attention, June 20, to fresh clauses for conferring additional powers on the commissioners, and enabling them to examine the boundaries of counties as well as boroughs. He at the same time announced the names of seven noblemen and gentlemen, whom it was proposed to place on the commission.* Mr. Bright objected to this list, and complained that—

While you send these gentlemen, who are nearly all practically of one political party, with a roving commission to examine into the maps and boundaries of all the boroughs of the kingdom, they have no power to contract the boundaries, and they have no power whatever to shut out great portions of land which have no business whatever in fifty boroughs. These commissioners have no power to contract; they have only power to enlarge; they may go down to hear such evidence and make such report as they please; and when their report is made, the House may then feel it is almost hopeless to deal with the subject.

Mr. Denman also complained—

That in this Commission the urban interest distinguished from the county interest was not sufficiently represented.†

A few days later (June 25), the Chancellor of the Exchequer produced another list which was more generally acceptable, and was finally adopted by the House. By amendments which have been incorporated in the Act, the Commissioners are invested with larger powers than were assigned by the original Bill. They are empowered to examine the temporary boundaries of new boroughs, and—

* *Hansard*, vol. 188, col. 170.   † *Ibid.*, vol. 188, col. 277.

Inquire into the boundaries of every other borough in England and Wales, except such boroughs as are wholly disfranchised by this Act, with a view to ascertain whether the boundaries should be enlarged, so as to include within the limits of the borough all premises which ought, due regard being had to situation or other local circumstances, to be included therein for the purpose of conferring upon the occupiers thereof the Parliamentary franchise for such borough.

The same authority is also directed to inquire into the divisions of counties constituted by the Act,

With a view to ascertain whether, having regard to the natural and legal divisions in each county, and the distribution of the population therein, any and what alterations should be made in such divisions or places.*

The adoption, rejection, or modification of any of the boundaries recommended is left to the future decision of Parliament, before whom the Commissioners' reports are to be laid.

In the course of the debate on this subject, Mr. Gladstone adverted to the provisions of the Bill of 1866 for the prospective enlargement of the boundaries of boroughs for electoral purposes. The government of 1866 recommended that wherever the *municipal* boundary was or should subsequently become more extensive than the *parliamentary* limits, the latter should be made the same as those of the municipal borough. This plan had considerable advantages. It substantially revived the ancient law which knew of no distinctions between a municipal and parliamentary borough, and made both absolutely conterminous. Moreover, the plan of the former Liberal Ministry would have established a general rule, whereas that of 1867 provides merely for a particular occasion. There is at least a possibility that the enlargement of an electoral area, adopted mainly on the recommendation of a special Commission, may be determined by the interests of political parties anxious to add or subtract populous

* 30 & 31 Vict. c. 102, s. 48.

areas, in order to increase their own influence in the counties. It will be observed that the only direction given to the Commissioners under the Act of 1867, with reference to boroughs, is to recommend changes which 'ought' to be made, 'due regard being had to situation and other local circumstances.' But what is meant by 'ought?' Does that vague word imply considerations of local convenience only, or of political expediency also? By the plan of 1866, persons resident in the places affected, might take the initiative in suggesting alterations. A clause of the Redistribution of Seats Bill provided that where a municipal borough may have its limits extended under a local Act or Provisional Order, 'any place situate beyond the limits of the parliamentary borough, but within the limits of such town, place, or borough, as so assigned or extended, shall form part of the parliamentary borough.' But these local Acts and Provisional Orders are made on the application of the residents. Consequently the suggested arrangement embodied the constitutional principle of self-government, which is the soul of English institutions. The people of the districts proposed to be connected are entitled to a supreme voice in the matter, for they are more directly concerned than any one else. They have a better right than all the rest of the world to decide such questions, and their more intimate topographical knowledge affords better means of deciding properly. The new rule which Mr. Gladstone suggested in 1866 was unhappily rejected. It was based upon a principle calculated to avoid the local quarrels and discontent which must almost inevitably result from any system of forcible annexation. The desire to purify counties from the suburban element, and thus to make the rearrangement of the political map subservient to temporary political purposes, can scarcely be held to justify an arbitrary and wholesale removal of ancient landmarks.

CHAPTER XVI.

THE REFORM BILL OF 1867.—THE THIRD READING.

Lord Cranbourne and Mr. Lowe strongly condemn the Bill, 244.—*Objections to it generally expressed in the debate,* 248.—*Mr. Disraeli's statement that the Conservative Government was in favour of Household Suffrage in* 1859, 253. —*The statement contradicted by the Earl of Carnarvon,* 255.

On July 9 the Representation of the People Bill, which had been in committee thirteen weeks, passed through that stage, and was reported to the House. The amended Bill was considered July 12, and on this occasion several additions and corrections in matters of detail were introduced. The third reading took place Monday, July 15, and gave rise to a long and animated debate. It is very remarkable that nearly all the principal speakers, Liberal and Conservative, either absolutely condemned the measure about to be passed, or spoke of it in terms of apology and apprehension.

Foremost among the uncompromising denunciations of the Bill were those uttered by Lord Cranbourne and Mr. Lowe. The former commenced his speech by showing that of the ten alterations in the Bill which Mr. Gladstone required, nine had been adopted. The enumeration was the same as that given in a previous page. Lord Cranbourne quoted several remarkable passages from the speeches of Mr. Disraeli and Lord Stanley, in which they had declared their determined opposition to a reduction of the suffrage, and then proceeded—

After all, our theory of government is not that a certain number of statesmen should place themselves in office and do whatever the House of Commons bids them. Our theory of government is, that on each side of the House there should be men supporting definite opinions, and that what they have supported in opposition they should adhere to in office; and that every one should know from the fact of their being in office that those particular opinions will be supported. If you reverse that, and declare that no matter what a man has supported in opposition, the moment he gets into office it shall be open to him to reverse and repudiate it all—you practically destroy the whole basis on which our form of government rests, and you make the House of Commons a mere scrambling place for office. You practically banish all honourable men from the political arena; and you will find in the long run that the time will come when your statesmen will become nothing but political adventurers, and that professions of opinion will be looked upon only as so many political manœuvres for the purpose of obtaining office. In using this language I naturally speak with much regret. The Conservative party, whose opinions have had my most sincere approval, have to my mind dealt themselves a fatal blow by the course which they have adopted. . . I for one deeply regret that the Conservative party should have committed themselves to such a course. I regret that I should be precluded from following any line of policy which they may pursue. Against that course, however, in which they have now entered, I deem it my duty to protest, because I wish, whatever may happen in the future, to record my own deep and strong feeling on this subject. I desire to protest, in the most earnest language which I am capable of using, against the political morality on which the manœuvres of this year have been based. If you borrow your political ethics from the ethics of the political adventurer, you may depend upon it the whole of your representative institutions will crumble beneath your feet. It is only because of that mutual trust in each other by which we ought to be animated, it is only because we believe that expressions and convictions expressed, and promises made, will be followed by deeds, that we are enabled to carry on this party government, which has led this country to so high a pitch of greatness. I entreat hon. gentlemen opposite not to believe that my feelings on this subject are dictated simply by my hostility to this particular measure, though I object to it most strongly, as the House is aware. But even if I took a contrary view, if I deemed it to be most advantageous,

I still should deeply regret that the position of the Executive should have been so degraded as it has been in the present session. I should deeply regret to find that the House of Commons has applauded a policy of legerdemain, and I should, above all things, regret that this great gift to the people, if gift you think it, should have been purchased at the cost of a political betrayal which has no parallel in our parliamentary annals, which strikes at the root of all mutual confidence, which is the very soul of our party government, and on which only the strength and freedom of our representative institutions can be sustained.*

Language of much stronger condemnation is rarely heard in the House of Commons, but Mr. Lowe's speech, which immediately followed, was if possible still more severe. He treated with ridicule the idea that the Bill was a settlement of the Reform question, and maintained that it 'contained the germs of endless agitation.' The hon. member for Calne thus met the charge that he himself had 'had a good deal to do with occasioning the passing of the Bill.' He had opposed the measure of the past year, and therefore materially contributed to the defeat of Lord Russell's administration; but how, he asked, could he have anticipated, that by helping to put the Tories in power, he would promote a democratic extension of the suffrage?

If I was not deceived, I must have been a prophet—a character to which I have no claims—for how was it possible that I, who was daily in confidential communication with the right hon. gentlemen opposite when they held widely different opinions, could ever have believed that after their declarations last year, and after their condescending to accept from us help they could not have done without, they would have done what they have done? Was it in human foresight to have imagined such a thing? Let us look a little further. Was it to be conceived that right hon. gentlemen, who had given no indications of the extreme facility of changing their opinions and lending themselves to the arts of treachery, would, for the sake of keeping a few of them in office for a short time and giving some

* *Hansard*, vol. 188, col. 1520.

small patronage to half a dozen lawyers, have been prepared to
sacrifice all the principles, all the convictions, and all the traditions of their lives, while others were prepared to turn round
on their order and on the institutions of the country, merely
for the purpose of sitting behind those right hon. gentlemen,
and hearing, with the knowledge that it is all true, language
such as that the noble lord (Viscount Cranbourne) has used tonight?

> Egregiam sane laudem et spolia ampla refertis.

You are well rewarded. How was I to foresee that the middle
classes, which to the great benefit of the country have been
entrusted with the electoral power, would so tamely and miserably give it up and allow it to be transferred to the poorer
classes? How was I to foresee that the right hon. gentleman,
with a body-guard of ducal families, would come forward to
overthrow the moderate system under which we live? And
yet, unless I had foreseen all this, I am not in any sense guilty,
because if right hon. gentlemen had been true to what they
said and pledged themselves to last year we should never have
seen what we have—not only a union of the two extremes of
society, the highest and the lowest, but the union of the two
parties for the same purpose, both hating and detesting each
other, the one tied by pledges, the other by party alliances.
Therefore, I say no one has a right to reproach me if I stood
alone. The disgrace is not on me, but on those who believing
what I say never ventured to say one word on the subject.

From this remarkable passage we learn that Mr.
Lowe repented but was not penitent. We learn
also that he was in daily confidential communication
with the Conservative leaders in 1866, and acted in
concert with them in opposing the Reform Bill of that
year. It is material to add that when the Whig Ministry resigned, overtures were made to the right hon.
member for Calne to join the Conservative government.
Much to the disappointment of that party, and greatly
to his own honour, he absolutely refused to have any connection with them. Of the sincerity and integrity of his
motives in 1866 there could be no question. His opposition to the Whig Reform Bill was founded upon
profound conviction. But in the passage just quoted

Mr. Lowe insists further, that his conduct in trusting the Conservative leaders was not devoid of prudence. Nothing but superhuman prescience, he contends, could have enabled him to foresee that they would deceive him. The obvious answer to this defence is that he was at that period placing his confidence in two of the most astute and least scrupulous masters of political strategy. We have seen

<blockquote>By what by-paths and indirect crook'd ways</blockquote>

they attained to power. Lord Russell, in announcing his resignation (June 26, 1866), said the Bill of that year had been met at every turn by 'surprises and unexpected tactics.' The fact was then patent, but it must have been known to Mr. Lowe long before it was patent to the world. He was admitted to the council of war: he therefore knew the spirit in which it was carried on. He knew how the ambuscades and camisades were prepared; and he might have conjectured that the men who were ready to deceive others would have no scruple in deceiving him when it suited their purpose.

Besides, once before Mr. Disraeli had suddenly changed his politics and affected Liberalism, in order to retain office. In 1859 the Conservative Government, as we have seen, was defeated on a motion which condemned their Reform Bill of that year, because they refused to lower the suffrage. They then appealed to the country, and in the new Parliament endeavoured unsuccessfully to avert a vote of want of confidence by a tardy offer to reduce the suffrage. Of course, if they were ready to make such sacrifices of principle in 1859, it required no particular sagacity to anticipate that they would pursue a similar flexible policy on any future occasion which might require it.

The bitterness of the philippic pronounced by Mr. Lowe on the third reading of the Reform Bill of 1867 was intensified by the feeling that he had been used as a tool—that his very efforts to stay the tide of democracy had speeded the flood. This was the peroration of a speech which has the ring of true English eloquence:

> England that was wont to conquer other nations has now gained a shameful victory over herself. And oh, that a man would rise in order that he might set forth in words that could not die, the shame, the rage, the scorn, the indignation, and the despair with which this measure is viewed by every cultivated Englishman who is not a slave to the trammels of party, or who is not dazzled by the glare of a temporary and ignoble success.*

Mr. Bright, who spoke next, vindicated himself from a charge made in the preceding speech that he had been 'agitating the country for household suffrage, but not meaning—as we see by his conduct this session—to get it.' He recurred to the history of his own Reform Bill of 1859 as conclusive proof that he had been long opposed to an indiscriminate reduction of the franchise:

> In the course of the discussions which have taken place upon the subject, I have said that in deference to the opinions of many persons and because I believed there was a class of householders in this country who were so dependent, and I am sorry to say so ignorant, that it was not likely that they would be independent electors, or would give strength to any constituency, it would be desirable to draw a line, and I believe the line I proposed was houses that were rented at 4*l.* or 3*l.* per annum. That however is perfectly consistent with what I have said before. I say now, what I have said all along, that the permanent foundation of the borough franchise should be the household suffrage. I do not complain of the passing of this Bill or of the House having adopted it in its entirety. But I have said that, looking at the prevailing opinion of powerful classes in this country, who regarded such a step with fear and alarm, and also to the fact, lamentable undoubtedly, but which no man can deny, that *there is a class which I hope is constantly decreasing, to whom the extension of the franchise at present can possibly be of no advantage either to themselves or the country,* I

---

* *Hansard,* vol. 188, col. 1550.

should for the present have been willing to consent to some proposition which fell short of household suffrage pure and simple.

Lord Elcho was in duty bound to speak favourably of the measure which was about to pass the third reading, for he was one of the chiefs of that section of the 'Liberals' who had given the Derby Government a majority in the House of Commons. Yet even he 'damns with faint praise':—

What its effect may be no one can predict. I think you must admit that some measure could not be avoided. Those very members who have opposed the present Bill so strenuously have failed to point out how the question could more satisfactorily be dealt with. They all fail to show how a safe resting place could be found between 10*l*. and household suffrage. The Bill was inevitable. Possible evils may arise; but I confess I am willing to accept this measure frankly and in a kindly spirit towards that class of the people who are about to be enfranchised.

Mr. Bernal Osborne replied to this speech, and denied that it represented the opinions of the Liberal party.

I believe my noble friend calls himself a moderate man. Well, he is a moderate man; but in what does his moderation consist? His moderation consists in having thrown out the Bill of last year, which was a safe gradual extension of the franchise; and in now having come forward with bold voice, (but I think with half-hearted feelings), and given his support to a measure which is no lateral extension of the suffrage but that degradation of it which hon. gentlemen opposite have so long and so loudly denounced. Let us have no more hypocrisy on this subject. We know what those gentlemen of the Cave are. We know what that 'unerring instinct' is by which they were guided—an instinct to turn out the late Government and put the noble lord's secret friends in their place. I for one, however I may have supported this Bill, regret that the Government of the day have abdicated their proper functions. When my noble friend talks of the right hon. member for South Lancashire as having been the means of throwing over all the securities that were to be given us, let me ask, if he did throw over those securities, what was the plain duty of the Government? It was to throw over a Bill which they could not sanction, as the right hon. gentleman the member for South Lancashire did in similar circumstances, and resign office. I take it that was the plain constitutional duty of the Government, and not even the noble lord can contradict that. . . .

Why, Sir, the most cogent argument for the reform of this House has been the conduct of this House. What can it be called but conduct vacillating in the extreme to have thrown out a Bill last year because it was too great, and this year to pass one which is twice as great? This House is condemned by its conduct on the Bill; and whatever may turn out, I do not think we shall get a worse than the present. We have heard something to-night about the paternity of this Bill. There is no doubt who is its father. The Chancellor of the Exchequer is no doubt its putative father, but he is not the real father. This offspring is a stolen child. The right hon. gentleman has stolen it, and then, as the *School for Scandal* has it, he has treated it as the gipsies do stolen children—he has disfigured it to make it pass for his own. But the real author of this Bill is the gentleman who sits below me, the Member for Birmingham. . . . It is all very well to speak of this as a Conservative measure. Why, Sir, the hands that brought in the Bill are the hands of Lord Derby, but the voice was the voice of John Bright.

A little later Mr. Newdegate swelled the chorus of lamentations over the Session's work. The honourable member for North Warwickshire has been, throughout his political career, a consistent Conservative; yet this was all he could say in favour of the *magnum opus* of the party:—

The Government had been forced into a measure of household suffrage for the boroughs, which was much more extensive than they originally intended, and even more extensive than the Liberal party intended, merely by their obstinate determination to preserve the gross anomaly which the very small boroughs represented. This obstinate adherence to the maintenance of those small boroughs for the purposes which they no longer answered, since with few though honourable exceptions, they no longer returned distinguished politicians, had carried the House further in the reduction of the franchise than they ever intended to go.

These extracts are given at some length, because they illustrate the general feelings of the House in reviewing the great achievement of the Session. The speakers are representatives of every party in Parliament—members who had, throughout their public lives, professed Conservatism, members of the last Whig Ministry, extreme Liberals, and the section led by Lords Elcho and Grosvenor. It is very remarkable that all these different speakers, without one exception, advert to the Bill either in terms of most fervid condemnation, or at least in the language of disparagement and apprehension. Not one of them praises it heartily for its own merits. Even those who declare their approval speak in lugubrious tones, and commend the measure, not heartily for its own sake, but because it was an inevitable necessity.

To this series of speeches, which had the depressing character of funeral orations, the Chancellor of the Exchequer replied. He chiefly occupied himself in an endeavour to vindicate the consistency of the Conservative Cabinet. For this purpose he gave a strange version of some passages in very modern history. In the course of his speech he said:—

> There is another feature in the policy of the Government of 1859 with regard to this question which I have a right to refer to, and indeed am bound to refer to in vindication of the conduct of that Government. Whatever difference of opinion might have existed in the Cabinet of Lord Derby in 1859 on the question of establishing the borough franchise on the principle of rated household suffrage, there was no difference upon one point. The Cabinet was unanimous, after the utmost deliberation and with the advantage of very large information on the subject, that if we attempted to reduce the borough qualification which then existed *we must have recourse to household suffrage*, whatever might be the condition. Upon that conclusion we acted.*

A little further on occurs this passage:—

> We still adhered to the policy of 1859, and still believed if you reduced the borough qualification—and some reduction

---

* *Hansard*, vol. 188, col. 1002.

was now inevitable—*there was no resting-place until you came to rating household suffrage.*'*

For the dignity of Parliament itself, it were to be hoped that this speech has been misreported. Among other serious objections to it, is the assumption of an utter obliviousness on the part of the audience to whom it was addressed. It is almost superfluous to remark, that the Tory Reform Bill of 1859 not only was not based on household suffrage, but did not in the slightest degree approximate to it. The 10*l.* qualification of householders in boroughs was maintained; and the new classes proposed to be enfranchised were persons of the same rank, such as lodgers paying 20*l.* annual rent, and persons in the receipt of Government pensions to the same amount. After the measure was rejected, and a new Parliament summoned, a vote declaratory of want of confidence in the ministry was proposed. Under that pressure, Mr. Disraeli made a tardy offer to reduce the amount of the borough qualification. But that offer was diametrically opposed to the principle of household suffrage; and in the speeches of the Conservative leaders at that period there was not a hint or suggestion that they would ever look upon household suffrage with favour. Then it was almost treason to utter the terrible phrase, and even the Radicals pronounced it with bated breath.

But in 1867 the Chancellor of the Exchequer tells the astounded House of Commons that eight years previously the Conservative Government had resolved, 'that if we attempted to reduce the borough qualification we must have recourse to household suffrage.' It would be easy to multiply extracts from his earlier speeches which directly contradict this statement. The following passage, cited in a former page of this work,

* *Hansard*, vol. 188, col. 1004.

is conclusive. Upon the introduction of the Bill of 1859 the Chancellor of the Exchequer said:—

It certainly would be most injudicious, not to say intolerable, when we are guarding ourselves against the predominance of a territorial aristocracy, that we should reform Parliament *by securing the predominance of a household democracy.**

Eight years after Mr. Disraeli declared his continued faith in the lateral extension of the franchise. He said in his speech on Mr. Baines's Borough Franchise Bill, May 8, 1865:—

All the results of my reflections lead me to this more and more, that the principle upon which the constituencies of this country should be increased is one not of radical, but I would say of lateral, reform.†

Again we have indisputable and irresistible evidence, that so late as the 11th of February 1867 the Chancellor of the Exchequer was not in favour of household suffrage or anything like it; on that day he proposed his Thirteen Resolutions. The second, referring to the increase of the number of electors in counties and boroughs, declares—

' That such increase may best be effected by both *reducing the value of the qualifying tenements* in counties and boroughs, and by adding other franchises not dependent on such value.'

The standard of value of the qualifying tenements was to be lowered—not abrogated; the test of pecuniary value, which is essentially repugnant to the principle of household suffrage, was to be maintained.

If in 1859 the Ministry were in favour of household suffrage they kept their secret longer and more closely than even Cabinet secrets are usually kept. If at the moment when he declared his objections to 'household democracy,' Mr. Disraeli and his colleagues really admired 'household suffrage,' people not adept in

---

* *Hansard*, vol. 152. col. 985 (Feb. 28, 1859.)
† *Ibid.*, vol. 177, col. 1702.

dialectical distinctions will be disposed to think that—to use the mildest expression—they dissembled. But one of those colleagues has indignantly repudiated this imputation. In his place in the House of Lords, Earl Carnarvon, as we shall see in the next chapter, contradicted point-blank Mr. Disraeli's statement that in 1859 the Conservative Ministry were in favour of household suffrage. This conflict of assertions is among the most painful and humiliating incidents of modern Parliamentary debate. That a peer of the realm should in his place in the House of Lords impute to a minister of the Crown a deliberate mis-statement, and that such a charge should remain unanswered—these are incidents which tend to lower the high parliamentary standard of honour; and there is some consolation, consequently, in knowing them to be unparalleled.

CHAPTER XVII.

THE REFORM BILL OF 1867 IN THE HOUSE OF LORDS.

Two nights' debate on the second reading in the House of Lords, 256.—*Lord Cairns's argument for enfranchising householders of all classes,* 259.—*Series of speeches condemning the Bill,* 261.

IN the House of Lords the second reading of the Reform Bill was moved by the Earl of Derby on the 22nd of July, 1867. After a general recapitulation of the history of former measures for the amendment of the suffrage, the Premier explained the reasons which induced the Government to adopt the proposed borough franchise:—

Having come to the conclusion that the 10*l.* standard could not be maintained, we looked about to see whether it was possible to take any other stand-point within that of household suffrage. ... What were the restrictions by which it might be thought satisfactory to guard that household suffrage? It might be feared that household suffrage pure and simple would introduce to the franchise a class of persons very unfit to exercise it intelligently and independently; but we were of opinion that instead of estimating the qualification of a man by the amount of rent he paid for his house—which in point of fact was adopted in 1832 as a rough-and-ready way of drawing a line between different classes and making a sort of compromise with public opinion—a far better test was to be found in a man's having for a considerable time been an inhabitant of a borough in which he sought to have a vote, and in his having during that time faithfully and punctually discharged the duties which devolved upon him by the payment of the rates and taxes to which he was liable. In adopting that principle we did not introduce any new qualification nor one unknown to the history of the country. We were introducing the old English qualification of scot and lot, which prevailed in about forty boroughs before the amendment of the representation of the people in 1832.*

We have here an authentic exposition by the head of the Administration of the fundamental principle of the new borough suffrage. The conditions of long residence and payment of rates and taxes, it is argued, eliminate persons incapable of exercising the franchise 'intelligently and independently.' That argument would be cogent if it were based on facts. But the conditions to which the noble Earl refers are not in the Bill. With respect to the term of residence, the new voters will be generally on the same footing as the 10*l*. householders, who must occupy their tenements for twelve months in order to be qualified under the Reform Act of 1832. Again, with respect to the 'payment of rates and taxes,' the Reform Act does not adopt any new conditions. With the payment of 'taxes' it does not even profess to deal; the payment of rates, it has been abundantly shown in these pages, may be made by the landlord as heretofore. In fact the Conservative Attorney-General,† at a later period admitted in the House of Commons that this view of the law is correct. Therefore the two conditions which, in the estimation of the Premier, distinguished the suffrage established under his Bill from 'household suffrage pure and simple' are imaginary.

Again, the inference from the history of scot and lot is incorrect, because it assumes that a system which answered well in one condition of society is applicable

* *Hansard*, vol. 188, col. 1787.

† In answer to a question by Mr. Forster in the House of Commons (Nov. 29, 1867) the Attorney-General said:—'If the landlord is the authorised agent of the tenant there is nothing to prevent him, as there is nothing to prevent any other person, paying the rate on his behalf. All that is forbidden by the Act of last session is the corrupt payment of rates with a view to influence votes.'

to other and altogether different social circumstances. It is quite true that before 1832 the scot and lot suffrage existed in many boroughs; it is also true that when the borough representation was first regularly established, in the reign of Edward I., the principle was adopted, that all persons *liable* to scot and lot in towns should participate in the municipal and electoral franchises. But until 1832 the actual payment of scot and lot, or rates, was never a *condition precedent* to the exercise of those privileges. If a man were in arrear with those payments the laws could enforce them as debts; but it did not until 1832 superadd disfranchisement as a penalty for want of punctuality. Prepayment of rates, as a political test, was an invention of the Whig Government of that period.

A more material consideration is this: that the scot and lot system was adapted to a condition of society now unknown. In the reign of Edward I., and for centuries afterwards, bribery was never practised: and for this simple reason, that there was no motive for bribery. The office of member of Parliament was not coveted as it is now; and the person elected had to find manucaptors or sureties for his due appearance in Parliament. The duty was as little desired as that of a juryman is at the present day. The electoral franchise was regarded, not as a privilege, but a burden; and there are still extant among the public records many ancient petitions from boroughs praying to be excused from making returns.* Until long after the establishment of the rule of scot and lot there is not a trace of bribery and corruption at elections. Indeed it would have been all but impracticable to bribe; for until the reign of James I. the election was made by the 'view' or show of hands; the electors were not polled; and therefore

---

* Prynne. *Brevia Parlia mentaria Rediviva*, p. 230-41.

the briber would rarely have had the means of ascertaining that he got the vote for which he bargained.* But how different are the conditions now! The statutes against bribery are numbered by the hundred, and yet notoriously they are to a great extent ineffectual. To point out the enormous injury produced by bribery, the pernicious effect upon the voter himself, the degradation of morals in the constituency where corruption prevails, the effect in lowering the dignity of Parliament, we must repeat truisms. But when fundamental and old established principles are attacked, truisms return to their original rank of truths. By reverting to the scot and lot system in modern times, when individual votes have acquired a pecuniary value, we place a purchaseable commodity in the hands of the poorest inhabitants of towns, and at least expose them to a temptation to sell that which they cannot barter away without injury to themselves and the whole community.

The indiscriminate lowering of the franchise has been recommended to the Conservative party by private arguments which would scarcely bear public discussion. Thus it has been suggested that the Bill of 1866 would have introduced a Radical class of electors, while that of 1867, by enfranchising the lowest orders, gives the suffrage to persons who are amenable to the influence of their superiors. Lord Cairns, who strenuously supported the Ministry, relied upon this argument. He said (July 23):—

The peculiar vice of the 7*l.* franchise was that it would have brought into existence a number of voters about equal to the 10*l.* voters, and it would have brought in first that section of

* It is somewhat remarkable that the advocates of the ballot have not made use of this argument. Beyond all doubt, voting in ancient times must have been secret in the majority of cases. When a multitude held up a forest of hands at the election (which we now call 'nomination') the mode in which individuals voted must have been generally indistinguishable. Whether it would be expedient to recur to an equivalent practice in modern times is an altogether different question.

voters below 10*l.* who would be most likely to pull together to *outvote those above them.* I say that is the difference between a franchise of 7*l.* and a franchise spread widely over all the rate-paying householders throughout the country. I agree with the noble duke that it is idle to suppose that all the voters below 10*l.* would run together on ordinary occasions; but the section which the 7*l.* franchise would have brought in would be more likely to run that way. We know that on most subjects there is a considerable difference of opinion between what are called the higher artisan classes and those below them.*

This was an argument better fitted to be used *in camerâ* than in the presence of Parliament and the nation. We know what it means. If the new voters had been selected from the 7*l.* rank, they would have combined to outvote their superiors. The 'higher artisan classes' are assumed to be hostile to Conservative interests, but if we go lower in the social scale the Party may still be saved. Is it, then, sunk so low as that? Must it rely upon the protection of the most indigent and least educated portion of the community? Are penury and ignorance to be henceforth the great bulwarks of Conservatism? If that hope induced county gentlemen to support household suffrage they leant upon a broken reed. They assume that they can 'influence,' to use a delicate euphemism, the cottagers who occupy houses at eighteenpence or two shillings a week. But if that be so, they must expect to meet with competitors who will use the same ignoble means. If it is to be a struggle of two parties to outbid each other for the favour of Demos, which is most likely to succeed: the gentleman who is trammeled by a code of honour, or the upstart who wants to get into Parliament for commercial purposes, and is ready to adopt any political creed—Whig, Tory, or Radical—to serve his own interests? If an election is to be won by bluster, bullying, and beer, who is most likely to be victorious:

* *Hansard,* vol. 188, col. 2001.

the man who retains his self-respect, or the unscrupulous adventurer? When it comes to a quarrel between patrician and parvenu, and the weapons are such as can be firmly grasped only by dirty hands, the parvenu is pretty sure to win.

The security of the Conservative party rests upon firmer ground. It rests, in the first place, upon that principle of Conservatism—respect for ancient laws and reverence for a glorious history—which influences more or less all Englishmen, of every grade and every shade of political opinion. The universality of this feeling will always produce a gravitation towards the party which chiefly represents it. Again, a large permanent influence is possessed by the Conservative party because it includes probably the majority of the country gentry —families which for generations have occupied the halls and country seats of England—men whose traditions and code of honour have procured for them a merited power and traditional authority which no other class enjoys. A Conservative true to himself and his own principles would rather rely upon these legitimate advantages than upon the hope of being able to practise bribery and intimidation more extensively than the plebeian capitalist or stockjobber.

In the protracted debate on the second reading of the Reform Bill in the House of Lords, nearly every speaker referred to the measure in terms of disparagement and regret. The House of Commons had dismissed the Bill to the upper House with 'a world of sighs,' and the Peers received it in a similar mood. The debates of this period exhibit a remarkable, probably a unique, phenomenon in the history of Parliament—that of an Act passed by both branches of the legislature with almost unanimous disapproval.

Earl Grey was the first of a long list of Peers who

successively took up their parable against the measure. He moved an amendment declaring that the Bill was not calculated to 'effect a permanent settlement of this important question or to promote the future good government of the country.' Lord Ravensworth expressed an apprehension that 'there would be a greater opportunity for bribery under the present Bill than ever existed under the present law, because there would be a large extension of the franchise among persons in humble life, and who were, of course, open to the temptation of being influenced by pecuniary motives.'

The Earl of Morley acutely remarked:—

It seemed to him that the various parishes, alive to the present system of collecting their rates, would commence to agitate, and perhaps, at no very late date obtain, a restoration of the system of collection, but with the proviso that the representative system should in consequence be in no way affected. Then the country would be landed in household suffrage, pure and simple, and the last checks which had been devised would have melted away.

The Duke of Rutland said:—

One by one every safeguard—the dual vote, voting papers, and two years' residence—had been thrown overboard, and the Bill was now a pure and simple proposition for household suffrage, clothed only in slight garments of the payment of rates and a year's residence. He hoped their lordships would send it back to the other House more decently attired.

The Earl of Camperdown suggested that—

When this session was finished the personal payment of rates would have had its day; it would have discharged the purpose for which it had been so prominently brought forward; and was it likely that Ministers in future sessions would attach any extraordinary value to a provision which had now been a most useful stalking horse? They would see the compound householder rise again, like a new phœnix from his ashes.

The Earl of Carnarvon, in an elaborate speech, condemned the Bill in language of the gravest and most severe reprehension. Among other things, he said:—

There is no doubt whatever as to the tendency—I will not

say tendency, I will say of the certain result—of the Bill, to swamp, as my noble friends on the Treasury Bench would call it—for the word was often in their mouths last year—property and education by the vast numerical preponderance of the artisan class.

In the following remarkable passage he denied emphatically the statement that household suffrage 'has always been the esoteric doctrine of the Conservative party and the secret faith of the Conservative Cabinet.' Mr. Disraeli had stated a few days before that in 1859 the Conservative Cabinet was unanimous, 'that if we then attempted to reduce the borough qualification which existed we must have recourse to household suffrage.' Lord Carnarvon, who was in the Cabinet at the same period, now makes a directly contrary statement. This conflict of assertions on the part of eminent members of the same Administration is at least a novelty in our parliamentary experiences. This is what Lord Carnarvon says on the subject:—

But now we are told on very eminent authority in the House of Commons that the Crown, the Church, and the House of Lords never were safer than now, that democracy in England is a bugbear and an impossibility, and that household suffrage has always been the esoteric doctrine of the Conservative party and the secret faith of Conservative Cabinets. My Lords, whatever others may say or do, and though I stand alone, a mere unit, I repudiate and protest against this statement. I protest against it not only as being inconsistent with fact but as being a gross and palpable insult to my understanding. My Lords, I am not a convert to this new faith, and I will not stultify by any act or word of mine my own course of action. I will not stultify the very existence of the Conservative party; for if this indeed were so, if household suffrage really be the secret faith of Conservative Cabinets and of the Conservative party, and has been for years; if during the time we have been opposing successive Reform Bills as they were introduced; if whilst last year we denounced a 7*l*. rental franchise as leading directly and immediately to revolution, we all the while cherished the hope of uniform household suffrage, why, my Lords, I would heap ashes on my head, and would acknowledge with all humility, but yet with all sincerity, that the whole life of the great party to which I thought I had the honour to belong was nothing but an organised hypocrisy.*

Earl Granville was one of the few who approved of the new borough franchise, yet even his praise was given subject to a most important deduction :—

I certainly should have preferred it if the franchise had excluded what has been frequently spoken of as ' the residuum.' But when household suffrage has been adopted by the House of Commons and proposed by a Minister of the Crown, I, for one, should not think for a moment of withdrawing my support from it.

The Duke of Marlborough, Lord President of the Council, made a speech in which he insisted that the measure had been forced upon the Government :—

I can say, and I believe my noble friend said it for himself, that he would have been glad that the settlement arrived at in 1832 had been left undisturbed; that the working classes, as they rose higher and higher in the scale, should adapt themselves to the franchise, not Parliament adapt the franchise to them. But was it possible for any Government to stand still in the matter? . . . No doubt the Government was obliged to yield to the times. Public opinion, the majority of the House of Commons, and the general march of events rendered the passing of a Reform Bill an imperative necessity.†

The debate on the second reading was resumed the next day (July 23), and the funeral dirge was continued by a fresh set of mourners. The Earl of Shaftesbury said :—

To proceed, as is done by this Bill, to lift by the sudden jerk of an Act of Parliament the whole residuum of society up to the level of the honest thrifty working man is, I believe, distasteful to the working men themselves. I am sure it dishonours the suffrage, and that you are throwing the franchise broadcast over the heads of men who will accept it, but who will misuse it.

An answer to the Earl of Shaftesbury was delivered

* *Hansard*, vol. 188, col. 1841. † *Ibid.*, vol. 188, col. 1807.

by the Lord Chancellor, but even he objected to the principal feature of the Bill, and concluded—

I should have been much better s.tisfied if the clause copied from the Reform Act had remained in the Bill, and the compound householder could only have procured himself to be put on the rate on the terms prescribed by the Reform Act.

The Duke of Argyll spoke with ability conspicuous even in a debate adorned by admirable oratory from both sides of the House of Lords. His speech contains this passage:—

Let us however at least be honest with ourselves, and do not let us conceal from ourselves the magnitude of the changes to which we are now about to give our assent. It is no matter of opinion, I apprehend, but matter of simple fact, that we are about to agree to the second reading of a Bill which, not twelve months, but six months ago, at the beginning of this session, no member of this House would have ventured to propose, and which, if it had been proposed, would have been met by your lordships with a unanimous shout of *non-content*.

A favourable opinion of the Bill was expressed by the Marquis of Clanricarde, but he added this material qualification:

He objected to portions of the Bill having reference to the compound householder and the redistribution of seats, but he was not prepared to reject it as a whole.

Lord Houghton fully acknowledged the necessity of an amendment of the representation, but thus declared his misgivings with respect to the present measure:—

What I fear, and what seems to me to give a gloomy aspect to what otherwise may be regarded as a joyful anticipation of bringing within the Constitution such large masses of the people, is that in future, certain difficulties and collisions may arise between the upper classes in this country and the interest of the lower classes of the community as they will be represented in Parliament under the new order of things.

The Earl of Harrowby

thought no one could dispute the fact that they were about to inaugurate a democracy. Now they knew what democracy elsewhere had been, and they could not flatter themselves that its consequences in England would be entirely different from what the world had ever seen before. Their lordships were told that they might rely on the social condition of the country; but then that social condition was in a great measure dependent on the political condition; and one of the first efforts of democracy would be to employ its power to get rid of those social influences on which alone reliance was now rested, having first got rid of all their constitutional safeguards.

The Earl Russell, who, during an arduous and honourable parliamentary career extending over fifty-five years * has been the uniform advocate of popular government, even he who has longest served in the cause of Reform, recoiled from the prospect of an indiscriminate suffrage, and thus gave utterance to his fears:—

My belief is that this measure will give rise to a great deal more treating and more bribery than we have ever had at elections in this country before; and I suppose that will be the case because the lowest class of householders are a very ignorant class; and it is with ignorant persons who do not know or care what political measures are carried or what candidates may succeed at elections that treating and bribery have their effect. These are the persons who are open to bribery and treating, and therefore I believe that these evils will be greater under this Bill than they have been heretofore. I do not apprehend that the throne will be destroyed or the Established Church annihilated. I have no fears of that kind; but I do think that the household suffrage now proposed is a change which is very much for the worse, and one which may therefore be expected to have its effect on the House of Commons.

These extracts from the speeches on the second reading have been given at some length because they have a historical value. They illustrate in a remarkable manner one of the most singular passages in our parliamentary annals: the strange phenomenon of a Bill passed through its final stages in both Houses without a division, and yet all but unanimously condemned. Why,

* Lord John Russell entered the House of Commons as member for Tavistock in 1813.

it will be asked in future times, did men of all shades of opinion—Whigs, Tories and Radicals—in both assemblies, disapprove of the measure, and yet consent to it? The answer is easy, if we consider by what steps the legislature had been brought into the narrow pass from which there was no escape but by going through it to the end. The Government had at the beginning of the session adopted their rating principle, supposing that it would effect only a moderate extension of the suffrage. But they had not examined the details. When Mr. Gladstone and others demonstrated the intolerable and absurd irregularities which would follow, Parliament and the country felt that he was in the right. The Ministry perceived though they did not acknowledge this feeling, and sought by a series of unsuccessful devices to palliate the original vice of their Bill. At last Mr. Hodgkinson—*deus ex machinâ*— showed them a way of escape at the expense of granting a suffrage which let in the very lowest class of householders indiscriminately. Mr. Disraeli eagerly clutched at the proposal as a *tabula ex naufragio*, and compelled his affrighted adherents to follow his example. On the other side of the House of Commons, Mr. Gladstone accepted the perilous change with distinctly avowed reluctance. Clearly, it was beyond his power to resist a proposal supported by the combined influence of Radicals and Tories. Lastly, the House of Lords passed the Bill because the Commons had passed it, because the measure was recommended by a Conservative Government, and because the Peers were not prepared to repeat the exploit of 1831, and reject another Reform Bill which had received the sanction of the representatives of the people.

CHAPTER XVIII.

THE LORDS' AMENDMENTS OF THE REFORM BILL, 1867.

Amendments with respect to copyholders' qualification, voting papers and representation of minorities, 268.—All these amendments rejected by the Commons excepting those relating to the representation of minorities, 270.—Arguments for and against such a system of representation, 271.

The House of Lords went into committee upon the Bill to amend the representation July 29, when Lord Halifax ineffectually brought forward a motion condemning the proposed redistribution of seats as inadequate. Upon the occasion of moving the second reading, the Earl of Derby himself had plainly indicated that this part of the Reform Bill was unsatisfactory. He said—

I proceed now to the question of redistribution. I am aware that in the minds of many, the scheme has not been so extensive as could be desired. But we were desirous not to carry the principle of disfranchisement further than was necessary for the purpose of enfranchisement.

It will not however be necessary to describe particularly all the unsuccessful motions offered to the committee. The amendments which are material to this history are these four: Firstly, Lord Cairns's amendment (July 29) to raise the lodgers' qualification to 15*l.* per annum; secondly, Lord Harrowby's modification (July 29) of the clause respecting the 5*l.* copyhold franchise, and restoring the old qualification; thirdly, Lord Cairns's proposal (July 30) for the representation of minorities; and fourthly, the Marquis of Salisbury's scheme (August 2) for the employment of voting papers at elections.

To the proposal of Lord Cairns, raising the annual amount of the lodgers' qualification to 15*l*., the Earl of Malmesbury, in the absence of Lord Derby, gave assent on the part of the Government, and on a division the modification was adopted by a considerable majority; on the question for retaining the original sum of 10*l*. the numbers were, contents 89, non-contents 121. This decision was however reversed by the House after the Bill had passed through committee. On the motion for receiving the report Earl Russell moved that the figure 15 should be expunged and the figure 10 restored. The Earl of Derby, who had resumed his seat in the House after a temporary absence from indisposition, considered that discontent would be occasioned among the working men of London if any increase took place in the original figures, and recommended an abandonment of the alteration made in the Bill in this respect. The House agreed to Lord Russell's motion, and thus the lodger franchise was restored to the amount at which it was fixed by the House of Commons.

The reduction of the copyhold qualification adopted in the House of Commons was opposed by Lord Harrowby, who proposed to revert to the former qualification. His motion for that purpose was carried by a majority of 63. The numbers were, for the clause as it stood in the Bill, 56 ; against it, 119.

On July 30 Lord Cairns moved important amendments with respect to those constituencies which are severally represented by three members, and the City of London, which is represented by four. He moved that 'at a contested election for any county or borough represented by three members, no person shall vote for more than two candidates.' And this amendment was carried by a majority of 91: contents 142; non-contents 51. A subsequent amendment provided that at elections for the City of London no person should vote for more than three candidates.

On the 2nd of August, the Marquis of Salisbury carried, by a majority of 36, a motion to insert the following clause:—

Any voter for a county or borough may, in compliance with the provisions hereinafter contained, give his vote by a voting paper instead of personally.

The Bill was read a third time in the House of Lords, and passed August 6, and on the 9th the Lords' amendments were taken into consideration by the Commons. Mr. Disraeli recommended that the use of voting papers should be allowed so far as related to county elections, and that on various grounds of expediency the amendments respecting copyholds and representation of minorities should be accepted. The lower House did not follow his advice, except with reference to the representation of minorities. The Lords' amendment respecting copyhold suffrage was rejected by a majority of 47. The question that the House should disagree to the clauses concerning voting papers, was carried in the affirmative by a majority of 52. But the amendment, with respect to votes in boroughs having three members, met with a different fate, and after debate was accepted in a very full House by a majority of 49, the numbers being, for the motion that 'This House doth disagree with the Lords in the said amendment,' ayes, 204; noes, 253. By another vote immediately following it was determined that in contested elections for the City of London no person should vote for more than three candidates.

Consequently the provisions adopted by the Lords with respect to *the representation of minorities* now stand part of the Act of 1867.

In coming to this decision the House of Commons in

effect reversed a former vote on a motion by Mr. Lowe by which it was proposed, though in a somewhat different form, to increase the voting power of minorities. The honourable member for Calne moved:—

> At any contested election for a county or borough represented by more than two members and having more than one seat vacant, every voter shall be entitled to a number of votes equal to the number of vacant seats, and may give all such votes to one candidate, or may distribute them among the candidates, as he thinks fit.

This motion, after a debate extending over two nights, was rejected by a majority of 141; the numbers being—ayes, 173; noes, 314. The more successful amendments of Lord Cairns agree with that of Mr. Lowe in this respect, that they affect only the constituencies which have more than two members, and that they enable a minority of the voters to procure the return of at least one candidate at a general election.

Of all the questions brought before Parliament during the discussion of the Reform Bill, there was no other debated so independently of the ordinary distinctions of parties. Mr. Gladstone, Mr. Disraeli, and Mr. Bright vigorously opposed the representation of minorities, while Mr. Lowe, Mr. Mill, Lord Cairns, and Earl Russell advocated that principle.

Mr. Lowe in bringing forward his proposition (July 4), relied upon it as a means of mitigating the evils of democracy.

> All our other arrows have been shot. Not one remains in the quiver, so that if this does not hit, there will be nothing left but one simple uniform franchise to be entrusted to and left in the hands of the lowest class of society.*

He further argued upon the abstract justice of allowing the distribution of votes contemplated by his motion.

* *Hansard,* vol. 188, col. 1037.

Suppose the usage to be the contrary way to the present, in the three-cornered constituency each elector would have three votes and would be allowed to dispose of them as he wished. Suppose some hon. gentlemen should interpose and say that this ought not to be; I maintain that if the voter does not distribute but consolidate, he should have only one vote. The present system works fairly well when there is only one vacancy, but it does not work fairly where there is more than one vacancy. The tendency of the present system is to make that stronger which is already strong, and that weaker which is already weak.

Undoubtedly. But if we consider the reason why a constituency is allowed to have three members, it seems apparent that the stronger ought to have the strength, and the weaker the weakness of which Mr. Lowe complains. Under the earliest constitution of the House of Commons, it has been already stated in these pages, the number of members returned by each constituency was regarded almost with indifference. But experience of Parliamentary government soon showed that the distribution of seats was a matter of moment. So early as the reign of Henry VIII., the necessity of apportioning the number of representatives with reference to the supposed importance of the constituencies appears to have been recognised. In the Act of the 27th year of his reign for settling the laws and government of Wales, *two* knights of the shire were allotted to the county of Monmouth, *one* to every other shire, and *one* burgess to each of the represented boroughs of Wales. It was considered, whether rightly or wrongly, that the boroughs of Wales and all the shires, except one, were entitled to less weight in the national councils than those of England. This principle, as we know, has been greatly extended in modern times. Manchester will henceforth have three votes in Parliament, and Thetford only one, because the one place is much more populous and wealthy than the other. But if in Manchester the minority is enabled to return one candidate, whose vote in Parliament is opposed to the votes of the other two, the great town is again put on an equality with the small one. On a critical question, respecting which there has been 'an appeal to the country,'—say, the question of carrying on a war, or of free-trade,—the very object of giving three votes to Manchester is defeated, if two of its representatives vote one way and the third the other. The third representative, instead of increasing the power of the borough, diminishes it.

The common way of arguing for the right of minorities to have a member of their own, is as follows:—Say that there are 20,000 in the majority and 15,000 in the minority; how unjust is it that the 20,000 should choose all the representatives, and the 15,000 should go unrepresented! This argument however depends upon a peculiar sense, attributed to the word 'representation.' It assumes that the electors who do not return a man of their own choice, are unrepresented. But clearly it would be impossible that every section should return a man of their own choice. A constituency is never divided absolutely into two distinct factions, and two only. In every controverted question of great public interest, there will be always two extremes and a mean; the Right, the Left, and the Centre, probably also the extreme Right and the extreme Left. It would be evidently impracticable to represent the whole community in the sense intended by the advocates for a representation of minorities.

An objection to the proposed system which has never yet been answered, is its partial character; it is applied only to constituencies which have more than two members. This objection was put by Mr. Disraeli:—

> If you adopt the principle of the cumulative vote—that is, that a man shall do what he likes with all his votes—you cannot confine the application of the principle to places repre-

sented by three members. It is a good principle or a bad
principle. If good, you must apply it to all constituencies; if
bad, why apply it to any? This appears to me an argument
unanswerable. And what would be the consequence of apply-
ing the principle generally, as you would have to do either
immediately or eventually? The result must be that you
would effectually neutralise the great bulk of the representative system. By far the greater number of places in the
country are represented by two members, and if you adopt
this principle, the consequence is that opinion is neutralised in
all those places.*

The common answer to this argument is clearly insufficient. It is said that the representation of minorities
is not applicable in constituencies which have either one
member or two, because if it were extended to them,
the minority would become as powerful as, or more
powerful than, the majority. But an evil is not the less
real because a remedy cannot be discovered; a wrong
does not cease to be a wrong because it remains
unredressed. If the unrepresented minority suffers
injustice in the three-cornered constituency, so do the
minorities in those which have only two members, or
only one member. The advocates of the peculiar method
of representation say—that their principle cannot be
worked out except where there are more than two
members—and thence they infer that it is not needed
elsewhere. This argument involves a fallacy which is
precisely equivalent to the following. A physician has
two patients, he can cure the one but not the other;
therefore the one who is beyond the reach of his art is
free from disease.

Much the clearest way of considering the abstract
question of right and wrong is to refer, not as Mr. Disraeli does, to places having two members, but to those
which have only *one*. Take a borough which has the
right of electing a single representative. A. and B. are

* *Hansard*, vol. 188, col. 1110.

candidates—A. gets 1,000 votes, and B. gets 900; will anybody contend that the 900 suffer any injustice by the return of A.? But unless there be injustice in this simple case, there is none in the more complicated case of the three-cornered constituency. Before we discuss the question of remedy, this antecedent question of grievance must be determined; the two subjects are distinct, and unless they are kept distinct, all speculation upon them is worthless.

In his speech in the House of Lords (July 30), on the plan of representation ultimately adopted, Lord Cairns greatly relied on the consideration that the represented minority would include the most intelligent portion of the constituency. But why? Why should we assume that the choice of the minority will necessarily be superior to that of the majority? It is supposed that the better educated portion of a community will band together to select a candidate who would not gain the favour of the mob; and in this way the evils of democracy will be mitigated. That is to say—we have so ill managed the electoral system, have put political power into the hands of persons so unfit to exercise it properly, that it is expedient to give a select body the right of choosing a superior set of representatives. By this course we begin the work of amending the representation at the wrong end; first, enfranchise those who are supposed to be untrustworthy and then partially reverse our own decision, in order to lessen the apprehended mischief. Such an expedient is but a palliative; and like other palliatives, leaves the real disease untouched. Clearly the proper way of remedying the evil—supposing it to exist—is to give the suffrage only to those who are worthy of it; then there would be no need to correct the errors of the majority by the supplemental vote of the minority. Besides, the hypothesis that the smaller portion of the community is more trustworthy than the major portion, is an unproved assumption. The argument founded upon it proves too much; for if the minority is best fitted to choose members of Parliament, it follows logically that the best House of Commons would be one chosen by minorities exclusively.

CHAPTER XIX.

THE FINAL STAGES OF THE REFORM BILL, 1867.

The Premier's description of the Bill, 277.—*The Reform Act of* 1832 *and that of* 1867 *contrasted,* 281.

AFTER the sense of the House of Commons had been taken upon the subjects mentioned in the last chapter, a committee was appointed in due course, to draw up reasons for disagreeing with the rejected amendments. These reasons were taken into consideration by the Lords, Monday, August 12, when the Earl of Derby moved that they should not insist upon their amendments, except one or two corrections of a verbal character. The motion was adopted; and three days afterwards (August 15, 1867), the 'Act further to amend the Laws relating to the Representation of the People in England and Wales,' received the Royal assent.

Upon the Bill, at its final stage in the House of Lords, the Prime Minister pronounced this remarkable valediction:—

Although I cannot say the Bill is altogether such as I should wish to see it, yet I expect that it will prove a settlement of a question of paramount importance.

On the third reading, the Premier concluded the debate with still more ominous language:—

No doubt we are making a great experiment, and taking a *leap in the dark.* But I have the greatest confidence in the sound sense of my fellow-countrymen, and I entertain a strong hope that the extended franchise which we are about conferring upon them will be the means of placing the institutions of this country on a firmer basis, and that the passing of this measure will tend to increase the loyalty and contentment of a great portion of her Majesty's subjects.

This, then, was the result of all the deliberations upon Parliamentary Reform; of the two years' debate, the statistical returns, the speeches, pamphlets, essays, newspaper articles, and discussions innumerable about Reform—'a leap in the dark.' A great experiment is to be tried with the institutions of England, and the experimenter 'hopes' that it will turn out well. The ship of the State is to navigate unknown waters without a chart, and the pilot 'hopes' that it will not founder upon rocks or quicksands.

Why the experiment should be made—why the leap in the dark should be taken—is not explained. Mr. Gladstone's Bill of 1866, whatever other objections might be attributed to it, at least had not this element of uncertainty. At least we knew how many voters, and what kind of voters would be introduced by the 7l. franchise. Their number was well ascertained, and nobody pretends that the tenant who pays a rent of 7l. differs materially from the ten-pound householder with whom we have long been familiar. The 'hard and fast line' might be only temporary, as its opponents were never weary of asserting, but at all events, so long as it lasted, we knew with sufficient accuracy the proportion in which political power would be shared by different classes of the community.

But when the leap in the dark is made, when the franchise is given to cottagers who pay a weekly rent of eighteen pence, when we have—not merely household suffrage—but hovel suffrage also—nobody knows who are to be the future governors of England. Hopeful Tories think the very poor class will be amenable to the influence of their superiors, and so the country will be saved from democracy. Others trust that only a small proportion of the 'residuum' will be actually registered. But confessedly the matter is left in absolute uncertainty. The Earl of Derby 'hopes' that all will turn out well. Adventurous gamesters are always hoping for luck; that the right card will be dealt, the right number turn up on the dice, the right horse win. But hitherto it has not been considered good statesmanship to commit the destinies of our empire unreservedly to Fortune. We have been content to advance from precedent to precedent, to pass from the known to the unknown by slow and heedful steps. The policy of political 'leaps' remained to be invented by a government which calls itself Conservative.

One of the most remarkable characteristics of the Reform Act of 1867 is the strong contrasts between its different parts. Some of the changes which it effects are utterly inadequate, others moderate, others extravagant. The clauses respecting the distribution of seats have been drawn in a spirit of stolid repugnance to Reform; the extension of the county suffrage is liberal, though temperate; the enactment of the new borough franchise is equivalent to a *coup d'état*.

A *coup d'état* struck without premeditation. Nobody believes that Mr. Disraeli intended it when he brought in his Reform Bill; he accompanied the borough suffrage by conditions—the dual vote, the prolonged residence, the oppressive formalities of registration—which rendered the extension of the franchise less than it would have been under Mr. Gladstone's Bill of the preceding year. One by one the conditions disappeared. They were abandoned because the Government itself found them to be intolerable. The Bill originally produced was so full of incongruities and absurd consequences, that it is quite certain that the Ministry were not originally aware of the nature of their own measure. Consequently, from the commencement of the session they were in a false position, and the parliamentary campaign was a continued series of retreats.

Doubtless the chief explanation of the blunders found in the Reform Bill of 1867 was the inconsiderate manner in which it was brought forward. We know, upon unimpeachable evidence—that of the Prime Minister—that it was produced in extreme haste. Narrating the proceedings of the Government with respect to this question, the Earl of Derby stated (March 4, 1867) that—

We determined in the first instance not to proceed by a Bill, but by introducing a series of Resolutions through which we had hoped to elicit from the House of Commons the views they took upon the main questions which would be necessarily involved in the Reform Bill.

He then proceeded to inform the House that upon the withdrawal of these Resolutions—

It became the duty of the Cabinet to consider immediately, and without a minute's delay, the provisions of such a Bill, as they thought they could lay upon the table of the House. Of course, the main provisions of a Bill had been the subject of anxious inquiry in the Cabinet for some time past, but we had not, up to that period, actually framed a Bill, and it therefore became necessary to consider what the provisions of the Bill should be. Two schemes were under the consideration of the Cabinet, varying from each other in that very essential particular, the amount of the extension of the franchise. One of these schemes was more extensive than the other.*

That is, not only the form but also the substance, of the Reform Bill were undetermined and under consideration at the end of February 1867. At that period Lord Derby and his colleagues proposed to contrive, 'without a minute's delay,' a scheme to amend the representation, and to deal with the intricacies of the electoral system, and the law and practice of rating. Newton might almost as well have proposed to write the *Principia* without a minute's delay.

This admission on the part of Lord Derby is the more remarkable, because he was a member of the Governments which produced the Reform Bills of 1831 and 1832. He took an active part in the discussion of those

* *Hansard*, vol. 185, col. 1285.

measures, and therefore knew by experience the enormous difficulties and complications which attend any effort to amend the Representation. It is impossible to find a greater contrast in legislation than that presented by a comparison of the Act of 1832 and the recent statute. The modern Bill was, in its original form, so crude and full of incongruities that, like a bad school-exercise, it had to be almost re-written.* The Act of 1832, on the contrary, is almost identical with the Bill on which it was founded; examine the measure proposed with the actual enactment, clause by clause, and you will find that in nearly every material particular the original scheme was ultimately adopted. This remarkable characteristic of the great statute of William IV. is undoubtedly due to the care and labour originally bestowed upon it. The first Reform Bill of 1831 was drawn up by a committee of the Cabinet, including the Earl of Durham, whose speech in the House of Lords, May 28, 1831, demonstrates the extent of the researches and labour which he devoted to the subject.† The second Reform Bill was produced in the following Session with still more scrutinous care; various defects of detail, which existed in the first measure, were corrected by means of elaborate returns from the municipal officers of various boroughs, procured by

---

* The appendix to this work contains a copy of the original Reform Bill of March 1867, printed so as to show the clauses subsequently omitted, or materially altered, and the clauses borrowed from the Franchise Bill and the Redistribution of Seats Bill of 1866.

Mr. Disraeli's measure consisted of forty-three clauses; of these, twenty-one have been omitted or materially altered; of the remaining twenty-two, eighteen have been taken substantially or verbatim from the Franchise Bill and the Redistribution of Seats Bill, introduced by Mr. Gladstone, in 1866. The remaining four are exclusively the work of the Conservative Government; they are:—Clause 1. The Title of the Act; 8. Disfranchisement of Totnes, Reigate, Yarmouth, and Lancaster; 30. Penalty for corrupt payment of Rates; 38. Provision for vacancies before completion of new Registers. The Act in its ultimate form comprises sixty-one sections.

† *Hansard*, vol. 3, col. 1014. Roebuck, History of the Whig Ministry, vol. 2, p. 129.

the Home Office, and a mass of information collected by a Royal Commission.* But the principal features of the first Bill—all its admirable machinery for registration, the revision of boundaries, the regulations with respect to polling and the main provisions with respect to redistribution of seats and the qualifications of electors, were sedulously preserved. The measure elaborated so critically, carefully, and cautiously, is a durable monument of legislative wisdom, which has borne the test of time, and produced incalculable benefits to this kingdom. It was not perfect; for it was the work of human hands. But the great Act of 1832, which we owe to the labours of a generation of illustrious statesmen, who happily are not all passed away—to Earl Grey, Lord John Russell, Lord Brougham, Lord Stanley, Lord Althorp, and the Earl of Durham—was so wisely conceived and prudently prepared, that its influence upon the laws and institutions of England will probably endure for ages.

Compared with that exploit of noble statesmanship, the history of the ephemeral Reform Bill of March 1867, is ignominious and humiliating. It was the scheme of uninstructed sciolists, who needed, step by step, to be set right by their opponents. The Act of 1832 was a grand effort to adapt our ancient parliamentary institutions to modern uses, and therefore was the prototype and progenitor of the more recent production. But while the earlier work stands before the world invested with the dignity of knowledge and patient thought; the successor

> Comes not
> Like his father's greatness; his approach,
> So out of circumstance and sudden, tells us
> 'Tis not a visitation fram'd, but forc'd
> By need and accident.

* *Hansard*, vol. 9. Appendix, p. 30.

AN ABSTRACT

OF THE

REPRESENTATION OF THE PEOPLE ACT, 1867.*

[*The additions to, and material variations from, the original Bill of March* 1867, *are designated by Italics.*]
[*Of the unaltered clauses of the original Bill, those which are taken from the Franchise Bill and the Redistribution of Seats Bill of* 1866, *are indicated by notes in brackets; but, besides these, a large number of clauses, introduced in committee, were also taken from the Bills of* 1866.]

1. The Act to be cited as the 'Representation of the People Act, 1867.'
2. The Act not to apply to Scotland or Ireland, or elections for the Universities of Oxford or Cambridge.
[Same as clause 2 of the Franchise Bill, 1866.]

PART I.—FRANCHISES.

3. *In and after the year one thousand eight hundred and sixty-eight*, a man may be a voter for a borough,
Who for *twelve months* preceding July 31, in any year, is an inhabitant occupier of any dwelling-house in the borough, and
During such occupation has been rated *as an ordinary occupier* in respect of such premises to all rates for the relief of the poor, and
Has, on or before July 20, paid *an equal amount in the pound to that payable by other ordinary occupiers in respect of poor rates payable by him* up to January 5.
No man to be entitled to vote under this section as a joint occupier of any dwelling-house.

* Received the Royal assent, 15th August, 1867.

4. *In and after the year one thousand eight hundred and sixty-eight a man may be a voter for a borough,*

Who as a lodger has occupied in the borough as sole tenant for twelve months preceding July 31, lodgings of a clear yearly value, if let unfurnished, of ten pounds or upwards, and

Has resided in the lodgings during the twelve months, and claimed to be registered.

5. *In and after the year one thousand eight hundred and sixty-eight, a man may be a voter for a county,*

Who is tenant for life, or lives of, or has a larger estate in freehold, copyhold, or other lands or tenements, of the clear yearly value of five pounds; or holder of a lease, for not less than sixty years originally, of lands or tenements of the clear yearly value of five pounds.

6. *In and after the year one thousand eight hundred and sixty-eight, a man may be a voter for a county,*

Who for twelve months preceding July 31, has been occupier, as owner, or tenant, of lands or tenements in the county of the rateable value of *twelve pounds,* and

Has during such occupation been rated for the premises to the relief of the poor, and

Has before July 20 paid all poor rates payable by him up to January 5.

7. *Owners shall cease to be rated instead of occupiers, in respect of dwellings in parishes wholly or partly within a borough.*

The full rateable value of every separate tenement; the full rate in the pound; and the name of the occupier shall be entered in the rate-book:

Saving existing compositions up to Michaelmas 1867.

Saving existing rates.

The owner of a tenement 'which has been let to him free from rates,' may deduct from his rent the rates paid by him.

8. *At first registration after 1867, an occupier of premises for which the owner was previously rated may be registered, though not rated before Michaelmas 1867, if he be subsequently rated and pay by July 20, 1868, rates due up to January 5 preceding.*

9. *At a contested election for any county or borough represented by three members, no person shall vote for more than two candidates.*

10. *At a contested election for the city of London, no person shall vote for more than three candidates.*

11. *An elector employed for reward as agent, &c., for a candidate not entitled to vote.*

12. The boroughs of Totnes, Reigate, Yarmouth, and Lancaster to cease to return members to Parliament.

13. *Persons reported by Royal Commission guilty of bribery not to vote for South Devon, in respect of property at Totnes.*

14. *Analogous provision with respect to Yarmouth.*

15. *Analogous provision with respect to Lancaster.*

16. *Analogous provision with respect to Reigate.*

PART II.—DISTRIBUTION OF SEATS.

17. Boroughs in Schedule A, *with population of less than 10,000 at census of 1861, shall return one member each—thirty-eight* boroughs.

18. *Manchester, Liverpool, Birmingham, and Leeds to return three members each.*

19. *New boroughs in schedule B to return one member each.*

20. Registers to be formed for new boroughs.
[Same as clause 10 of the Seats Bill of 1866.]

21. *Merthyr Tydfil and Salford to return two members each.* Tower Hamlets to be divided into two divisions. Tower Hamlets and Hackney, each to have two members.
[Substantially the same as clause 13 of the Seats Bill, 1866.]

22. Registers to be formed for Hackney and Tower Hamlets.
[Substantially the same as clause 13 of the Seats Bill, 1866.]

23. *Division of counties in schedule D.*

24. University of London to return one member.
[Same as clause 20 of Seats Bill, 1866.]

25. Graduate members of the convocation to be elected for the University of London.
[Same as clause 21 of Seats Bill, 1866.]

PART III.—SUPPLEMENTAL PROVISIONS.

26. Different premises occupied in immediate succession by any owner or tenant may qualify him to vote for a county or borough.
[Same as in clause 6 of the Franchise Bill, 1866.]

27. In a county joint occupiers may vote, if the aggregate value of the premises be sufficient. *Proviso as to more than two joint occupiers.*
[Same as in clause 6 of the Franchise Bill, 1866, so far as relates to counties, excepting proviso.]

28. *Where the poor rate of a borough occupier is in arrear, the overseer is to give him notice before June* 20. *An overseer*

withholding such notice, with intent to keep the occupier off the register, deemed guilty of a breach of duty.

29. *Overseers to make out lists of arrears of rates which shall be open to perusal without fee.*

30. Overseers to make out lists of occupiers entitled to vote for the county, in the same way that borough lists of ten-pound householders are made out under the Registration Act.

[Same as in clause 10 of Franchise Bill, 1866.]

Persons claiming to vote as lodgers to make their claims in a prescribed form between July 31 and August 25. Lists of such claims to be published before September 1.

The regulations of the Registration Act of 1843 respecting publication of claims, proofs, and objections to be applicable to lodgers.

31. *Definition of ' expenses of registration.'*

32. *Provision as to duties of Clerks of Peace in parts of Lincolnshire.*

33. *Places for elections for counties in schedule D.*

34. *County Justices empowered to increase the number of polling places.*

The Town Council or other 'Local Authority' empowered to divide a borough into polling districts. Lists of voters to be made out accordingly.

35. *Alterations of polling places to be advertised.*

36. *Payment of the expenses of conveying voters to the poll in any borough illegal, excepting Retford, Shoreham, Cricklade, Wenlock, and Aylesbury.*

37. *At contested elections the polling to take place at a building instead of a booth, if practicable.*

38. *Time of transmitting register of voters to returning officers. The register to take effect from Jan. 1 in each year.*

39. *Form of oath of poll clerk.*

40. *Receipt of parochial relief a disqualification of electors in counties as well as boroughs.*

41. In the University of London, Vice-Chancellor to be the returning officer.

[Same as clause 22 of Seats Bill, 1866.]

42. Time for elections in University of London.

[Same as clause 23 of Seats Bill, 1866.]

43. Polling in University of London may continue *five* days.

[Same as clause 24 of Seats Bill, 1866, except as to duration of the Poll.]

44. Power of Vice-Chancellor to appoint poll clerks.

[Same as clause 25 of the Seats Bill, 1866.]

45. *Votes may be recorded in elections for the University of London by voting papers.*

46. *Residents within twenty-five miles of the City of London may, if otherwise qualified, vote for the city.*

47. Who are to be the returning officers of new boroughs.

[Same as clause 19 of the Seats Bill, 1866.]

48. Certain persons named appointed Commissioners, to examine the boundaries of boroughs constituted by the Act, *and all other boroughs and the divisions of counties constituted by the Act,* and to report if enlargement necessary. Their reports to be laid before Parliament.

49. Corrupt payment of rates punishable as bribery.

50. *Any returning officer acting as agent for a candidate deemed guilty of misdemeanour.*

51. *The Parliament in being at any future demise of the Crown shall not be thereby dissolved.*

52. A member of Parliament holding one of the offices mentioned *in Schedule H,* shall not vacate his seat by accepting another of those offices.

53. *Printed copies of Commissioners' Reports respecting Totnes, Yarmouth, Lancaster, and Reigate to be evidence.*

54. Temporary provision with respect to the registers of the counties and the boroughs divided under the Act.

55. Temporary provision consequent on the formation of new boroughs. *The revising barrister to mark in county lists cases where property in new boroughs ceases to qualify for the county.*

[The first part of this clause is the same as clause 17 of Seats Bill, 1866.]

56. The franchises conferred by this Act shall be in addition to existing franchises, and the laws relating to representation and registration to remain in full force.

[Substantially the same as clause 29 of the Seats Bill, 1866.]

57. *Writs for elections in the County Palatine of Lancaster to be issued as in counties not Palatine.*

58. Parliamentary writs and other documents to be framed in accordance with this Act.

[Same as clause 30 of the Seats Bill, 1866.]

59. The Act to be construed as one with existing Acts relating to representation *and registration. The provisions of the Reform Act* 1832, *relating to county votes in respect of freeholds, copyholds, leaseholds, and tenancies in boroughs extended to franchises under this Act.*

60. *In the event of a vacancy or dissolution of Parliament before Jan.* 1, 1869, *elections to take place as heretofore except as to the boroughs disfranchised.*

61. Interpretation clause.

[Same as clause 3 of the Franchise Bill of 1866, omitting the definition of 'clear yearly value.']

Of the sixty-one sections of this Act, forty-one are additions to, or comprise material variations from, the original Bill. Of the remaining twenty clauses of the original Bill which have been retained without substantial alteration, sixteen are borrowed from the Franchise Bill, and the Seats Bill, introduced by Mr. Gladstone in 1866. The sections of the Act of 1867, which are the work of the Conservative Ministry exclusively, are these four.

Section 1. The title of the Act.
    12. The total disfranchisement of four boroughs.
    49. Penalty for corrupt payment of rates.
    54. Temporary provisions respecting registers of divided counties and boroughs.

The extent to which the Reform Act of 1867 differs from the Bill originally introduced will further appear from the following copy of the original Bill, in which the provisions subsequently struck out or materially altered, are designated by italics.

THE REFORM BILL,

INTRODUCED MARCH 1867.

A Bill further to amend the Laws relating to the Representation of the People in England and Wales.*

[*The parts of this Bill subsequently omitted or materially altered are designated by Italics.*]
[*The clauses taken verbatim or substantially from the Franchise Bill and Seats Bill of 1866, are indicated by notes in brackets.*]

Whereas it is expedient to amend the Laws relating to the Representation of the People in England and Wales:

Be it further enacted by the Queen's most Excellent Majesty, by and with the Advice and Consent of the Lords Spiritual and Temporal, and Commons, in this present Parliament assembled, .nd by the Authority of the same, as follows:

1. This Act shall be cited for all Purposes as ' The Representation of the People Act, 1867.'
2. This Act shall not apply to Scotland or Ireland, nor to the Universities of Oxford or Cambridge.
[Same as clause 2 of the Franchise Bill, 1866.]

PART 1.—FRANCHISES.

3. Every Man shall be entitled to be registered as a Voter, and, when registered, to vote for a Member or Members to serve in Parliament for a Borough, who is qualified as follows; that is to say:

1. Is of full Age, and not subject to any legal incapacity: and

* Ordered by the House of Commons to be printed, March 18, 1867.

U

2. *Is on the last Day of July in any Year and has during the whole of the preceding Two Years been an Inhabitant Occupier, as Owner or Tenant, of any Dwelling House within the Borough;* and
3. Has during the time of such Occupation been rated in respect of the Premises so occupied by him within the Borough to all Rates (if any) made for the Relief of the Poor in respect of such Premises; and
4. *Has before the Twentieth Day of July in the same Year paid all Poor Rates that have become payable by him in respect of the said Premises up to the preceding Fifth Day of January.*

4. Every Man shall be entitled to be registered as a Voter, and, when registered, to vote for a Member or Members to serve in Parliament for *a County*, who is qualified as follows; that is to say:

1. Is of full Age, and not subject to any legal incapacity; and
2. Is on the *last day of July* in any Year and has during the *Twelve Months* immediately preceding been the Occupier, as Owner or Tenant, of Premises of any Tenure, within the County of the *rateable value of Fifteen Pounds or upwards;* and
3. Has during the Time of such Occupation been rated in respect to the Premises so occupied by him to all Rates (if any) made for the Relief of the Poor in respect of the said Premises; and
4. Has before the *Twentieth Day of July* in the same Year paid all Poor Rates that have become payable by him in respect of the said Premises up to the preceding *Fifth Day of January.*

5. *Every Man shall be qualified to be registered, and, when registered, to vote at the Election of a Member or Members to serve in Parliament for a County or Borough, who is of full Age, and not subject to any legal incapacity, and is on the last Day of July in any Year and has during the Year immediately preceding been resident in such County or Borough, and is possessed of any One or more of the Qualifications following; that is to say:*

1. *Is, and has been during the Period of such Residence, a Graduate or Associate in Arts of any University of the United Kingdom; or a Male Person who has passed at any Senior Middle Class Examination of any University of the United Kingdom:*

2. *Is, and has been during the Period aforesaid, an ordained Priest or Deacon of the Church of England;* or
3. *Is, and has been during the Period aforesaid a Minister of any other Religious Denomination appointed either alone or with not more than One Colleague to the Charge of any registered Chapel or Place of Worship, and is, and has been during such Period, officiating as the Minister thereof;* or
4. *Is, and has been during the Period aforesaid, a Serjeant-at-Law or Barrister-at-Law in any of the Inns of Court in England, or a Certificated Pleader or Certificated Conveyancer ;* or
5. *Is, and has been during the Period aforesaid, a Certificated Attorney or Solicitor or Proctor in England or Wales ;* or
6. *Is, and has been during the Period aforesaid, a duly qualified Medical Practitioner registered under the Medical Act,* 1858 ; or
7. *Is, and has been during the Period aforesaid, a Schoolmaster holding a Certificate from the Committee of Her Majesty's Council on Education:*

Provided that no Person shall be entitled to be registered as a Voter or to vote in respect of any of the Qualifications mentioned in this Section in more than One Place.

6. *Every Man shall be entitled to be registered, and, when registered, to vote at the Election of a Member or Members to serve in Parliament for a County or Borough, who is of full Age, and not subject to any legal Incapacity, and is on the First Day of July in any Year, and has during the Two Years immediately preceding been resident in such County or Borough, and is possessed of any One or more of the Qualifications following ; that is to say :*

1. *Has on the First Day of July in any Year, and has had during the Two Years immediately preceding, a Balance of not less than Fifty Pounds deposited in some Savings' Bank in his own sole Name and for his own Use ;* or
2. *Holds on the First Day of July in any Year, and has held during the Two Years immediately preceding, in the Books of the Governor and Company of the Bank of England or Ireland in his own sole Name and for his own Use any Parliamentary Stocks or Funds of the United Kingdom to the Amount of not less than Fifty Pounds ;* or
3. *Has during the Twelve Months immediately preceding the Fifth Day of April in any Year been charged with a*

Sum of not less than Twenty Shillings in the whole by the Year for Assessed Taxes and Income Tax, or either of such Taxes, and has before the Twentieth Day of July in that Year paid all such Taxes due from him up to the preceding Fifth day of January:

Provided, first, that every Person entitled to vote in respect of any of the Qualifications mentioned in this Section shall on or before the Twentieth Day of July in each Year claim to be registered as a Voter; secondly, that no Person shall be entitled to be registered as a Voter or to vote in respect of any of the Qualifications mentioned in this Section for more than One Place.

7. *A Person registered as a Voter for a Borough by reason of his having been charged with and paid the requisite amount of Assessed Taxes and Income Tax, or either of such Taxes, shall not by reason of being so registered lose any Right to which he may be entitled (if otherwise duly qualified) to be registered as a Voter for the same Borough in respect of any Franchise involving Occupation of Premises and Payment of Rates, and when so registered in respect of such double Qualification he shall be entitled to give Two Votes for the Member, or (if there be more than One) for each Member to be returned to serve in Parliament for the said Borough.*

Part II.—Distribution of Seats.

8. From and after the End of this present Parliament the Boroughs of Totnes, Reigate, Great Yarmouth, and Lancaster shall respectively cease to return any Member or Members to serve in Parliament.

9. From and after the End of this present Parliament *each of the Boroughs enumerated in Schedule (A.)* to this Act annexed shall return One Member and no more to serve in Parliament.

10. *Each of the Places named in Schedule (B.)* to this Act annexed shall be a Borough, and shall each return One Member to serve in future Parliaments, and until otherwise directed by Parliament each such Borough shall comprise such Places as are specified and described in connexion with the Name of each such Borough in the said Schedule (B.)

11. Registers of Voters shall be formed in and after the Year One thousand eight hundred and sixty-eight, notwithstanding the Continuance of this present Parliament, for or in respect of

the Boroughs constituted by this Act, in like Manner as if before the passing of this Act they respectively had been Boroughs returning Members to serve in Parliament.

[Substantially the same as clause 10 of the Seats Bill of 1866.]

12. From and after the End of the present Parliament the Borough of the Tower Hamlets shall be divided into Two Divisions, and each Division shall in all future Parliaments be a separate Borough, returning Two Members to serve in Parliament.

Each of the said Divisions, until otherwise directed by Parliament, shall comprise the Places mentioned in connexion with each such Division in Schedule (C.) hereto annexed, and shall be called by the Name of the Northern and Southern Division of the Tower Hamlets respectively.

[Same as clause 13 of the Seats Bill, 1866.]

13. Registers of Voters shall be formed in and after the Year One thousand eight hundred and sixty-eight, notwithstanding the Continuance of this present Parliament, in respect of the Divisions of the said Borough of the Tower Hamlets constituted under this Act, in like Manner as if such Divisions had previously to the passing of this Act been separate Boroughs returning Members to serve in Parliament.

[Substantially the same as clause 13 of the Seats Bill, 1866.]

14. From and after the End of the present Parliament *each County named in the First Column of Schedule (D)* to this Act annexed shall be divided into the Two Divisions named in the Second Column of the said Schedule, and each of such Divisions shall consist of the Hundreds, Lathes, Wapentakes, and Places mentioned in the Third Column of the said Schedule.

In all future Parliaments there shall be Two Members to serve for each of the Divisions specified in the said Second Column, and such Members shall be chosen in the same Manner and by the same Description of Voters, and in respect of the same Rights of Voting, as if each such Division were a separate County.

[Same as in clause 6 of the Seats Bill, 1866.]

All Enactments relating to Divisions of Counties returning Members to serve in Parliament shall be deemed to apply to the Divisions constituted as aforesaid.

[Same as in clause 6 of the Seats Bill, 1866.]

Registers of Voters shall be formed in and after the Year One thousand eight hundred and sixty-eight, notwithstanding the Continuance of this present Parliament, for or in respect of the Divisions of Counties constituted by this Act, in like Manner as if before the passing of this Act they had respectively been Counties returning Members to serve in Parliament.

[Same as clause 10 of Seats Bill, 1866, with respect to county proposed to be divided.]

15. In all future Parliaments the University of London shall return One Member to serve in Parliament.

[Same as clause 20 of the Seats Bill.]

16. Every person whose name is for the time being on the Register of Graduates constituting the Convocation of the University of London shall, if of full Age, and not subject to any legal Incapacity, be entitled to vote in the Election of a Member to serve in any future Parliament for the said University.

[Same as clause 21 of the Seats Bill.]

PART III.—SUPPLEMENTAL PROVISIONS.

Incidents of Franchise.

17. Different Premises occupied in succession by any Person as Owner or Tenant shall have the same effect in qualifying such Person to vote for a County or Borough as a continued Occupation of the same Premises.

[Same as in clause 6 of the Franchise Bill.]

18. In a County where Premises are in the joint Occupation of several Persons as Owners or Tenants, and the aggregate rateable value of such Premises is such as would, if divided amongst the several Occupiers, so far as the Value is concerned, confer on each of them a Vote, then each of such joint Occupiers shall, if otherwise qualified, and subject to the Conditions of this Act, be entitled to be registered as a Voter, and, when registered, to vote at an Election for the County.

[Same as in clause 6 of the Franchise Bill, so far as relates to counties.]

Registration of Voters.

19. The following Regulations shall be observed with respect to the Registration of Voters:

1. The Overseers of every Parish or Township shall make out or cause to be made out a List of all Persons on whom a Right to vote in respect of the Occupation of Premises is conferred by this Act, in the same Manner and subject to the same Regulations, as nearly as Cir-

cumstances admit, in and subject to which the Overseers of Parishes and Townships in Boroughs are required by the Registration Acts to make out or cause to be made out a List of all Persons entitled to vote for a Member or Members for a Borough in respect of the Occupation of Premises of a clear yearly Value of not less than Ten Pounds:
   [Same as in clause 10 of the Franchise Bill.]
2. *The Claim of any Person desirous of being registered as a Voter for any County or Borough, and hereinbefore required to make a Claim shall be made in the Form marked 1. in Schedule (E.) annexed hereto, or as near thereto as Circumstances admit:*
3. *The Claim of a Person claiming to be registered in respect of a Deposit in a Savings Bank shall not be received by the Overseers unless it have annexed thereto a Certificate in the Form marked 2. in the said Schedule, or as near thereto as Circumstances will admit, and is signed, in the case of a Post Office Savings Bank, by some Officer authorised to sign the same by the Postmaster General, and in the case of any other Savings Bank by Two of the Trustees or Managers of such Savings Bank, or by some Officer authorised by them:*
4. *The Claim of any Person claiming to be registered in respect of the holding of any Parliamentary Stocks or Funds of the United Kingdom to the amount of not less than Fifty Pounds shall not be received by the Overseers unless it have annexed thereto a Certificate in the Form marked 3. in the said Schedule, or as near thereto as Circumstances admit, and signed by an Officer of the Governor and Company of the Bank of England, or, as the case may require, by an Officer of the Governor and Company of the Bank of England.*
5. *The Claim of any Person claiming to be registered in respect of the Payment of Assessed Taxes and Income Tax, or either of such Taxes shall not be received unless it have annexed thereto a Certificate in the Form marked 4. in the said Schedule, or as near thereto as Circumstances admit, and signed by One of the Commissioners or Collectors acting in relation to the Tax in respect of which such Certificate is required:*
6. *The Overseers of Parishes and Townships in Counties and Boroughs shall annually give notice directing all Persons who are required by this Act to make their Claim to send*

in their Claims to them, such Notice to be given in the same Manner so far as Circumstances admit, in which Overseers give notice in Counties under the Law in force at the time of the passing of this Act to Persons desirous of being placed on the list of County Voters:

7. *Upon the Receipt of a Claim by any such person as aforesaid, having annexed thereto such Certificates as aforesaid, the Overseers may make all such Objections to the Claim so made as Overseers in Counties are empowered to make on receiving Claims of Voters, but subject thereto shall place the Claimant on the List of Voters for the Parish or Township in which the Residence of the Voter is situate.*

20. *If any Person whose Certificate is required under this Act in support of the Claim of a Person to vote wilfully refuses to give such Certificate, he shall on summary Conviction be liable to a Penalty not exceeding Five Pounds.*

21. *If any Person is guilty of any of the following offences, that is to say,—*
    1. *Wilfully gives any Certificate required by this Act falsely;*
    2. *Forges, counterfeits, or fraudulently alters any such Certificate, or any Signature thereto;*
    3. *Knowingly makes use of, in support of a Claim to be registered or to vote, any false Certificate, or any Certificate forged, counterfeited, or altered as aforesaid;*

Such Person shall be guilty of a Misdemeanour, and on being convicted thereof shall be liable to Imprisonment, with or without Hard Labour, for a Term not exceeding Two Years.

Places for Election, and Polling Places.

22. *The Court for the Election of Members for each of the Divisions mentioned in the Second Column of the said Schedule (D.) shall be holden at the Places named for that purpose in the Fourth column of the same Schedule.*

23. In every County the Justices of the Peace having Jurisdiction therein, assembled at some Court of General or Quarter Sessions not later than the first holden after the Dissolution of the present Parliament, shall appoint proper and convenient Places for polling in their County, *so that there may be a Polling Place in every Parish or Township in which there are not less than Two hundred resident Electors, and a Polling Place for every Two or more adjoining Parishes or Townships in either of which separately there may be less than Two hundred resident Electors, at some central or convenient point at which*

as nearly as possible Two hundred Voters from such smaller Parishes or Townships may most conveniently attend to record their Votes; and the places so selected by the Justices as the future Polling Places of the County shall forthwith be duly advertised in such manner as the Justices think fit; and the said Justices may from time to time at any Court of General or Quarter Sessions alter such Polling Places as they may think expedient; but it shall not be incumbent upon any Revising Barrister to attend at any Polling Place at which less than *Five hundred* Voters are appointed to poll.

24. At every contested Election *for any County*, unless some Building or Place belonging *to the County* is provided by the Justices for that Purpose, the Sheriff shall, whenever it is practicable so to do, instead of erecting a Booth, hire a Building or Room for the purpose of taking the Poll *at the Places so appointed by the Justices as aforesaid; and the Expenses incurred by the said Sheriff in the Hire of Rooms, or Erecting Booths for Polling, shall be paid to him by the Justices for such County out of the County Rate.*

Where in any Place there is any Room, the Expense of maintaining which is payable out of any Rates levied in such Place, such Room may, with the Consent of the Person or Corporation having the Control over the same, be used for the Purpose of taking the Poll at such Place.

Election in University of London.

25. The Vice Chancellor of the University of London shall be the Returning Officer for such University, and the Writ for any Election of a Member to serve in Parliament for such University shall be directed to such Vice Chancellor.

[Same as clause 22 of the Seats Bill.]

26. The Vice Chancellor of the University of London shall proceed to Election in pursuance of any Writ to be directed to him, as herein-before mentioned, within Six Days after the Receipt of such Writ, giving Three clear Days' Notice of the Day and Place of Election, exclusive of the Day of Proclamation and the Day of Election; and the Vice Chancellor shall, after such Election, certify the same, together with such Writ, according to the Directions thereof.

[Same as clause 23 of the Seats Bill.]

27. At every contested Election of a Member or Members to serve in Parliament for the University of London the Polling shall commence at Eight o'clock in the Morning of the Day next

ollowing the Day fixed for the Election, *and may continue for not more than Three Days*, Sunday, Christmas Day, and Good Friday being excluded, but no Poll shall be kept open later than Four o'clock in the Afternoon.

[Same as clause 24 of the Seats Bill.]

28. At every Election of a Member to serve in Parliament for the University of London the Vice Chancellor shall appoint the Polling Place, and also shall have power to appoint Two or more Pro-Vice Chancellors, any One of whom may receive the Votes and decide upon all Questions during the Absence of such Vice Chancellor, and such Vice Chancellor shall have Power to appoint Poll Clerks and other Officers, by One or more of whom the Votes may be entered in the Poll Book or such Number of Poll Books as may be judged necessary by such Vice Chancellor; and such Vice Chancellor shall, not later than Two o'clock in the Afternoon of the Day next following the Close of the Poll, openly declare the State of the Poll and make Proclamation of the Member chosen.

[Same as clause 25 of the Seats Bill.]

Voting Papers.

29. *Any Elector may give his Vote by a Voting Paper in the same Manner and subject to the same Conditions in and subject to which an Elector of any of the Universities of Oxford, Cambridge, or Dublin, may give his Vote, and all the Provisions of the Act of the Session of the Twenty-fourth and Twenty-fifth Years of the Reign of Her present Majesty, Chapter Fifty-three, shall, with the requisite Variations, apply accordingly; and in construing the said Act 'the Returning Officer' shall be substituted for 'the Vice Chancellor of the University,' and the Expression 'University' shall be taken to mean the County or Borough for which the Elector votes.*

Miscellaneous.

30. In any Borough named in Schedules (B.) and (C.) to this Act annexed, which is or includes a Municipal Borough, the Mayor of such Municipal Borough shall be the Returning Officer, and in other Cases the Returning Officer shall be appointed in the same manner as if such Places were included amongst the Boroughs mentioned in Schedules (C.) and (D.) of the Act of the Second Year of His late Majesty William the Fourth, Chapter Forty-five, for which no Persons are mentioned in such Schedules as Returning Officers.

[Same as clause 19 of the Seats Bill.]

31. The following Persons, that is to say,

shall be appointed Boundary Commissioners for England and Wales, and they shall, immediately after the passing of this Act, name special Assistant Commissioners, who shall examine the Boundaries *of the Boroughs constituted by this Act,* (including the Divisions of the Borough of the Tower Hamlets,) and of every other Borough in England and Wales.

The Assistant Commissioners so appointed shall give Notice, by Public Advertisement, of their Intention *to visit such Boroughs,* and shall appoint a Time for receiving the Statements of any Persons who may be desirous of giving Information as to the Boundaries or other local Circumstances *of such Boroughs,* and shall, by personal Inspection and such other Means as they shall think necessary, possess themselves of such Information as will enable them to make such Report and Recommendation as hereinafter mentioned.

Upon the Completion of such Examination by the said Assistant Commissioners, the Inclosure Commissioners shall report to One of Her Majesty's Principal Secretaries of State whether any Enlargement of the Boundaries *of such Boroughs* is necessary in order to include within the area thereof the Population properly belonging *to such Boroughs* respectively, and in such Report shall propose such new Boundaries (if any) as in their Judgment would effect that Object, but such Report shall be of no Validity until it has been confirmed by Parliament.

[Same as clause 28 of the Seats Bill, except the names of the Commissioners.]

32. *Every Person claiming to vote in respect of any Franchise conferred by this Act, other than one involving Occupation of Premises and Payment of Rates, shall vote at the Booth at which he would vote if he were registered as a Voter in respect of the House in which he resides.*

33. *There shall be repealed so much of the Seventy-ninth Section of the Act of the Sixth Year of the Reign of Her present Majesty, Chapter Eighteen, as relates to the Residence of Voters at the Time at which they give their votes.*

34. *Where the Owner is* rated *in respect of a Dwelling House instead of the Occupier, the Occupier may claim to be rated for the Purpose of acquiring the Franchise in the same Manner and subject to the same Conditions in and subject to which an Occupier may claim to be registered under the existing Acts of Parlia-*

ment *for the Purpose of acquiring the Franchise in respect of the Occupation of Premises of a clear yearly Value of not less than Ten Pounds, and all the Provisions of the said Acts shall apply accordingly; provided that the Rates to be paid by such Occupier in order to entitle him to the Franchise shall be Rates calculated on the full Rateable Value of the Premises.*

35. *Where any Occupier of a Dwelling House in respect of which the Owner is rated instead of the Occupier at the Time of the passing of this Act would be entitled to be registered, in pursuance of this Act, at the First Registration of Parliamentary Voters to be made after the passing of this Act, if he had paid Rates for the required Period, such Occupier shall, notwithstanding he may not have paid such Rates, be entitled to be registered, subject to the following Conditions:*

1. *That he makes a Claim to be rated in manner in which such Claims are required by the existing Law to be made, within One Month after the passing of this Act:*
2. *That he pays all Rates due in respect of such House at the Time of making his Claim, and further pays all Rates becoming due in respect of such House between the Date of his Claim being made and the Date of his Name being placed on the Register of Parliamentary Voters, such last-mentioned Rates to be calculated on the full Rateable Value of the Premises.*

36. Any Candidate or other Person, either directly or indirectly, corruptly paying any Rate on behalf of any Voter for the Purpose of enabling him to be registered as a Voter, or for the Purpose of inducing him to vote, shall be guilty of Bribery, and be punishable accordingly; and any Person on whose Behalf and with whose Privity any such Payment is made shall also be guilty of Bribery, and punishable accordingly.

37. Whereas by the Act of the Sixth Year of the Reign of Queen Anne, Chapter Seven, all Persons appointed to Offices of Profit under the Crown, and thereafter duly elected as Members of the House of Commons, are required to vacate their Seats upon their Acceptance of any other Office of Profit under the Crown, and it is expedient to alter the Laws in this respect: Be it therefore enacted, That if any Person appointed *to any Office of Profit under the Crown*, and thereafter duly returned as a Member of the House of Commons, accepts, while he continues to be such Member, *any other Office of Profit under the Crown* (*except an Office which by Law incapacitates the Holder thereof from being elected or from voting in Parliament*), the Acceptance of such other Office shall not

render the Election of such Person void, nor shall any Writ thereupon issue for a new Election.

38. Where separate Registers of Voters have been directed to be made in any County or Borough divided by this Act, if a Vacancy take place in the representation of the said County or Borough before the summoning of a future Parliament, and after the Completion of such separate Registers, such last-mentioned Registers shall, for the purpose of any Election to fill up such Vacancy, be deemed together to form the Register for the County or Borough.

39. Nothing in this Act contained shall affect the Rights of Persons whose Names are for the Time being on the Register of Voters for any County in which the Boroughs constituted by this Act are situate to vote in any Election for such County in respect of any Vacancy that may take place before the summoning of a future Parliament, but after such summoning no Person shall be entitled to be registered as a Voter or to vote in any Election for any such County who would not be entitled to be so registered or to vote in case the Boroughs constituted by this Act were before the passing of this Act Boroughs returning Members to Parliament.

[Same as clause 17 of the Seats Bill.]

40. The Franchises conferred by this Act shall be in addition to and not in substitution for any existing Franchises; and, subject to the Provisions of this Act, all Laws, Customs, and Enactments now in force conferring any Right to vote or otherwise relating to the Representation of the People in England and Wales shall remain in full Force, and shall apply, as nearly as Circumstances admit, to any Constituency hereby authorised to return a Member or Members to Parliament as if it had heretofore returned such Members to Parliament.

[Same as clause 14 of the Franchise Bill.]

41. All writs to be issued for the Election of Members to serve in Parliament, and all Mandates, Precepts, Instruments, Proceedings, and Notices consequent upon such Writs, shall be framed and expressed in such Manner and Form as may be necessary for the carrying the Provisions of this Act into effect.

[Same as clause 30 of the Seats Bill.]

42. This Act, so far as is consistent with the Tenor thereof, shall be construed as One with the Enactments for the Time being in force relating to the Representation of the People.

[Same as clause 31 of the Seats Bill.]

43. The following Terms shall in this Act have the Meanings hereinafter assigned to them, unless there is something in the Context repugnant to such Construction; (that is to say,) 'Month' shall mean Calendar Month: 'Member' shall include a Knight of the Shire: 'Election' shall mean an Election of a Member or Members to serve in Parliament: 'County' shall not include a County of a City or County of a Town, but shall mean any County, Riding, Parts or Division of a County returning a Member or Members to serve in Parliament: 'Borough' shall mean any Borough, City, Place, or Combination of Places, not being a County as herein-before defined, returning a Member or Members to serve in Parliament: 'The Registration Acts' shall mean the Act of the Sixth Year of the Reign of Her present Majesty, Chapter Eighteen, and the Act of the Twenty-eighth Year of the Reign of Her present Majesty, Chapter Thirty-six, and any other Acts or Parts of Acts relating to the Registration of Persons entitled to vote at and Proceedings in the Election of Members to serve in Parliament for England and Wales.

[Same as clause 3 of Franchise Bill, omitting definition of 'clear yearly value.']

Of the forty-three clauses of this Bill, twenty-one were subsequently omitted or materially altered. Of the twenty-two which have been retained unaltered eighteen have been taken from the Franchise Bill and the Seats Bill introduced by Mr. Gladstone in 1866. The clauses which are exclusively the work of the Conservative Government are these four:— Clause 1, the Title; clause 8, the Disfranchisement of Reigate and three other boroughs; clause 36, the Penalty for corrupt payment of rates; and clause 38, Temporary provision respecting the Registers of divided counties and boroughs.

By the same Author.

In One thick Volume. 8vo. Price £1. 4s. cloth,

THE INSTITUTIONS OF THE ENGLISH GOVERNMENT;

BEING AN ACCOUNT OF THE CONSTITUTION, POWERS, AND PROCEDURE OF ITS LEGISLATIVE, JUDICIAL AND ADMINISTRATIVE DEPARTMENTS,

WITH

COPIOUS REFERENCES TO ANCIENT AND MODERN AUTHORITIES.

CONTENTS AND ARRANGEMENT OF THE WORK.

BOOK I.—*Legislature.*—Chapter I. Divisions of Government.—II. The Authority of Parliament.—III. The Origin of Parliament.—IV. The Acts of Parliament.—V. Legislative Prerogatives of the Crown.—VI. The Parliamentary Powers of the Crown.—VII. The Constitution of the House of Lords.—VIII. The Constitution of the House of Commons.—IX. Procedure in Parliament.—X. The Privy Council and Cabinet Council.—XI. The Rights of Petition, Public Meetings and the Press.

BOOK II.—*Judicature.*—Chapter I. Divisions of the Judicature.—II. Origin of the Courts of Law.—III. Judicial Offices.—IV. Procedure in Courts of Justice generally.—V. The Supreme Power of the Law.—VI. The Judicature of Parliament and the Lords.—VII. The Judicature of the Privy Council.—VIII. The Court of Chancery.—IX. The Superior Courts of Common Law.—X. Courts of Criminal Jurisdiction.—XI. Courts of Special Civil Jurisdiction.

BOOK III.—*Administrative Government.*—Chapter I. Division of Administrative Offices.—II. Administrative Prerogatives of the Crown.—III. The Title of the Crown.—IV. Origin and Distribution of Administrative Offices.—V. The Privy Council and its Committees.—VI. The Secretarial Departments.—VII. The Fiscal Administrative Offices.—VIII. Military and Naval Offices.—IX. Local Administrative Government.

General Index—Index of Statutes—Addenda et Corrigenda—Table of Authorities cited—Analysis of the Work.

OPINIONS OF THE PRESS.

'It is a clear, concise, well ordered and well executed exposition of the present state of the British Commonwealth........in nearly everything a model of good workmanship. Mr. Cox's style is graceful and intelligible; his learning is great and varied, and his skill in setting forth the materials which he has spent many years in collecting, always from original authorities, is highly to be praised.' EXAMINER.

'A better text-book on the English Constitution can hardly be looked for.'
EXAMINER (*Second Notice*).

'The work before us is a bold and ambitious effort of a thoughtful and able man. There are already numerous works which occupy more or less of the ground which Mr. Homersham Cox has selected for his learned researches, but none of them of the same comprehensive and scientific character as his book.' SOLICITORS' JOURNAL.

'Such is the plan of Mr. Cox's work which has been ably carried into execution by its author. It is written in a clear style, contains a vast amount of constitutional knowledge, and is calculated to give a good idea of the working of our political system; while merely party questions have been carefully eschewed.' JURIST, *Sept.* 3, 1864.

'We have for the first time the anatomy and physiology of the body politic displayed by an able demonstrator, and also for the first time, on a complete plan, exhaustive in its scope, well divided and arranged, and for all but technical purposes sufficiently minute in detail. ....In no single book, and scarcely in any one private library, could we, however well skilled in research, find all the information that is collected in this handsome volume of 750 pages.' MORNING HERALD.

'He has made a careful study of every direct or collateral source of information within his reach, has drawn together a mass of valuable information, and has arranged it in a way both scholarly and attractive.........Of the three sections into which Mr. Cox's book is divided, that detailing the duties and responsibilities of the legislature is perhaps the most valuable for its summing-up of much reading among varied and contradictory authorities in a little space; while the account of the administrative government is specially noteworthy for its information on subjects little understood and nowhere properly explained.'
READER.

'One part of the matter, also, though not perhaps absolutely new, must have been collected with much difficulty from the obscure receptacles in which alone it is to be found, and it has certainly been set forth by Mr. Cox in a very judicious and forcible way......... It is no less true than singular that till the present work was published no easily accessible account of the Executive Government of England existed in our own language.'
SATURDAY REVIEW.

'Das dritte von der Administration handelnde Buch ist wohl der schätzenswertheste Theil des ganzen, sehr umfassenden und wohlgeordneten Werkes, und enthält eine Menge wichtigster Daten aus Originalquellen. Während der Inhalt des Werkes sich einer streng historischen Methode anschliesst, ist der Styl klar und gefällig, ein Vorzug, der bei Schriften dieser Art nicht gar zu häufig ist.' NATIONAL ZEITUNG.

'It contains the largest amount of information on the subjects of which it treats which is anywhere to be obtained within the same compass, and which in fact can only be found elsewhere in a variety of works; whilst with respect to the administrative institutions which form the subject of one of the divisions of the treatise, the same information is not to be found in any other book.........A most admirable compendium; accurate, full, clear, and exceedingly well arranged.' LAW MAGAZINE.

'Im Jahre 1763 resolvirten namentlich beide Häuser, dass das "privilege of parliament" sich auf die Abfassung und Veröffentlichung von aufrührerischen Schriften *nicht* beziehe. Andere Privilegien werden von den beiden Häusern als *Körperschaften* in Anspruch genommen, namentlich Freiheit der Debatte von jeder Controlle durch die Krone (welche Controlle, wie wir seiner Zeit nachgewiesen haben, ursprünglich nicht darauf gerichtet war, wie die einzelnen Mitglieder sich ausdrückten, sondern mit welchen Gegenständen sich das Parlament befasste) und Strafgewalt über die Mitglieder und über andere. Auf diese letztere, die Jurisdiction über Dritte und auf den Conflict mit der Jurisdiction der Gerichte bezieht sich die anzuführende Stelle aus Homersham Cox, "The Institutions of the English Government," London, 1863, einem Werke, das wir allen angelegentlich empfehlen, denen es um eine rechtsverständige und ungefärbte Darstellung dessen, was man englische Verfassung nennt, zu thun ist.' NORDDEUTSCHE ALLGEMEINE ZEITUNG, *April* 22, 1866.

London: H. SWEET, 3 Chancery Lane, Fleet Street.   1863.

By the same Author.

8vo. pp. 214, price 8*s.* 6*d.* cloth,

ANTIENT
PARLIAMENTARY ELECTIONS:

A HISTORY SHEWING HOW PARLIAMENTS WERE CONSTITUTED AND REPRESENTATIVES OF THE PEOPLE ELECTED IN ANTIENT TIMES.

CONTENTS:—Chapter 1. The Rural Population of the Middle Ages. 2. Social Order of the Middle Ages. 3. The Saxon County Court. 4. The County Court after the Conquest. 5. The Origin of Parliaments. 6. The County Suffrage after the Fourteenth Century. 7. Procedure at Elections. 8. The Representation of Boroughs. 9. The Borough Electors.

Appendix:—Particulars taken from Manuscript Cartularies in the Record Office, showing the tenures and services of tenants of various manors in the fourteenth and fifteenth centuries.

A few years ago the compilation of a satisfactory history of Antient Parliamentary Elections would have been almost impracticable. Some of the most important documents relating to the subject were but little known, and others entirely unknown. For example, when the elaborate *Report on the Dignity of a Peer* was published in 1820, the writers were not acquainted with the returns for the very first regularly constituted and complete House of Commons ever convened in this country—that which sat in the twenty-third year of the reign of EDWARD I. Those returns have since been published in the magnificent collection of Parliamentary Writs, edited by Sir FRANCIS PALGRAVE. The publication of that, and of the other great works issued by the Record Commission, marks a new era in the study of Constitutional History. But the very magnitude and number of the volumes, and the obscurity of the language in which they are written, render them inaccessible to all but the most diligent and determined inquirers. In another branch of the subject discussed in the present work—the Saxon polity—most important additions to our means of knowledge have been made within the last few years. In order to investigate accurately the original suffrage, either in counties or boroughs, a knowledge of English political institutions before the Conquest is requisite. It was not until 1840 that the *Antient Laws and Institutes of England* during the Anglo-Saxon period were made fully accessible by the publication of a collection of those laws, edited by Mr. THORPE, under the direction of the Commissioners of

Mr. Cox subsequently gives a singular instance of an appeal to the county court even from the king himself, and as a matter of right, not of favour:—

'A charter of the reign of Æthelred, some time before 995, relates to a claim of land brought in the first instance before that king on the application of one claimant Wynficed and subsequently, at the instance of the other claimant, Leofwine, referring to the county court. The king having heard Wynficed, who produced her title, "sent forthwith by the archbishop and by those who were there to witness with him to Leofwine, and made this known to him. Then he would not [comply] unless it were carried to the shire-mote. And they did so. Then the king sent by Abbot Ælfere his brief to the mote at Cuckhamslow, and greeted all the witan who were there assembled. That was Æthelsige bishop, and Æscwig bishop, and Ælfric abbot, and all the shire. And prayed and commanded that they should reconcile Wynficed and Leofwine as justly as might ever seem to them most just.'

The Saxon tribunals would seem, from the following curious account of a purchase by the Abbey of Ely, to have been largely used as a machinery for the transfer of land. The Abbey had purchased land at Bluntesham from Winothus for thirty pounds:—

'Five pounds were paid to him at Ely, and "the xxv. pounds which remained were paid to him before the King Edgar and his wise men; which being done, Winothus in their presence delivered Bluntesham to the bishop with a deed." But afterwards the title of Winothus was disputed by one Boge, who asserted a prior title, alleging that the land had descended to him from his grandmother. The narrative proceeds: "After these things there was assembled the whole county of Huntingdon by Beornotho the alderman and by Afwold and by Ædric. Forthwith there was a very great assembly. Wifnoth is summoned and brings with him faithful men, namely all the better men (meliores) of vi Hundreds, and Lessius, now of Ely, produced there the deed of Bluntesham, who being all gathered together they explained the claim and ventilated (ventilaverunt) and discussed the cause; and the truth of the matter being known they by their judgment took the land from the sons of Bogan. . . . . Then Winoth produced more than a thousand men, that by their oath he might assert his title to that land; but the sons of Bogan were unwilling to take the oath, and so all determined that Winoth should have Bluntesham, and faithfully promised to be his helpers in this matter and to bear witness what they had done if ever at any other time he or any of his heirs had need. And when all this was done Bishop Œdelwood gave to Winoth xl shillings and an armlet worth iii marks because he had laboured much in this and was about to go beyond the sea in the service of God."'

It is as the assemblies in which representatives were chosen to serve in Parliament that the county courts have after all most interest for us, and to that branch of his subject and the ancient suffrages in counties and boroughs and the changes wrought in them, Mr. Cox devotes the greater share of his attention. It is remarkable that as late as the reign of Philip and Mary, Parliamentary candidates dissatisfied with the sheriff's decision as to a majority by show of hands had no right to call for a poll. In 1554 an action was brought by Sir Richard Buckley against Rice Thomas, the sheriff of Anglesea, for refusing him a poll at the county election in the first year of Queen Mary's reign, and the three judges before whom the case came agreed that the right did not exist. In the reign of James I. a more enlightened view of the subject was entertained, and it was decided that the sheriff was bound to take the poll. An account of the mode in which an election was conducted at York, a few years afterwards, shows the means taken for polling the electors to have been by no means of the most satisfactory description:—

'The sheriff was charged—1. That upon his view, without poll, he gave his judgment for Sir Tho. Wentworth and Sir Tho. Fairfax, to be knights; when Sir Jo. Savyle most voices; 2ly, That when the poll required, he said it was only of courtesy to grant it; 3ly, That he began the poll, but having polled about thirty-five, brake it off....That upon Tuesday last he by his counsel alleged that the day of the election after eight of the clock he made proclamation and read the writ at the usual place. That the writ being read, he caused the gates to be shut; he took a view of the freeholders, and returning, said he thought Sir Tho. Wentworth and Sir Tho. Fairfax were double the voices of Sir Jo. Savyle. That he chose to take the poll at the postern gate, and having polled about thirty-five, heard the fore gate was broken open, and many freeholders gone out upon Sir John Savyle's persuasion that the poll would last many days. That thereupon he brake off the poll.'

Although the reputation which Mr. Homersham Cox's previous work upon the English Constitution has acquired is of itself sufficient to secure for the book before us a large share of public attention, there are in almost every page indications of a research and painstaking labour which are alone sufficient to obtain for it the thorough appreciation of every one interested in the subject.

London: LONGMANS and CO. 1868.

39 PATERNOSTER ROW, E.C.
LONDON: *January* 1867.

GENERAL LIST OF WORKS

PUBLISHED BY

Messrs. LONGMANS, GREEN, READER, and DYER.

ARTS, MANUFACTURES, &c. 12	MISCELLANEOUS and POPULAR METAPHYSICAL WORKS 6
ASTRONOMY, METEOROLOGY, POPULAR GEOGRAPHY, &c. 7	MUSICAL PUBLICATIONS 11
BIOGRAPHY AND MEMOIRS 3	NATURAL HISTORY and POPULAR SCIENCE 7
CHEMISTRY, MEDICINE, SURGERY, and the ALLIED SCIENCES 9	POETRY and THE DRAMA 17
COMMERCE, NAVIGATION, and MERCANTILE AFFAIRS 19	RELIGIOUS AND MORAL WORKS 13
CRITICISM, PHILOLOGY, &c. 4	RURAL SPORTS, &c. 18
FINE ARTS and ILLUSTRATED EDITIONS 11	TRAVELS, VOYAGES, &c. 15
HISTORICAL WORKS 1	WORKS OF FICTION 16
INDEX .... 21—24	WORKS OF UTILITY and GENERAL INFORMATION 19
KNOWLEDGE for the YOUNG 20	

Historical Works.

Lord Macaulay's Works. Complete and uniform Library Edition. Edited by his Sister, Lady TREVELYAN. 8 vols. 8vo. with Portrait, price £5 5s. cloth, or £8 8s. bound in tree-calf by Rivière.

The History of England from the Fall of Wolsey to the Death of Elizabeth. By JAMES ANTHONY FROUDE, M.A. late Fellow of Exeter College, Oxford. VOLS. I. to X. in 8vo. price £7 2s. cloth.

VOLS. I. to IV. the Reign of Henry VIII. Third Edition, 54s.

VOLS. V. and VI. the Reigns of Edward VI. and Mary. Second Edition, 28s.

VOLS. VII. & VIII. the Reign of Elizabeth, VOLS. I. & II. Fourth Edition, 28s.

VOLS. IX. and X. the Reign of Elizabeth. VOLS. III. and IV. 32s.

The History of England from the Accession of James II. By Lord MACAULAY.
LIBRARY EDITION, 5 vols. 8vo. £4.
CABINET EDITION, 8 vols. post 8vo. 48s.
PEOPLE'S EDITION, 4 vols. crown 8vo. 16s.

Revolutions in English History. By ROBERT VAUGHAN, D.D. 3 vols. 8vo. 45s.
VOL. I. Revolutions of Race, 15s.
VOL. II. Revolutions in Religion, 15s.
VOL. III. Revolutions in Government, 15s.

An Essay on the History of the English Government and Constitution, from the Reign of Henry VII. to the Present Time. By JOHN EARL RUSSELL. Fourth Edition, revised. Crown 8vo. 6s.

The History of England during the Reign of George the Third. By the Right Hon. W. N. MASSEY. Cabinet Edition, 4 vols. post 8vo. 24s.

The Constitutional History of England, since the Accession of George III. 1760—1860. By Sir THOMAS ERSKINE MAY, K.C.B. Second Edit. 2 vols. 8vo. 33s.

Brodie's Constitutional History of the British Empire from the Accession of Charles I. to the Restoration. Second Edition. 3 vols. 8vo. 36s.

Historical Studies. I. On Precursors of the French Revolution; II. Studies from the History of the Seventeenth Century; III. Leisure Hours of a Tourist. By HERMAN MERIVALE, M.A. 8vo. 12s. 6d.

Lectures on the History of England. By WILLIAM LONGMAN. VOL. I. from the Earliest Times to the Death of King Edward II. with 6 Maps, a coloured Plate, and 53 Woodcuts. 8vo. 15s.

A

History of Civilization in England and France, Spain and Scotland. By HENRY THOMAS BUCKLE. Fifth Edition of the entire work, complete in 3 vols. crown 8vo. price 24s. cloth; or 42s. bound in treecalf by Rivière.

The History of India, from the Earliest Period to the close of Lord Dalhousie's Administration. By JOHN CLARK MARSHMAN. 3 vols. crown 8vo.
[*Nearly ready.*]

Democracy in America. By ALEXIS DE TOCQUEVILLE. Translated by HENRY REEVE, with an Introductory Notice by the Translator. 2 vols. 8vo. 21s.

The Spanish Conquest in America, and its Relation to the History of Slavery and to the Government of Colonies. By ARTHUR HELPS. 4 vols. 8vo. £3. VOLS. I. & II. 28s. VOLS. III. & IV. 16s. each.

History of the Reformation in Europe in the Time of Calvin. By J. H. MERLE D'AUBIGNÉ, D.D. VOLS. I. and II. 8vo. 28s. VOL. III. 12s. and VOL. IV. price 16s. VOL. V. in the press.

Library History of France, in 5 vols. 8vo. By EYRE EVANS CROWE. VOL. I. 14s. VOL. II. 15s. VOL. III. 18s. VOL. IV. 18s.

Lectures on the History of France. By the late Sir JAMES STEPHEN, LL.D. 2 vols. 8vo. 24s.

The History of Greece. By C. THIRLWALL, D.D. Lord Bishop of St. David's. 8 vols. fcp. with Vignette-titles, 28s.

The Tale of the Great Persian War, from the Histories of Herodotus. By GEORGE W. COX, M.A. late Scholar of Trin. Coll. Oxon. Fcp. 7s. 6d.

Greek History from Themistocles to Alexander, in a Series of Lives from Plutarch. Revised and arranged by A. H. CLOUGH. Fcp. with 44 Woodcuts, 6s.

Critical History of the Language and Literature of Ancient Greece. By WILLIAM MURE, of Caldwell. 5 vols. 8vo. £3 9s.

History of the Literature of Ancient Greece. By Professor K. O. MÜLLER. Translated by the Right Hon. Sir GEORGE CORNEWALL LEWIS, Bart. and by J. W. DONALDSON, D.D. 3 vols. 8vo. 36s.

History of the City of Rome from its Foundation to the Sixteenth Century of the Christian Era. By THOMAS H. DYER, LL.D. 8vo. with 2 Maps, 15s.

History of the Romans under the Empire. By CHARLES MERIVALE, B.D. Chaplain to the Speaker. Cabinet Edition, with Maps, complete in 8 vols. post 8vo. 48s.

The Fall of the Roman Republic: a Short History of the Last Century of the Commonwealth. By the same Author. 12mo. 7s. 6d.

The Conversion of the Roman Empire; the Boyle Lectures for the year 1864, delivered at the Chapel Royal, Whitehall. By the same. 2nd Edition. 8vo. 8s. 6d.

The Conversion of the Northern Nations; the Boyle Lectures for 1865. By the same Author. 8vo. 8s. 6d.

Critical and Historical Essays contributed to the *Edinburgh Review*. By the Right Hon. Lord MACAULAY.
  LIBRARY EDITION, 3 vols. 8vo. 36s.
  CABINET EDITION, 4 vols. post 8vo. 24s.
  TRAVELLER'S EDITION, in 1 vol. 21s.
  POCKET EDITION, 3 vols. fcp. 21s.
  PEOPLE'S EDITION, 2 vols. crown 8vo. 8s.

History of the Rise and Influence of the Spirit of Rationalism in Europe. By W. E. H. LECKY, M.A. Third Edition. 2 vols. 8vo. 25s.

The History of Philosophy, from Thales to the Present Day. By GEORGE HENRY LEWES. Third Edition, partly rewritten and greatly enlarged. In 2 vols. VOL. I. *Ancient Philosophy*; VOL. II. *Modern Philosophy*. [*Nearly ready.*]

History of the Inductive Sciences. By WILLIAM WHEWELL, D.D. F.R.S. late Master of Trin. Coll. Cantab. Third Edition. 3 vols. crown 8vo. 24s.

Egypt's Place in Universal History; an Historical Investigation. By C. C. J. BUNSEN, D.D. Translated by C. H. COTTRELL, M.A. With many Illustrations. 4 vols. 8vo. £5 8s. VOL. V. is nearly ready, completing the work.

Maunder's Historical Treasury; comprising a General Introductory Outline of Universal History, and a Series of Separate Histories. Fcp. 10s.

Historical and Chronological Encyclopædia, presenting in a brief and convenient form Chronological Notices of all the Great Events of Universal History. By B. B. WOODWARD, F.S.A. Librarian to the Queen. [*In the press.*

History of the Christian Church, from the Ascension of Christ to the Conversion of Constantine. By E. Burton, D.D. late Regius Prof. of Divinity in the University of Oxford. Eighth Edition. Fcp. 3s. 6d.

Sketch of the History of the Church of England to the Revolution of 1688. By the Right Rev. T. V. Short, D.D. Lord Bishop of St. Asaph. Seventh Edition. Crown 8vo. 10s. 6d.

History of the Early Church, from the First Preaching of the Gospel to the Council of Nicæa, A.D. 325. By the Author of 'Amy Herbert.' Fcp. 4s. 6d.

History of Wesleyan Methodism. By George Smith, F.A.S Fourth Edition, with numerous Portraits. 3 vols. crown 8vo. 7s. each.

The English Reformation. By F. C. Massingberd, M.A. Chancellor of Lincoln. Fourth Edit. revised. Fcp. 7s. 6d.

Biography and Memoirs.

Life and Correspondence of Richard Whately, D.D. late Archbishop of Dublin. By E. Jane Whately, Author of 'English Synonymes.' With 2 Portraits. 2 vols. 8vo. 28s.

Extracts of the Journals and Correspondence of Miss Berry, from the Year 1783 to 1852. Edited by Lady Theresa Lewis. Second Edition, with 3 Portraits. 3 vols. 8vo. 42s.

The Diary of the Right Hon. William Windham, M.P. From 1783 to 1809. Edited by Mrs. H. Baring. 8vo. 18s.

Life of the Duke of Wellington. By the Rev. G. R. Gleig, M.A. Popular Edition, carefully revised; with copious Additions. Crown 8vo. with Portrait, 5s.

Life of the Duke of Wellington, partly from M. Brialmont, partly from Original Documents (Intermediate Edition). By Rev. G. R. Gleig, M.A. 8vo. with Portrait, 15s.

Brialmont and Gleig's Life of the Duke of Wellington (the Parent Work). 4 vols. 8vo. with Illustrations, £2 14s.

Life of Robert Stephenson, F.R.S. By J. C. Jeaffreson, Barrister-at-Law; and William Pole, F.R.S. Member of the Institution of Civil Engineers. With 2 Portraits and 17 Illustrations on Steel and Wood. 2 vols. 8vo. 32s.

History of my Religious Opinions. By J. H. Newman, D.D. Being the Substance of Apologia pro Vitâ Suâ. Post 8vo. 6s.

Father Mathew: a Biography. By John Francis Maguire, M.P. Popular Edition, with Portrait. Crown 8vo. 3s. 6d.

Rome; its Rulers and its Institutions. By the same Author. New Edition is in preparation.

Letters and Life of Francis Bacon, including all his Occasional Works. Collected and edited, with a Commentary, by J. Spedding, Trin. Coll. Cantab. Vols. I. and II. 8vo. 24s.

Some Account of the Life and Opinions of a Fifth-Monarchy Man, chiefly extracted from the Writings of John Rogers, preacher. Edited by the Rev. Edward Rogers, M.A. Student of Christ Church, Oxford. Crown 4to.
[*Nearly ready.*

Life of Amelia Wilhelmina Sieve- king, from the German. Edited, with the Author's sanction, by Catherine Winkworth. Post 8vo. with Portrait, 12s.

Mozart's Letters (1769-1791), translated from the Collection of Dr. Ludwig Nohl by Lady Wallace. 2 vols. post 8vo. with Portrait and Facsimile, 18s.

Beethoven's Letters (1790-1826), from the Two Collections of Drs. Nohl and Von Köchel. Translated by Lady Wallace. 2 vols. post 8vo. Portrait, 18s.

Felix Mendelssohn's Letters from *Italy and Switzerland,* and *Letters from 1833 to 1847,* translated by Lady Wallace. With Portrait. 2 vols. crown 8vo. 5s. each.

Recollections of the late William Wilberforce, M.P. for the County of York during nearly 30 Years. By J. S. Harford, F.R.S. Second Edition. Post 8vo. 7s.

Memoirs of Sir Henry Havelock, K.C.B. By John Clark Marshman. Second Edition. 8vo. with Portrait, 12s. 6d.

Miscellaneous Works and Popular Metaphysics.

Recreations of a Country Parson. By A. K. H. B. First Series, with 41 Woodcut Illustrations from Designs by R. T. Pritchett. Crown 8vo. 12s. 6d.

Recreations of a Country Parson. Second Series. Crown 8vo. 3s. 6d.

The Commonplace Philosopher in Town and Country. By the same Author. Crown 8vo. 3s. 6d.

Leisure Hours in Town; Essays Consolatory, Æsthetical, Moral, Social, and Domestic. By the same. Crown 8vo. 3s. 6d.

The Autumn Holidays of a Country Parson; Essays contributed to *Fraser's Magazine* and to *Good Words*. By the same. Crown 8vo. 3s. 6d.

The Graver Thoughts of a Country Parson, Second Series. By the same. Crown 8vo. 3s. 6d.

Critical Essays of a Country Parson, selected from Essays contributed to *Fraser's Magazine*. By the same. Post 8vo. 9s.

Sunday Afternoons at the Parish Church of a University City. By the same. Crown 8vo. 3s. 6d.

A Campaigner at Home. By Shirley, Author of 'Thalatta' and 'Nugæ Criticæ.' Post 8vo. with Vignette, 7s. 6d.

Studies in Parliament: a Series of Sketches of Leading Politicians. By R. H. Hutton. (Reprinted from the *Pall Mall Gazette*.) Crown 8vo. 4s. 6d.

Lord Macaulay's Miscellaneous Writings.
Library Edition, 2 vols. 8vo. Portrait, 21s.
People's Edition, 1 vol. crown 8vo. 4s. 6d.

The Rev. Sydney Smith's Miscellaneous Works; including his Contributions to the *Edinburgh Review*. People's Edition, 2 vols. crown 8vo. 8s.

Elementary Sketches of Moral Philosophy, delivered at the Royal Institution. By the same Author. Fcp. 6s.

The Wit and Wisdom of the Rev. Sydney Smith: a Selection of the most memorable Passages in his Writings and Conversation. 16mo. 5s.

Epigrams, Ancient and Modern: Humorous, Witty, Satirical, Moral, and Panegyrical. Edited by Rev. John Booth, B.A. Cambridge. Second Edition, revised and enlarged. Fcp. 7s. 6d.

The Folk-Lore of the Northern Counties of England and the Borders. By William Henderson. With an Appendix on Household Stories by the Rev. S. Baring-Gould. Crown 8vo. with Coloured Frontispiece, 9s. 6d.

From Matter to Spirit: the Result of Ten Years' Experience in Spirit Manifestations. By Sophia E. De Morgan. With a Preface by Professor De Morgan. Post 8vo. 8s. 6d.

Essays selected from Contributions to the *Edinburgh Review*. By Henry Rogers. Second Edition. 3 vols. fcp. 21s.

Reason and Faith, their Claims and Conflicts. By the same Author. New Edition, revised and extended, and accompanied by several other Essays, on related subjects. Crown 8vo. 6s. 6d.

The Eclipse of Faith; or, a Visit to a Religious Sceptic. By the same Author. Eleventh Edition. Fcp. 5s.

Defence of the Eclipse of Faith, by its Author. Third Edition. Fcp. 3s. 6d.

Selections from the Correspondence of R. E. H. Greyson. By the same Author. Third Edition. Crown 8vo. 7s. 6d.

Fulleriana, or the Wisdom and Wit of Thomas Fuller, with Essay on his Life and Genius. By the same Author. 16mo. 2s. 6d.

Occasional Essays. By Chandos Wren Hoskyns, Author of 'Talpa, or the Chronicles of a Clay Farm,' &c. 16mo. 5s. 6d.

An Essay on Human Nature; showing the Necessity of a Divine Revelation for the Perfect Development of Man's Capacities. By Henry S. Boase, M.D. F.R.S. and G.S. 8vo. 12s.

The Philosophy of Nature; a Systematic Treatise on the Causes and Laws of Natural Phenomena. By the same Author. 8vo. 12s.

The Secret of Hegel: being the Hegelian System in Origin, Principle, Form, and Matter. By James Hutchison Stirling. 2 vols. 8vo. 28s.

An Introduction to Mental Philosophy, on the Inductive Method. By J. D. Morell, M.A. LL.D. 8vo. 12s.

Elements of Psychology, containing the Analysis of the Intellectual Powers. By the same Author. Post 8vo. 7s. 6d.

Sight and Touch: an Attempt to Disprove the Received (or Berkeleian) Theory of Vision. By THOMAS K. ABBOTT, M.A. Fellow and Tutor of Trin. Coll. Dublin. 8vo. with 21 Woodcuts, 5s. 6d.

The Senses and the Intellect. By ALEXANDER BAIN, M.A. Prof. of Logic in the Univ. of Aberdeen. Second Edition. 8vo. 15s.

The Emotions and the Will, by the same Author. 8vo. 15s.

On the Study of Character, including an Estimate of Phrenology. By the same Author. 8vo. 9s.

Time and Space: a Metaphysical Essay. By SHADWORTH H. HODGSON. 8vo. pp. 588, price 16s.

The Way to Rest: Results from a Life-search after Religious Truth. By R. VAUGHAN, D.D. Crown 8vo. 7s. 6d.

Hours with the Mystics: a Contribution to the History of Religious Opinion. By ROBERT ALFRED VAUGHAN, B.A. Second Edition. 2 vols. crown 8vo. 12s.

The Philosophy of Necessity; or, Natural Law as applicable to Mental, Moral, and Social Science. By CHARLES BRAY. Second Edition. 8vo. 9s.

The Education of the Feelings and Affections. By the same Author. Third Edition. 8vo. 8s. 6d.

On Force, its Mental and Moral Correlates. By the same Author. 8vo. 5s.

Christianity and Common Sense. By Sir WILLOUGHBY JONES, Bart. M.A. Trin. Coll. Cantab. 8vo. 6s.

Astronomy, Meteorology, Popular Geography, &c.

Outlines of Astronomy. By Sir J. F. W. HERSCHEL, Bart, M.A. Eighth Edition, revised; with Plates and Woodcuts. 8vo. 18s.

Arago's Popular Astronomy. Translated by Admiral W. H. SMYTH, F.R.S. and R. GRANT, M.A. With 25 Plates and 358 Woodcuts. 2 vols. 8vo. £2 5s.

Saturn and its System. By RICHARD A. PROCTOR, B.A. late Scholar of St. John's Coll. Camb. and King's Coll. London. 8vo. with 14 Plates, 14s.

The Handbook of the Stars. By the same Author. Square fcp. 8vo. with 3 Maps. price 5s.

Celestial Objects for Common Telescopes. By T. W. WEBB, M.A. F.R.A.S. With Map of the Moon, and Woodcuts. 16mo. 7s.

A General Dictionary of Geography, Descriptive, Physical, Statistical, and Historical; forming a complete Gazetteer of the World. By A. KEITH JOHNSTON, F.R.S.E. 8vo. 31s. 6d.

M'Culloch's Dictionary, Geographical, Statistical, and Historical, of the various Countries, Places, and principal Natural Objects in the World. Revised Edition, with the Statistical Information throughout brought up to the latest returns. By FREDERICK MARTIN. 4 vols. 8vo. with coloured Maps, £4 4s.

A Manual of Geography, Physical, Industrial, and Political. By W. HUGHES, F.R.G.S. Prof. of Geog. in King's Coll. and in Queen's Coll. Lond. With 6 Maps. Fcp. 7s. 6d.

Hawaii: the Past, Present, and Future of its Island-Kingdom: an Historical Account of the Sandwich Islands. By MANLEY HOPKINS, Hawaiian Consul-General, &c. Second Edition, revised and continued; with Portrait, Map, and 8 other Illustrations. Post 8vo. 12s. 6d.

Maunder's Treasury of Geography, Physical, Historical, Descriptive, and Political. Edited by W. HUGHES, F.R.G.S. With 7 Maps and 16 Plates. Fcp. 10s. 6d.

Physical Geography for Schools and General Readers. By M. F. MAURY, LL.D. Fcp. with 2 Charts, 2s. 6d.

Natural History and Popular Science.

The Elements of Physics or Natural Philosophy. By NEIL ARNOTT, M.D. F.R.S. Physician Extraordinary to the Queen. Sixth Edition, rewritten and completed. 2 Parts, 8vo. 21s.

Volcanos, the Character of their Phenomena, their Share in the Structure and Composition of the Surface of the Globe, &c. By G. POULETT SCROPE, M.P. F.R.S. Second Edition. 8vo. with Illustrations, 15s.

Rocks Classified and Described.
By BERNHARD VON COTTA. An English Edition, by P. H. LAWRENCE (with English, German, and French Synonymes), revised by the Author. Post 8vo. 14s.

*** Lithology, or a Classified Synopsis of the Names of Rocks and Minerals, also by Mr. LAWRENCE, adapted to the above work, may be had, price 5s. or printed on one side only (interpaged blank), for use in Cabinets, price 7s.

Sound: a Course of Six Lectures delivered at the Royal Institution of Great Britain. By Professor JOHN TYNDALL, LL.D. F.R.S. 1 vol. crown 8vo.
[*Nearly ready.*

Heat Considered as a Mode of Motion. By Professor JOHN TYNDALL, LL.D. F.R.S. Second Edition. Crown 8vo. with Woodcuts, 12s. 6d.

A Treatise on Electricity, in Theory and Practice. By A. DE LA RIVE, Prof. in the Academy of Geneva. Translated by C. V. WALKER, F.R.S. 3 vols. 8vo. with Woodcuts, £3 13s.

The Correlation of Physical Forces. By W. R. GROVE, Q.C. V.P.R.S. Fifth Edition, revised by the Author, and augmented by a Discourse on Continuity. 8vo.

Manual of Geology. By S. HAUGHTON, M.D. F.R.S. Fellow of Trin. Coll. and Prof. of Geol. in the Univ. of Dublin. Second Edition, with 66 Woodcuts. Fcp. 7s. 6d.

A Guide to Geology. By J. PHILLIPS, M.A. Prof. of Geol. in the Univ. of Oxford. Fifth Edition. Fcp. 4s.

A Glossary of Mineralogy. By H. W. BRISTOW, F.G.S. of the Geological Survey of Great Britain. With 486 Figures. Crown 8vo. 12s.

The Elements: an Investigation of the Forces which determine the Position and Movements of the Ocean and Atmosphere. By WILLIAM LEIGHTON JORDAN. Vol. I. royal 8vo. with 13 maps, price 8s.

Phillips's Elementary Introduction to Mineralogy, re-edited by H. J. BROOKE, F.R.S. and W. H. MILLER, F.G.S. Post 8vo. with Woodcuts, 18s.

Van Der Hoeven's Handbook of ZOOLOGY. Translated from the Second Dutch Edition by the Rev. W. CLARK, M.D. F.R.S. 2 vols. 8vo. with 24 Plates of Figures, 60s.

The Comparative Anatomy and Physiology of the Vertebrate Animals. By RICHARD OWEN, F.R.S. D.C.L. 3 vols. 8vo. with upwards of 1,200 Woodcuts. VOLS. I. and II. price 21s. each, now ready. VOL. III. in the Spring.

The First Man and His Place in Creation, considered on the Principles of Common Sense from a Christian Point of View; with an Appendix on the Negro. By GEORGE MOORE, M.D. M.R.C.P.L. &c. Post 8vo. 8s. 6d.

The Lake Dwellings of Switzerland and other Parts of Europe. By Dr. F. KELLER, President of the Antiquarian Association of Zürich. Translated and arranged by J. E. LEE, F.S.A. F.G.S. Author of 'Isca Silurum.' With several Woodcuts and nearly 100 Plates of Figures. Royal 8vo. 31s. 6d.

Homes without Hands: a Description of the Habitations of Animals, classed according to their Principle of Construction. By Rev. J. G. WOOD, M.A. F.L.S. With about 140 Vignettes on Wood (20 full size of page). Second Edition. 8vo. 21s.

The Harmonies of Nature and Unity of Creation. By Dr. G. HARTWIG, 8vo. with numerous Illustrations, 18s.

The Sea and its Living Wonders. By the same Author. Third Edition, enlarged. 8vo. with many Illustrations, 21s.

The Tropical World. By the same Author. With 8 Chromoxylographs and 172 Woodcuts. 8vo. 21s.

Manual of Corals and Sea Jellies. By J. R. GREENE, B.A. Edited by J. A. GALBRAITH, M.A. and S. HAUGHTON, M.D. Fcp. with 39 Woodcuts, 5s.

Manual of Sponges and Animalculæ; with a General Introduction on the Principles of Zoology. By the same Author and Editors. Fcp. with 16 Woodcuts, 2s.

Manual of the Metalloids. By J. APJOHN, M.D. F.R.S. and the same Editors. 2nd Edition. Fcp. with 38 Woodcuts, 7s. 6d.

Sketches of the Natural History of Ceylon. By Sir J. EMERSON TENNENT, K.C.S. LL.D. With 82 Wood Engravings. Post 8vo. 12s. 6d.

Ceylon. By the same Author. 5th Edition; with Maps, &c. and 90 Wood Engravings. 2 vols. 8vo. £2 10s.

The Wild Elephant, its Structure and Habits, with the Method of Taking and Training it in Ceylon. By the same Author. Fcp. 8vo. with Illustrations.

A Familiar History of Birds.
By E. STANLEY, D.D. late Lord Bishop of Norwich. Fcp. with Woodcuts, 3s. 6d.

Kirby and Spence's Introduction to Entomology, or Elements of the Natural History of Insects. Crown 8vo. 5s.

Maunder's Treasury of Natural History, or Popular Dictionary of Zoology. Revised and corrected by T. S. COBBOLD, M.D. Fcp. with 900 Woodcuts, 10s.

The Elements of Botany for Families and Schools. Tenth Edition, revised by THOMAS MOORE, F.L.S. Fcp with 154 Woodcuts, 2s. 6d.

The Treasury of Botany, or Popular Dictionary of the Vegetable Kingdom; with which is incorporated a Glossary of Botanical Terms. Edited by J. LINDLEY, F.R.S. and T. MOORE, F.L.S. assisted by eminent Contributors. Pp. 1,274, with 274 Woodcuts and 20 Steel Plates. 2 Parts, fcp. 20s.

The British Flora; comprising the Phænogamous or Flowering Plants and the Ferns. By Sir W. J. HOOKER, K.H. and G. A. WALKER-ARNOTT, LL.D. 12mo. with 12 Plates, 14s. or coloured, 21s.

The Rose Amateur's Guide. By THOMAS RIVERS. New Edition. Fcp. 4s.

The Indoor Gardener. By Miss MALING. Fcp. with Frontispiece, 5s.

Loudon's Encyclopædia of Plants; comprising the Specific Character, Description, Culture, History, &c. of all the Plants found in Great Britain. With upwards of 12,000 Woodcuts. 8vo. 42s.

Loudon's Encyclopædia of Trees and Shrubs; containing the Hardy Trees and Shrubs of Great Britain scientifically and popularly described. With 2,000 Woodcuts. 8vo. 50s.

Bryologia Britannica; containing the Mosses of Great Britain and Ireland, arranged and described. By W. WILSON. 8vo. with 61 Plates, 42s. or coloured, £4 4s.

Maunder's Scientific and Literary Treasury; a Popular Encyclopædia of Science, Literature, and Art. New Edition, thoroughly revised and in great part re-written, with above 1,000 new articles, by J. Y. JOHNSON, Corr. M.Z.S. Fcp. 10s. 6d.

A Dictionary of Science, Literature, and Art. Fourth Edition, re-edited by the late W. T. BRANDE (the Author) and GEORGE W. COX, M.A. 3 vols. medium 8vo. price 63s. cloth.

Essays on Scientific and other subjects, contributed to Reviews. By Sir H. HOLLAND, Bart. M.D. Second Edition. 8vo. 14s.

Essays from the Edinburgh and *Quarterly Reviews*; with Addresses and other Pieces. By Sir J. F. W. HERSCHEL, Bart. M.A. 8vo. 18s.

Chemistry, Medicine, Surgery, and the Allied Sciences.

A Dictionary of Chemistry and the Allied Branches of other Sciences. By HENRY WATTS, F.C.S. assisted by eminent Contributors. 5 vols. medium 8vo. in course of publication in Parts. VOL. I. 31s. 6d. VOL. II. 26s. VOL. III. 31s. 6d. and VOL. IV. 24s. are now ready.

A Handbook of Volumetrical Analysis. By ROBERT H. SCOTT, M.A. T.C.D. Post 8vo. 4s. 6d.

Elements of Chemistry, Theoretical and Practical. By WILLIAM A. MILLER, M.D. LL.D. F.R.S. F.G.S. Professor of Chemistry, King's College, London. 3 vols. 8vo. £2 13s. PART I. CHEMICAL PHYSICS, Third Edition, 12s. PART II. INORGANIC CHEMISTRY, 21s. PART III. ORGANIC CHEMISTRY, Third Edition, 24s.

A Manual of Chemistry, Descriptive and Theoretical. By WILLIAM ODLING, M.B. F.R.S. PART I. 8vo. 9s.

A Course of Practical Chemistry, for the use of Medical Students. By the same Author. Second Edition, with 70 new Woodcuts. Crown 8vo. 7s. 6d.

Lectures on Animal Chemistry Delivered at the Royal College of Physicians in 1865. By the same Author. Crown 8vo. 4s. 6d.

The Toxicologist's Guide: a New Manual on Poisons, giving the Best Methods to be pursued for the Detection of Poisons. By J. HORSLEY, F.C.S. Analytical Chemist. Post 8vo. 3s. 6d.

The Diagnosis and Treatment of the Diseases of Women; including the Diagnosis of Pregnancy. By GRAILY HEWITT, M.D. &c. New Edition, with Woodcut Illustrations, in the press.

Lectures on the Diseases of Infancy and Childhood. By CHARLES WEST, M.D. &c. 5th Edition, revised and enlarged. 8vo. 16s.

Exposition of the Signs and Symptoms of Pregnancy: with other Papers on subjects connected with Midwifery. By W. F. MONTGOMERY, M.A. M.D. M.R.I.A. 8vo. with Illustrations, 25s.

A System of Surgery, Theoretical and Practical, in Treatises by Various Authors. Edited by T. HOLMES, M.A. Cantab. Assistant-Surgeon to St. George's Hospital. 4 vols. 8vo. £4 13s.

Vol. I. General Pathology, 21s.
Vol. II. Local Injuries: Gun-shot Wounds, Injuries of the Head, Back, Face, Neck, Chest, Abdomen, Pelvis, of the Upper and Lower Extremities, and Diseases of the Eye. 21s.
Vol. III. Operative Surgery. Diseases of the Organs of Circulation, Locomotion, &c. 21s.
Vol. IV. Diseases of the Organs of Digestion, of the Genito-Urinary System, and of the Breast, Thyroid Gland, and Skin; with APPENDIX and GENERAL INDEX. 30s.

ectures on the Principles and Practice of Physic. By THOMAS WATSON, M.D. Physician-Extraordinary to the Queen. Fourth Edition. 2 vols. 8vo. 34s.

Lectures on Surgical Pathology. By J. PAGET, F.R.S. Surgeon-Extraordinary to the Queen. Edited by W. TURNER, M.B. 8vo. with 117 Woodcuts, 21s.

A Treatise on the Continued Fevers of Great Britain. By C. MURCHISON, M.D. Senior Physician to the London Fever Hospital. 8vo. with coloured Plates, 18s.

Anatomy, Descriptive and Surgical. By HENRY GRAY, F.R.S. With 410 Wood Engravings from Dissections. Fourth Edition, by T. HOLMES, M.A. Cantab. Royal 8vo. 28s.

The Cyclopædia of Anatomy and Physiology. Edited by the late R. B. TODD, M.D. F.R.S. Assisted by nearly all the most eminent cultivators of Physiological Science of the present age. 5 vols. 8vo. with 2,853 Woodcuts, £6 6s.

Physiological Anatomy and Physiology of Man. By the late R. B. TODD, M.D. F.R.S. and W. BOWMAN, F.R.S. of King's College. With numerous Illustrations. VOL. II. 8vo. 25s.

VOL. I. New Edition by Dr. LIONEL S. BEALE, F.R.S. in course of publication; PART I. with 8 Plates, 7s. 6d.

Histological Demonstrations; a Guide to the Microscopical Examination of the Animal Tissues in Health and Disease, for the use of the Medical and Veterinary Professions. By G. HARLEY, M.D. F.R.S. Prof. in Univ. Coll. London; and G. T. BROWN, M.R.C.V.S. Professor of Veterinary Medicine, and one of the Inspecting Officers in the Cattle Plague Department of the Privy Council. Post 8vo. with 223 Woodcuts, 12s.

A Dictionary of Practical Medicine. By J. COPLAND, M.D. F.R.S. Abridged from the larger work by the Author, assisted by J. C. COPLAND, M.R.C.S. and throughout brought down to the present state of Medical Science. Pp. 1,560, in 8vo. price 36s.

The Works of Sir B. C. Brodie, Bart. collected and arranged by CHARLES HAWKINS, F.R.C.S.E. 3 vols. 8vo. with Medallion and Facsimile, 48s.

Autobiography of Sir B. C. Brodie, Bart. printed from the Author's materials left in MS. Second Edition. Fcp. 4s. 6d.

A Manual of Materia Medica and Therapeutics, abridged from Dr. PEREIRA'S Elements by F. J. FARRE, M.D. assisted by R. BENTLEY, M.R.C.S. and by R. WARINGTON, F.R.S. 1 vol. 8vo. with 90 Woodcuts, 21s.

Dr. Pereira's Elements of Materia Medica and Therapeutics, Third Edition, by A. S. TAYLOR, M.D. and G. O. REES, M.D. 3 vols. 8vo. with Woodcuts, £3 15s.

Thomson's Conspectus of the British Pharmacopœia. Twenty-fourth Edition, corrected and made conformable throughout to the New Pharmacopœia of the General Council of Medical Education. By E. LLOYD BIRKETT, M.D. 18mo. 5s. 6d.

Manual of the Domestic Practice of Medicine. By W. B. KESTEVEN, F.R.C.S.E. Second Edition, thoroughly revised, with Additions. Fcp. 5s.

Sea-Air and Sea-Bathing for Children and Invalids. By WILLIAM STRANGE, M.D. Fcp. 3s.

The Restoration of Health; or, the Application of the Laws of Hygiene to the Recovery of Health: a Manual for the Invalid, and a Guide in the Sick Room. By W. STRANGE, M.D. Fcp. 6s.

Manual for the Classification, Training, and Education of the Feeble-Minded, Imbecile, and Idiotic. By P. MARTIN DUNCAN, M.B. and WILLIAM MILLARD. Crown 8vo. 5s.

The Fine Arts, and *Illustrated Editions.*

The Life of Man Symbolised by the Months of the Year in their Seasons and Phases; with Passages selected from Ancient and Modern Authors. By RICHARD PIGOT. Accompanied by a Series of 25 full-page Illustrations and numerous Marginal Devices, Decorative Initial Letters, and Tailpieces, engraved on Wood from Original Designs by JOHN LEIGHTON, F.S.A. 4to. 42s.

The New Testament, illustrated with Wood Engravings after the Early Masters, chiefly of the Italian School. Crown 4to. 63s. cloth, gilt top; or £5 5s. morocco.

Lyra Germanica; Hymns for the Sundays and Chief Festivals of the Christian Year. Translated by CATHERINE WINKWORTH; 125 Illustrations on Wood drawn by J. LEIGHTON, F.S.A. Fcp. 4to 21s.

Cats' and Farlie's Moral Emblems; with Aphorisms, Adages, and Proverbs of all Nations: comprising 121 Illustrations on Wood by J. LEIGHTON, F.S.A. with an appropriate Text by R. PIGOT. Imperial 8vo. 31s. 6d.

Shakspeare's Sentiments and Similes printed in Black and Gold, and illuminated in the Missal style by HENRY NOEL HUMPHREYS. In massive covers, containing the Medallion and Cypher of Shakspeare. Square post 8vo. 21s.

Half-Hour Lectures on the History and Practice of the Fine and Ornamental Arts. By W. B. SCOTT. Second Edition. Crown 8vo. with 50 Woodcut Illustrations, 8s. 6d.

The History of Our Lord, as exemplified in Works of Art. By Mrs. JAMESON and Lady EASTLAKE. Being the concluding Series of 'Sacred and Legendary Art.' Second Edition, with 13 Etchings and 281 Woodcuts. 2 vols. square crown 8vo. 42s.

Mrs. Jameson's Legends of the Saints and Martyrs. Fourth Edition, with 19 Etchings and 187 Woodcuts. 2 vols. 31s. 6d.

Mrs. Jameson's Legends of the Monastic Orders. Third Edition, with 11 Etchings and 88 Woodcuts. 1 vol. 21s.

Mrs. Jameson's Legends of the Madonna. Third Edition, with 27 Etchings and 165 Woodcuts. 1 vol. 21s.

Musical Publications.

An Introduction to the Study of National Music; Comprising Researches into Popular Songs, Traditions, and Customs. By CARL ENGEL, Author of 'The Music of the most Ancient Nations.' With Frontispiece and numerous Musical Illustrations. 8vo. 16s.

Six Lectures on Harmony. Delivered at the Royal Institution of Great Britain before Easter 1867. By G. A. MACFARREN. 8vo. [*In the press.*

Lectures on the History of Modern Music, delivered at the Royal Institution. By JOHN HULLAH. FIRST COURSE, with Chronological Tables, post 8vo. 6s. 6d. SECOND COURSE, the Transition Period, with 26 Specimens, 8vo. 16s.

Sacred Music for Family Use; A Selection of Pieces for One, Two, or more Voices, from the best Composers, Foreign and English. Edited by JOHN HULLAH. 1 vol. music folio, 21s. half bound.

Hullah's Part Music, Sacred and Secular, for Soprano, Alto, Tenor, and Bass. New Edition, with Pianoforte Accompaniments, in course of publication in Monthly Numbers, each number in Score, with Pianoforte Accompaniment, price 1s. and in separate Parts (Soprano, Alto, Tenor, and Bass), uniform with the Score in size, but in larger type, price 3d. each Part. Each Series (Sacred and Secular) to be completed in 12 Numbers, forming a Volume, in imperial 8vo.

Arts, Manufactures, &c.

Drawing from Nature; a Series of Progressive Instructions in Sketching, from Elementary Studies to Finished Views, with Examples from Switzerland and the Pyrenees. By GEORGE BARNARD, Professor of Drawing at Rugby School. With 18 Lithographic Plates and 108 Wood Engravings. Imp. 8vo. 25s.

Gwilt's Encyclopædia of Architecture. New Edition, revised, with alterations and considerable Additions, by WYATT PAPWORTH. With above 850 New Engravings and Diagrams on Wood by O. JEWITT, and upwards of 100 other Woodcuts. 8vo. [*Nearly ready.*

Tuscan Sculptors, their Lives, Works, and Times. With 45 Etchings and 28 Woodcuts from Original Drawings and Photographs. By CHARLES C. PERKINS. 2 vols. imp. 8vo. 63s.

The Grammar of Heraldry: containing a Description of all the Principal Charges used in Armory, the Signification of Heraldic Terms, and the Rules to be observed in Blazoning and Marshalling. By JOHN E. CUSSANS. Fcp. with 196 Woodcuts, 4s. 6d.

The Engineer's Handbook; explaining the Principles which should guide the young Engineer in the Construction of Machinery. By C. S. LOWNDES. Post 8vo. 5s.

The Elements of Mechanism. By T. M. GOODEVE, M.A. Prof. of Mechanics at the R. M. Acad. Woolwich. Second Edition, with 217 Woodcuts. Post 8vo. 6s. 6d.

Ure's Dictionary of Arts, Manufactures, and Mines. Re-written and enlarged by ROBERT HUNT, F.R.S., assisted by numerous Contributors eminent in Science and the Arts. With 2,000 Woodcuts. 3 vols. 8vo. [*Nearly ready.*

Treatise on Mills and Millwork. By W. FAIRBAIRN, C.E. F.R.S. With 18 Plates and 322 Woodcuts. 2 vols. 8vo. 32s.

Useful Information for Engineers. By the same Author. FIRST, SECOND, and THIRD SERIES, with many Plates and Woodcuts. 3 vols. crown 8vo. 10s. 6d. each.

The Application of Cast and Wrought Iron to Building Purposes. By the same Author. Third Edition, with 6 Plates and 118 Woodcuts. 8vo. 16s.

Iron Ship Building, its History and Progress, as comprised in a Series of Experimental Researches on the Laws of Strain; the Strengths, Forms, and other conditions of the Material; and an Inquiry into the Present and Prospective State of the Navy, including the Experimental Results on the Resisting Powers of Armour Plates and Shot at High Velocities. By W. FAIRBAIRN, C E. F.R.S. With 4 Plates and 130 Woodcuts, 8vo. 18s.

Encyclopædia of Civil Engineering, Historical, Theoretical, and Practical. By E. CRESY, C.E. With above 8,000 Woodcuts. 8vo. 42s.

The Practical Mechanic's Journal: An Illustrated Record of Mechanical and Engineering Science, and Epitome of Patent Inventions. 4to. price 1s. monthly.

The Practical Draughtsman's Book of Industrial Design. By W. JOHNSON, Assoc. Inst. C.E. With many hundred Illustrations. 4to. 28s. 6d.

The Patentee's Manual: a Treatise on the Law and Practice of Letters Patent for the use of Patentees and Inventors. By J. and J. H. JOHNSON. Post 8vo. 7s. 6d.

The Artisan Club's Treatise on the Steam Engine, in its various Applications to Mines, Mills, Steam Navigation, Railways, and Agriculture. By J. BOURNE, C.E. Seventh Edition; with 37 Plates and 546 Woodcuts. 4to. 42s.

A Treatise on the Screw Propeller, Screw Vessels, and Screw Engines, as adapted for purposes of Peace and War; illustrated by many Plates and Woodcuts. By the same Author. New and enlarged Edition in course of publication in 24 Parts, royal 4to. 2s. 6d. each.

Catechism of the Steam Engine, in its various Applications to Mines, Mills, Steam Navigation, Railways, and Agriculture. By J. BOURNE. C.E. With 199 Woodcuts. Fcp. 9s. The INTRODUCTION of 'Recent Improvements' may be had separately, with 110 Woodcuts, price 3s. 6d.

Handbook of the Steam Engine, by the same Author, forming a KEY to the Catechism of the Steam Engine, with 67 Woodcuts. Fcp. 9s.

The Art of Perfumery; the History and Theory of Odours, and the Methods of Extracting the Aromas of Plants. By Dr. PIESSE, F.C.S. Third Edition, with 53 Woodcuts. Crown 8vo. 10s. 6d.

Chemical, Natural, and Physical Magic, for Juveniles during the Holidays. By the same Author. Third Edition, enlarged with 38 Woodcuts. Fcp. 6s.

Talpa; or, the Chronicles of a Clay Farm. By C. W. HOSKYNS, Esq. With 24 Woodcuts from Designs by G. CRUIKSHANK. Sixth Edition. 16mo. 5s. 6d.

History of Windsor Great Park and Windsor Forest. By WILLIAM MENZIES, Resident Deputy Surveyor. With 2 Maps and 20 Photographs. Imp. folio, £8 8s.

Loudon's Encyclopædia of Agriculture: Comprising the Laying-out, Improvement, and Management of Landed Property, and the Cultivation and Economy of the Productions of Agriculture. With 1,100 Woodcuts. 8vo. 31s. 6d.

Loudon's Encyclopædia of Gardening: Comprising the Theory and Practice of Horticulture, Floriculture, Arboriculture, and Landscape Gardening. With 1,000 Woodcuts. 8vo. 31s. 6d.

Loudon's Encyclopædia of Cottage, Farm, and Villa Architecture and Furniture. With more than 2,000 Woodcuts. 8vo. 42s.

Bayldon's Art of Valuing Rents and Tillages, and Claims of Tenants upon Quitting Farms, both at Michaelmas and Lady-Day. Eighth Edition, revised by J. C. MORTON. 8vo. 10s. 6d.

Religious and *Moral Works.*

An Exposition of the 39 Articles, Historical and Doctrinal. By E. HAROLD BROWNE, D.D. Lord Bishop of Ely. Seventh Edition. 8vo. 16s.

The Pentateuch and the Elohistic Psalms, in Reply to Bishop Colenso. By the same. Second Edition. 8vo. 2s.

Examination-Questions on Bishop Browne's Exposition of the Articles. By the Rev. J. GORLE, M.A. Fcp. 8s. 6d.

The Acts of the Apostles; with a Commentary, and Practical and Devotional Suggestions for Readers and Students of the English Bible. By the Rev. F. C. COOK, M.A., Canon of Exeter, &c. New Edition, 8vo. 12s. 6d.

The Life and Epistles of St. Paul. By W. J. CONYBEARE, M.A. late Fellow of Trin. Coll. Cantab. and J. S. HOWSON, D.D. Principal of Liverpool Coll.

LIBRARY EDITION, with all the Original Illustrations, Maps, Landscapes on Steel, Woodcuts, &c. 2 vols. 4to. 48s.

INTERMEDIATE EDITION, with a Selection of Maps, Plates, and Woodcuts. 2 vols. square crown 8vo. 31s. 6d.

PEOPLE'S EDITION, revised and condensed, with 46 Illustrations and Maps. 2 vols. crown 8vo. 12s.

The Voyage and Shipwreck of St. Paul; with Dissertations on the Ships and Navigation of the Ancients. By JAMES SMITH, F.R.S. Crown 8vo. Charts, 10s. 6d.

Fasti Sacri, or a Key to the Chronology of the New Testament; comprising an Historical Harmony of the Four Gospels, and Chronological Tables generally from B.C. 70 to A.D. 70: with a Preliminary Dissertation and other Aids. By THOMAS LEWIN, M.A. F.S.A. Imp. 8vo. 42s.

A Critical and Grammatical Commentary on St. Paul's Epistles. By C. J. ELLICOTT, D.D. Lord Bishop of Gloucester and Bristol. 8vo.
Galatians, Third Edition, 8s. 6d.
Ephesians, Third Edition, 8s. 6d.
Pastoral Epistles, Third Edition, 10s. 6d.
Philippians, Colossians, and Philemon, Third Edition, 10s. 6d.
Thessalonians, Second Edition, 7s. 6d.

Historical Lectures on the Life of Our Lord Jesus Christ: being the Hulsean Lectures for 1859. By the same Author. Fourth Edition. 8vo. 10s. 6d.

The Destiny of the Creature; and other Sermons preached before the University of Cambridge. By the same. Post 8vo. 5s.

The Broad and the Narrow Way; Two Sermons preached before the University of Cambridge. By the same. Crown 8vo. 2s.

The Greek Testament; with Notes, Grammatical and Exegetical. By the Rev. W. WEBSTER, M.A. and the Rev. W. F. WILKINSON, M.A. 2 vols. 8vo. £2 4s.
VOL. I. the Gospels and Acts, 20s.
VOL. II. the Epistles and Apocalypse, 24s.

Rev. T. H. Horne's Introduction to the Critical Study and Knowledge of the Holy Scriptures. Eleventh Edition, corrected, and extended under careful Editorial revision. With 4 Maps and 22 Woodcuts and Facsimiles. 4 vols. 8vo. £3 13s. 6d.

Rev. T. H. Horne's Compendious Introduction to the Study of the Bible, being an Analysis of the larger work by the same Author. Re-edited by the Rev. JOHN AYRE, M.A. With Maps, &c. Post 8vo. 9s.

The Treasury of Bible Knowledge; being a Dictionary of the Books, Persons, Places, Events, and other Matters of which mention is made in Holy Scripture; intended to establish its Authority and illustrate its Contents. By Rev. J. AYRE, M.A. With Maps, 15 Plates, and numerous Woodcuts. Fcp. 10s. 6d.

Every-day Scripture Difficulties explained and illustrated. By J. E. PRESCOTT, M.A. VOL. I. *Matthew* and *Mark*; VOL. II. *Luke* and *John*. 2 vols. 8vo. 9s. each.

The Pentateuch and Book of Joshua Critically Examined. By the Right Rev. J. W. COLENSO, D.D. Lord Bishop of Natal. People's Edition, in 1 vol. crown 8vo. 6s. or in 5 Parts, 1s. each.

The Pentateuch and Book of Joshua Critically Examined. By Prof. A. KUENEN, of Leyden. Translated from the Dutch, and edited with Notes, by the Right Rev. J. W. COLENSO, D.D. Bishop of Natal. 8vo. 8s. 6d.

The Church and the World: Essays on Questions of the Day. By various Writers. Edited by Rev. ORBY SHIPLEY, M.A. Second Edition, revised. 8vo. 15s.

The Formation of Christendom. PART I. By T. W. ALLIES. 8vo. 12s.

Christendom's Divisions; a Philosophical Sketch of the Divisions of the Christian Family in East and West. By EDMUND S. FFOULKES, formerly Fellow and Tutor of Jesus Coll. Oxford. Post 8vo. 7s. 6d.

Christendom's Divisions, Part II. *Greeks and Latins*, being a History of their Dissensions and Overtures for Peace down to the Reformation. By the same Author. [*Nearly ready*.

The Life of Christ, an Eclectic Gospel, from the Old and New Testaments, arranged on a New Principle, with Analytical Tables, &c. By CHARLES DE LA PRYME, M.A. Revised Edition. 8vo. 5s.

The Hidden Wisdom of Christ and the Key of Knowledge; or, History of the Apocrypha. By ERNEST DE BUNSEN. 2 vols. 8vo. 28s.

The Temporal Mission of the Holy Ghost; or, Reason and Revelation. By the Most Rev. Archbishop MANNING. Second Edition. Crown 8vo. 8s. 6d.

Essays on Religion and Literature. Edited by the Most Rev. Archbishop MANNING. 8vo. 10s. 6d.

Essays and Reviews. By the Rev. W. TEMPLE, D.D. the Rev. R. WILLIAMS, B.D. the Rev. B. POWELL, M.A. the Rev. H. B. WILSON, B.D. C. W. GOODWIN, M.A. the Rev. M. PATTISON, B.D. and the Rev. B. JOWETT, M.A. 12th Edition. Fcp. 5s.

Mosheim's Ecclesiastical History. MURDOCK and SOAMES's Translation and Notes, re-edited by the Rev. W. STUBBS, M.A. 3 vols. 8vo. 45s.

Bishop Jeremy Taylor's Entire Works: With Life by BISHOP HEBER. Revised and corrected by the Rev. C. P. EDEN, 10 vols. £5 5s.

Passing Thoughts on Religion. By the Author of 'Amy Herbert.' New Edition. Fcp. 5s.

Thoughts for the Holy Week, for Young Persons. By the same Author. Third Edition. Fcp. 8vo. 2s.

Self-examination before Confirmation. By the same Author. 32mo. 1s. 6d.

Readings for a Month Preparatory to Confirmation from Writers of the Early and English Church. By the same. Fcp. 4s.

Readings for Every Day in Lent, compiled from the Writings of Bishop JEREMY TAYLOR. By the same. Fcp. 5s.

Preparation for the Holy Communion; the Devotions chiefly from the works of JEREMY TAYLOR. By the same. 32mo. 3s.

Principles of Education drawn from Nature and Revelation, and Applied to Female Education in the Upper Classes. By the same. 2 vols. fcp. 12s. 6d.

The Wife's Manual; or, Prayers, Thoughts, and Songs on Several Occasions of a Matron's Life. By the Rev. W. CALVERT, M.A. Crown 8vo. 10s. 6d.

Lyra Domestica; Christian Songs for Domestic Edification. Translated from the *Psaltery and Harp* of C. J. P. SPITTA, and from other sources, by RICHARD MASSIE. FIRST and SECOND SERIES, fcp. 4s. 6d. each.

Spiritual Songs for the Sundays and Holidays throughout the Year. By J. S. B. MONSELL, LL.D. Vicar of Egham. Fourth Edition. Fcp. 4s. 6d.

The Beatitudes: Abasement before God: Sorrow for Sin; Meekness of Spirit; Desire for Holiness; Gentleness; Purity of Heart; the Peace-makers; Sufferings for Christ. By the same. Third Edition. Fcp. 3s. 6d.

Lyra Sacra; Hymns, Ancient and Modern, Odes, and Fragments of Sacred Poetry. Edited by the Rev. B. W. SAVILE, M.A. Third Edition, enlarged. Fcp. 5s.

Lyra Germanica, translated from the German by Miss C. WINKWORTH. FIRST SERIES, Hymns for the Sundays and Chief Festivals; SECOND SERIES, the Christian Life. Fcp. 3s. 6d. each SERIES.

Hymns from Lyra Germanica, 18mo. 1s.

The Chorale Book for England; a complete Hymn-Book in accordance with the Services and Festivals of the Church of England: the Hymns translated by Miss C. WINKWORTH; the Tunes arranged by Prof. W. S. BENNETT and OTTO GOLDSCHMIDT. Fcp. 4to. 12s. 6d.

Congregational Edition. Fcp. 2s.

Lyra Eucharistica; Hymns and Verses on the Holy Communion, Ancient and Modern; with other Poems. Edited by the Rev. ORBY SHIPLEY, M.A. Second Edition. Fcp. 7s. 6d.

Lyra Messianica; Hymns and Verses on the Life of Christ, Ancient and Modern; with other Poems. By the same Editor. Second Edition, enlarged. Fcp. 7s. 6d.

Lyra Mystica; Hymns and Verses on Sacred Subjects, Ancient and Modern. By the same Editor. Fcp. 7s. 6d.

The Catholic Doctrine of the Atonement; an Historical Inquiry into its Development in the Church: with an Introduction on the Principle of Theological Developments. By H. N. OXENHAM, M.A. formerly Scholar of Balliol College, Oxford. 8vo. 8s. 6d.

From Sunday to Sunday; an Attempt to consider familiarly the Weekday Life and Labours of a Country Clergyman. By R. GEE, M.A. Fcp. 5s.

Our Sermons: an Attempt to consider familiarly, but reverently, the Preacher's Work in the present day. By the same Author. Fcp. 6s.

Paley's Moral Philosophy, with Annotations. By RICHARD WHATELY, D.D. late Archbishop of Dublin. 8vo. 7s.

Travels, Voyages, &c.

Ice Caves of France and Switzerland; a narrative of Subterranean Exploration. By the Rev. G. F. BROWNE, M.A. Fellow and Assistant-Tutor of St. Catherine's Coll. Cambridge, M.A.C. With 11 Woodcuts. Square crown 8vo. 12s. 6d.

Village Life in Switzerland. By SOPHIA D. DELMARD. Post 8vo. 9s. 6d.

How we Spent the Summer; or, a Voyage en Zigzag in Switzerland and Tyrol with some Members of the ALPINE CLUB. From the Sketch-Book of one of the Party. Third Edition, re-drawn. In oblong 4to. with about 300 Illustrations, 15s.

Beaten Tracks; or, Pen and Pencil Sketches in Italy. By the Authoress of 'A Voyage en Zigzag.' With 42 Plates, containing about 200 Sketches from Drawings made on the Spot. 8vo. 16s.

Map of the Chain of Mont Blanc, from an actual Survey in 1863-1864. By A. ADAMS-REILLY, F.R.G.S. M.A.C. Published under the Authority of the Alpine Club. In Chromolithography on extra stout drawing-paper 28in. x 17in. price 10s. or mounted on canvas in a folding case, 12s. 6d.

Transylvania, its Products and its People. By CHARLES BONER. With 5 Maps and 43 Illustrations on Wood and in Chromolithography. 8vo. 21s.

Explorations in South-west Africa, from Walvisch Bay to Lake Ngami and the Victoria Falls. By THOMAS BAINES, F.R.G.S. 8vo. with Maps and Illustrations, 21s.

Vancouver Island and British Columbia; their History, Resources, and Prospects. By MATTHEW MACFIE, F.R.G.S. With Maps and Illustrations. 8vo. 18s.

History of Discovery in our Australasian Colonies, Australia, Tasmania, and New Zealand, from the Earliest Date to the Present Day. By WILLIAM HOWITT. With 3 Maps of the Recent Explorations from Official Sources. 2 vols. 8vo. 20s.

The Capital of the Tycoon; a Narrative of a 3 Years' Residence in Japan. By Sir RUTHERFORD ALCOCK, K.C.B. 2 vols. 8vo. with numerous Illustrations, 42s.

Florence, the New Capital of Italy. By C. R. WELD. With several Engravings on Wood, from Drawings by the Author. Post 8vo.

The Dolomite Mountains. Excursions through Tyrol, Carinthia, Carniola, and Friuli in 1861, 1862, and 1863. By J. GILBERT and G. C. CHURCHILL, F.R.G.S. With numerous Illustrations. Square crown 8vo. 21s.

A Lady's Tour Round Monte Rosa; including Visits to the Italian Valleys. With Map and Illustrations. Post 8vo. 14s.

Guide to the Pyrenees, for the use of Mountaineers. By CHARLES PACKE. With Maps, &c. and Appendix. Fcp. 6s.

A Guide to Spain. By H. O'SHEA. Post 8vo. with Travelling Map, 15s.

Christopher Columbus; his Life, Voyages, and Discoveries. Revised Edition, with 4 Woodcuts. 18mo. 2s. 6d.

Captain James Cook; his Life, Voyages, and Discoveries. Revised Edition, with numerous Woodcuts. 18mo. 2s. 6d.

The Alpine Guide. By JOHN BALL, M.R.I.A. late President of the Alpine Club. Post 8vo. with Maps and other Illustrations.

Guide to the Eastern Alps. [Just ready.

Guide to the Western Alps, including Mont Blanc, Monte Rosa, Zermatt, &c. price 7s. 6d.

Guide to the Oberland and all Switzerland, excepting the Neighbourhood of Monte Rosa and the Great St. Bernard; with Lombardy and the adjoining portion of Tyrol. 7s. 6d.

Humboldt's Travels and Discoveries in South America. Third Edition, with numerous Woodcuts. 18mo. 2s. 6d.

Narratives of Shipwrecks of the Royal Navy between 1793 and 1857, compiled from Official Documents in the Admiralty by W. O. S. GILLY; with a Preface by W. S. GILLY, D.D. 3d Edition, fcp. 5s.

A Week at the Land's End. By J. T. BLIGHT; assisted by E. H. RODD, R. Q. COUCH, and J. RALFS. With Map and 96 Woodcuts. Fcp. 6s. 6d.

Visits to Remarkable Places: Old Halls, Battle-Fields, and Scenes illustrative of Striking Passages in English History and Poetry. By WILLIAM HOWITT. 2 vols. square crown 8vo. with Wood Engravings, 25s.

The Rural Life of England. By the same Author. With Woodcuts by Bewick and Williams. Medium 8vo. 12s. 6d.

Works of Fiction.

Atherstone Priory. By L. N. COMYN. 2 vols. post 8vo. 21s.

Ellice : a Tale. By the same. Post 8vo. 9s. 6d.

Stories and Tales by the Author of 'Amy Herbert,' uniform Edition, each Tale or Story complete in a single volume.

AMY HERBERT, 2s. 6d.
GERTRUDE, 2s. 6d.
EARL'S DAUGHTER, 2s. 6d.
EXPERIENCE OF LIFE, 2s. 6d.
CLEVE HALL, 3s. 6d.
IVORS, 3s. 6d.
KATHARINE ASHTON, 3s. 6d.
MARGARET PERCIVAL, 5s.
LANETON PARSONAGE, 4s. 6d.
URSULA, 4s. 6d.

A Glimpse of the World. By the Author of 'Amy Herbert.' Fcp. 7s. 6d.

The Six Sisters of the Valleys: an Historical Romance. By W. BRAMLEY-MOORE, M.A. Incumbent of Gerrard's Cross, Bucks. Fourth Edition, with 14 Illustrations. Crown 8vo. 5s.

Gallus; or, Roman Scenes of the Time of Augustus: with Notes and Excursuses illustrative of the Manners and Customs of the Ancient Romans. From the German of Prof. BECKER. New Edit. Post 8vo. 7s. 6d.

Charicles; a Tale illustrative of Private Life among the Ancient Greeks: with Notes and Excursuses. From the German of Prof. BECKER. New Edition, Post 8vo. 7s. 6d.

Icelandic Legends. Collected by JON. ARNASON. Selected and Translated from the Icelandic by GEORGE E. J. POWELL and E. MAGNUSSON. SECOND SERIES, with Notes and an Introductory Essay on the Origin and Genius of the Icelandic Folk-Lore, and 3 Illustrations on Wood. Crown 8vo. 21s.

The Warden: a Novel. By ANTHONY TROLLOPE, Crown 8vo. 2s. 6d.

Barchester Towers: a Sequel to 'The Warden.' By the same Author. Crown 8vo. 3s. 6d.

Tales from Greek Mythology. By GEORGE W. COX, M.A. late Scholar of Trin. Coll. Oxon. Second Edition. Square 16mo. 3s. 6d.

Tales of the Gods and Heroes. By the same Author. Second Edition. Fcp. 5s.

Tales of Thebes and Argos. By the same Author. Fcp. 4s. 6d.

The Gladiators: a Tale of Rome and Judæa. By G. J. WHYTE MELVILLE. Crown 8vo. 5s.

Digby Grand, an Autobiography. By the same Author. 1 vol. 5s.

Kate Coventry, an Autobiography. By the same. 1 vol. 5s.

General Bounce, or the Lady and the Locusts. By the same. 1 vol. 5s.

Holmby House, a Tale of Old Northamptonshire. 1 vol. 5s.

Good for Nothing, or All Down Hill. By the same. 1 vol. 6s.

The Queen's Maries, a Romance of Holyrood. By the same. 1 vol. 6s.

The Interpreter, a Tale of the War. By the same Author. 1 vol. 5s.

Poetry and *The Drama.*

Goethe's Second Faust. Translated by JOHN ANSTER, LL.D. M.R.I.A. Regius Professor of Civil Law in the University of Dublin. Post 8vo. 15s.

Tasso's Jerusalem Delivered, translated into English Verse by Sir J. KINGSTON JAMES, Kt. M.A. 2 vols. fcp. with Facsimile, 14s.

Poetical Works of John Edmund Reade; with final Revision and Additions. 3 vols. fcp. 18s. or each vol. separately, 6s.

Moore's Poetical Works, Cheapest Editions complete in 1 vol. including the Autobiographical Prefaces and Author's last Notes, which are still copyright. Crown 8vo. ruby type, with Portrait, 6s. or People's Edition, in larger type, 12s. 6d.

Moore's Poetical Works, as above, Library Edition, medium 8vo. with Portrait and Vignette, 14s. or in 10 vols. fcp. 3s. 6d. each.

Moore's Lalla Rookh, Tenniel's Edition, with 68 Wood Engravings from Original Drawings and other Illustrations. Fcp. 4to. 21s.

Moore's Irish Melodies, Maclise's Edition, with 161 Steel Plates from Original Drawings. Super-royal 8vo. 31s. 6d.

Miniature Edition of Moore's Irish Melodies, with Maclise's Illustrations, (as above) reduced in Lithography. Imp. 16mo. 10s. 6d.

Southey's Poetical Works, with the Author's last Corrections and copyright Additions. Library Edition, in 1 vol. medium 8vo. with Portrait and Vignette, 14s. or in 10 vols. fcp. 3s. 6d. each.

Lays of Ancient Rome; with *Ivry* and the *Armada*. By the Right Hon. LORD MACAULAY. 16mo. 4s. 6d.

Lord Macaulay's Lays of Ancient Rome. With 90 Illustrations on Wood, Original and from the Antique, from Drawings by G. SCHARF. Fcp. 4to. 21s.

Miniature Edition of Lord Macaulay's Lays of Ancient Rome, with Scharf's Illustrations (as above) reduced in Lithography. Imp. 16mo. 10s. 6d.

Poems. By JEAN INGELOW. Twelfth Edition. Fcp. 8vo. 5s.

Poems by Jean Ingelow. A New Edition, with nearly 100 Illustrations by Eminent Artists, engraved on Wood by the Brothers DALZIEL. Fcp. 4to. 21s.

Poetical Works of Letitia Elizabeth Landon (L.E.L.) 2 vols. 16mo. 10s.

Playtime with the Poets: a Selection of the best English Poetry for the use of Children. By a LADY. Crown 8vo. 5s.

Bowdler's Family Shakspeare, cheaper Genuine Edition, complete in 1 vol. large type, with 36 Woodcut Illustrations, price 14s. or, with the same ILLUSTRATIONS, in 6 pocket vols. 3s. 6d. each.

Arundines Cami, sive Musarum Cantabrigiensium Lusus Canori. Collegit atque edidit H. DRURY. M.A. Editio Sexta, curavit H. J. HODGSON, M.A. Crown 8vo. price 7s. 6d.

The Æneid of Virgil Translated into English Verse. By JOHN CONINGTON, M.A. Corpus Professor of Latin in the University of Oxford. Crown 8vo. 9s.

The Iliad of Homer Translated into Blank Verse. By ICHABOD CHARLES WRIGHT, M.A. late Fellow of Magdalen Coll. Oxon. 2 vols. crown 8vo. 21s.

The Iliad of Homer in English Hexameter Verse. By J. HENRY DART, M.A. of Exeter College, Oxford; Author of 'The Exile of St. Helena, Newdigate, 1838.' Square crown 8vo. price 21s. cloth.

Dante's Divine Comedy, translated in English Terza Rima by JOHN DAYMAN, M.A. [With the Italian Text, after *Brunetti*, interpaged.] 8vo. 21s.

Rural Sports, &c.

Encyclopædia of Rural Sports; a Complete Account, Historical, Practical, and Descriptive, of Hunting, Shooting, Fishing, Racing, &c. By D. P. BLAINE. With above 600 Woodcuts (20 from Designs by JOHN LEECH). 8vo. 42s.

Notes on Rifle Shooting. By Captain HEATON, Adjutant of the Third Manchester Rifle Volunteer Corps. Fcp. 2s. 6d.

Col. Hawker's Instructions to Young Sportsmen in all that relates to Guns and Shooting. Revised by the Author's SON. Square crown 8vo. with Illustrations, 18s.

The Rifle, its Theory and Practice. By ARTHUR WALKER (79th Highlanders), Staff, Hythe and Fleetwood Schools of Musketry. Second Edition. Crown 8vo. with 125 Woodcuts, 5s.

The Dead Shot, or Sportsman's Complete Guide; a Treatise on the Use of the Gun, Dog-breaking, Pigeon-shooting, &c. By MARKSMAN. Fcp. with Plates, 5s.

Hints on Shooting, Fishing, &c. both on Sea and Land and in the Fresh and Saltwater Lochs of Scotland. By C. IDLE, Esq. Second Edition. Fcp. 6s.

A Book on Angling: being a Complete Work on every branch of Angling practised in Great Britain. By FRANCIS FRANCIS. With numerous Explanatory Plates, coloured and plain, and the largest and most reliable List of Salmon Flies ever published. Post 8vo.

The Art of Fishing on the Principle of Avoiding Cruelty: being a brief Treatise on the Most Merciful Methods of Capturing Fish; describing certain approved Rules in Fishing, used during 60 Years' Practice. By the Rev. O. RAYMOND, LL.B. Fcp. 8vo.

Handbook of Angling: Teaching Fly-fishing, Trolling, Bottom-fishing, Salmon-fishing; with the Natural History of River Fish, and the best modes of Catching them. By EPHEMERA. Fcp. Woodcuts, 5s.

The Fly-Fisher's Entomology. By ALFRED RONALDS. With coloured Representations of the Natural and Artificial Insect. Sixth Edition; with 20 coloured Plates. 8vo. 14s.

The Cricket Field; or, the History and the Science of the Game of Cricket. By JAMES PYCROFT, B.A. 4th Edition. Fcp. 5s.

The Cricket Tutor; a Treatise exclusively Practical. By the same. 18mo. 1s.

Cricketana. By the same Author. With 7 Portraits of Cricketers. Fcp. 5s.

Youatt on the Horse. Revised and enlarged by W. WATSON, M.R.C.V.S. 8vo. with numerous Woodcuts, 12s. 6d.

Youatt on the Dog. (By the same Author.) 8vo. with numerous Woodcuts, 6s.

The Horse-Trainer's and Sportsman's Guide: with Considerations on the Duties of Grooms, on Purchasing Blood Stock, and on Veterinary Examination. By DIGBY COLLINS. Post 8vo. 6s.

Blaine's Veterinary Art: a Treatise on the Anatomy, Physiology, and Curative Treatment of the Diseases of the Horse, Neat Cattle, and Sheep. Seventh Edition, revised and enlarged by C. STEEL, M.R.C.V.S.L. 8vo. with Plates and Woodcuts, 18s.

On Drill and Manœuvres of Cavalry, combined with Horse Artillery. By Major-Gen. MICHAEL W. SMITH, C.B. commanding the Poonah Division of the Bombay Army. 8vo. 12s. 6d.

The Horse's Foot, and how to keep it Sound. By W. MILES, Esq. 9th Edition, with Illustrations. Imp. 8vo. 12s. 6d.

A Plain Treatise on Horse-shoeing. By the same Author. Post 8vo. with Illustrations, 2s. 6d.

Stables and Stable Fittings. By the same. Imp. 8vo. with 13 Plates, 15s.

Remarks on Horses' Teeth, addressed to Purchasers. By the same. Post 8vo. 1s. 6d.

The Dog in Health and Disease. By STONEHENGE. With 70 Wood Engravings. New Edition. Square crown 8vo. 10s. 6d.

The Greyhound. By the same Author. Revised Edition, with 24 Portraits of Greyhounds. Square crown 8vo. 21s.

The Ox, his Diseases and their Treatment; with an Essay on Parturition in the Cow. By J. R. DOBSON, M.R.C.V.S. Crown 8vo. with Illustrations, 7s. 6d.

Commerce, Navigation, and *Mercantile Affairs.*

The Commercial Handbook of France; Furnishing a detailed and comprehensive account of the Trade, Manufactures, Industry, and Commerce of France at the Present Time. By FREDERICK MARTIN. With Maps and Plans, including a Coloured Map showing the Seats of the Principal Industries. Crown 8vo.

Banking, Currency, and the Exchanges: a Practical Treatise. By ARTHUR CRUMP, Bank Manager, formerly of the Bank of England. Post 8vo. 6s.

The Theory and Practice of Banking. By HENRY DUNNING MACLEOD, M.A. Barrister-at-Law. Second Edition, entirely remodelled. 2 vols. 8vo. 30s.

A Dictionary, Practical, Theoretical, and Historical, of Commerce and Commercial Navigation. By J. R. M'CULLOCH. New Edition in preparation.

Practical Guide for British Shipmasters to United States Ports. By PIERREPONT EDWARDS, Her Britannic Majesty's Vice-Consul at New York. Post 8vo. 8s. 6d.

A Manual for Naval Cadets. By J. M'NEIL BOYD, late Captain R.N. Third Edition; with 240 Woodcuts, and 11 coloured Plates. Post 8vo. 12s. 6d.

The Law of Nations Considered as Independent Political Communities. By TRAVERS TWISS, D.C.L. Regius Professor of Civil Law in the University of Oxford. 2 vols. 8vo. 30s. or separately, PART I. *Peace,* 12s. PART II. *War,* 18s.

A Nautical Dictionary, defining the Technical Language relative to the Building and Equipment of Sailing Vessels and Steamers, &c. By ARTHUR YOUNG. Second Edition; with Plates and 150 Woodcuts. 8vo. 18s.

Works of Utility and *General Information.*

Modern Cookery for Private Families, reduced to a System of Easy Practice in a Series of carefully-tested Receipts. By ELIZA ACTON. Newly revised and enlarged; with 8 Plates, Figures, and 150 Woodcuts. Fcp. 7s. 6d.

On Food and its Digestion; an Introduction to Dietetics. By W. BRINTON, M.D. Physician to St. Thomas's Hospital, &c. With 48 Woodcuts. Post 8vo. 12s.

Wine, the Vine, and the Cellar. By THOMAS G. SHAW. Second Edition, revised and enlarged, with Frontispiece and 31 Illustrations on Wood. 8vo. 16s.

A Practical Treatise on Brewing; with Formulæ for Public Brewers, and Instructions for Private Families. By W. BLACK. Fifth Edition. 8vo. 10s. 6d.

How to Brew Good Beer: a complete Guide to the Art of Brewing Ale, Bitter Ale, Table Ale, Brown Stout, Porter, and Table Beer. By JOHN PITT. Revised Edition. Fcp. 4s. 6d.

The Billiard Book. By Captain CRAWLEY, Author of 'Billiards, its Theory and Practice,' &c. With nearly 100 Diagrams on Steel and Wood. 8vo. 21s.

Whist, What to Lead. By CAM. Third Edition. 32mo. 1s.

Short Whist. By MAJOR A. The Sixteenth Edition, revised, with an Essay on the Theory of the Modern Scientific Game by PROF. P. Fcp. 3s. 6d.

Two Hundred Chess Problems, composed by F. HEALEY, including the Problems to which the Prizes were awarded by the Committees of the Era, the Manchester, the Birmingham, and the Bristol Chess Problem Tournaments; accompanied by the SOLUTIONS. Crown 8vo. with 200 Diagrams, 5s.

The Cabinet Lawyer; a Popular Digest of the Laws of England, Civil, Criminal, and Constitutional. 22nd Edition, entirely recomposed, and brought down by the AUTHOR to the close of the Parliamentary Session of 1866. Fcp. 10s. 6d.

The Philosophy of Health; or, an Exposition of the Physiological and Sanitary Conditions conducive to Human Longevity and Happiness. By SOUTHWOOD SMITH, M.D. Eleventh Edition, revised and enlarged; with 113 Woodcuts. 8vo. 15s.

Hints to Mothers on the Management of their Health during the Period of Pregnancy and in the Lying-in Room. By T. BULL, M.D. Fcp. 5s.

The Maternal Management of Children in Health and Disease. By the same Author. Fcp. 5s.

Notes on Hospitals. By FLORENCE NIGHTINGALE. Third Edition, enlarged; with 13 Plans. Post 4to. 18s.

The Executor's Guide. By J. C. HUDSON. Enlarged Edition, revised by the Author, with reference to the latest reported Cases and Acts of Parliament. Fcp. 6s.

Hudson's Plain Directions for Making Wills. Fcp. 2s. 6d.

The Law relating to Benefit Building Societies; with Practical Observations on the Act and all the Cases decided thereon, also a Form of Rules and Forms of Mortgages. By W. TIDD PRATT, Barrister. 2nd Edition. Fcp. 3s. 6d.

C. M. Willich's Popular Tables for Ascertaining the Value of Lifehold, Leasehold, and Church Property, Renewal Fines, &c.; the Public Funds; Annual Average Price and Interest on Consols from 1731 to 1861; Chemical, Geographical, Astronomical, Trigonometrical Tables, &c. Post 8vo. 10s.

Thomson's Tables of Interest, at Three, Four, Four and a Half, and Five per Cent., from One Pound to Ten Thousand and from 1 to 365 Days. 12mo. 3s. 6d.

Maunder's Treasury of Knowledge and Library of Reference: comprising an English Dictionary and Grammar, Universal Gazetteer, Classical Dictionary, Chronology, Law Dictionary, Synopsis of the Peerage, useful Tables, &c. Fcp. 10s. 6d.

Knowledge for the *Young*.

The Stepping Stone to Knowledge: Containing upwards of 700 Questions and Answers on Miscellaneous Subjects, adapted to the capacity of Infant Minds. By a MOTHER. 18mo. price 1s.

The Stepping Stone to Geography: Containing several Hundred Questions and Answers on Geographical Subjects. 18mo. 1s.

The Stepping Stone to English History: Containing several Hundred Questions and Answers on the History of England. 1s.

The Stepping Stone to Bible Knowledge: Containing several Hundred Questions and Answers on the Old and New Testaments. 18mo. 1s.

The Stepping Stone to Biography: Containing several Hundred Questions and Answers on the Lives of Eminent Men and Women. 18mo. 1s.

Second Series of the Stepping Stone to Knowledge: containing upwards of Eight Hundred Questions and Answers on Miscellaneous Subjects not contained in the FIRST SERIES. 18mo. 1s.

The Stepping Stone to French Pronunciation and Conversation: Containing several Hundred Questions and Answers. By Mr. P. SADLIER. 18mo. 1s.

The Stepping Stone to English Grammar: containing several Hundred Questions and Answers on English Grammar. By Mr. P. SADLIER. 18mo. 1s.

The Stepping Stone to Natural History: VERTEBRATE OF BACKBONED ANIMALS. PART I. *Mammalia*; PART II. *Birds, Reptiles, Fishes.* 18mo. 1s. each Part.

INDEX.

ABBOTT on Sight and Touch	7
ACTON's Modern Cookery	19
ALCOCK's Residence in Japan	16
ALLIES on Formation of Christianity	14
Alpine Guide (The)	16
AFJOHN's Manual of the Metalloids	8
ARAGO's Biographies of Scientific Men	4
———— Popular Astronomy	7
ARNOLD's Manual of English Literature	5
ARNOTT's Elements of Physics	7
Arundines Cami	18
Atherstone Priory	16
Autumn Holidays of a Country Parson	6
AYRE's Treasury of Bible Knowledge	14
BACON's Essays, by WHATELY	4
———— Life and Letters, by SPEDDING	3
———— Works	4
BAIN on the Emotions and Will	7
——— on the Senses and Intellect	7
——— on the Study of Character	7
BAINES's Explorations in S.W. Africa	15
BALL's Guide to the Central Alps	12
———— Guide to the Western Alps	12
———— Guide to the Eastern Alps	16
BARNARD's Drawing from Nature	12
BAYLDON's Rents and Tillages	13
Beaten Tracks	15
BECKER's *Charicles* and *Gallus*	3
BEETHOVEN's Letters	3
BENFEY's Sanskrit-English Dictionary	5
BERRY's Journals	3
BLACK's Treatise on Brewing	19
BLACKLEY and FRIEDLANDER's German and English Dictionary	5
BLAINE's Rural Sports	18
———— Veterinary Art	18
BLIGHT's Week at the Land's End	16
BOASE's Essay on Human Nature	6
———— Philosophy of Nature	6
BONER's Transylvania	15
BOOTH's Epigrams	6
BOURNE on Screw Propeller	12
BOURNE's Catechism of the Steam Engine	12
———— Handbook of Steam Engine	12
———— Treatise on the Steam Engine	12
BOWDLER's Family SHAKSPEARE	18
BOYD's Manual for Naval Cadets	19
BRAMLEY-MOORE's Six Sisters of the Valleys	16
BRANDE's Dictionary of Science, Literature, and Art	9
BRAY's (C.) Education of the Feelings	7
———— Philosophy of Necessity	7
———— On Force	7
BRINTON on Food and Digestion	19
BRISTOW's Glossary of Mineralogy	8
BRODIE's Constitutional History	1

BRODIE's (Sir C. B.) Works	10
———— Autobiography	10
BROWNE's Ice Caves of France and Switzerland	15
———— Exposition 39 Articles	13
———— Pentateuch	13
BUCKLE's History of Civilization	2
BULL's Hints to Mothers	20
———— Maternal Management of Children	20
BUNSEN's Ancient Egypt	2
BUNSEN on Apocrypha	14
BURKE's Vicissitudes of Families	4
BURTON's Christian Church	3
Cabinet Lawyer	20
CALVERT's Wife's Manual	14
Campaigner at Home	6
CATS and FARLIE's Moral Emblems	11
Chorale Book for England	15
CLOUGH's Lives from Plutarch	2
COLENSO (Bishop) on Pentateuch and Book of Joshua	14
COLLINS's Horse Trainer's Guide	18
COLUMBUS's Voyages	16
Commonplace Philosopher in Town and Country	6
CONINGTON's Translation of Virgil's Æneid	18
CONTANSEAU's Two French and English Dictionaries	5
CONYBEARE and HOWSON's Life and Epistles of St. Paul	13
COOK's Acts of the Apostles	13
———— Voyages	16
COPLAND's Dictionary of Practical Medicine	10
Cox's Tales of the Great Persian War	2
———— Tales from Greek Mythology	17
———— Tales of the Gods and Heroes	17
———— Tales of Thebes and Argos	17
CRAWLEY's Billiard Book	19
CRESY's Encyclopædia of Civil Engineering	11
Critical Essays of a Country Parson	6
CROWE's History of France	2
CRUMP on Banking, &c	19
CUSSANS's Grammar of Heraldry	12
DART's Iliad of Homer	18
D'AUBIGNÉ's History of the Reformation in the time of CALVIN	2
DAYMAN's Dante's Divina Commedia	18
Dead Shot (The), by MARKSMAN	18
DE LA RIVE's Treatise on Electricity	8
DELMARD's Village Life in Switzerland	15
DE LA PRYME's Life of Christ	14
DE MORGAN on Matter and Spirit	6
DE TOCQUEVILLE's Democracy in America	2
DISRAELI's Speeches on Reform	5
DOBSON on the Ox	19

Duncan and Millard on Classification, &c. of the Idiotic............	11
Dyer's City of Rome............	2
Edwards's Shipmaster's Guide	19
Elements of Botany	9
Ellice, a Tale............	16
Ellicott's Broad and Narrow Way......	13
——— Commentary on Ephesians	13
——— Destiny of the Creature......	13
——— Lectures on Life of Christ	13
——— Commentary on Galatians	13
——————————— Pastoral Epist.	13
——————————— Philippians, &c.	13
——————————— Thessalonians	13
Engel's Introduction to National Music ..	11
Essays and Reviews	14
——— on Religion and Literature, edited by Manning	13
Fairbairn's Application of Cast and Wrought Iron to Building......	12
——————— Information for Engineers ..	12
——————— Treatise on Mills & Millwork	12
Fairbairn on Iron Ship Building	11
Farrar's Chapters on Language	5
Ffoulkes's Christendom's Divisions......	14
Francis's Fishing Book	18
Froude's History of England............	1
Gee's Our Sermons	15
——— Sunday to Sunday............	15
Gilbert and Churchill's Dolomite Mountains............	16
Gilly's Shipwrecks of the Navy	16
Goethe's Second Faust, by Anster......	17
Goodeve's Elements of Mechanism......	12
Gorle's Questions on Browne's Exposition of the 39 Articles............	13
Grant's Ethics of Aristotle	4
Graver Thoughts of a Country Parson......	6
Gray's Anatomy............	10
Greene's Corals and Sea Jellies	8
——— Sponges and Animalculae	8
Grove on Correlation of Physical Forces ..	8
Gwilt's Encyclopædia of Architecture	12
Handbook of Angling, by Ephemera......	18
Hare on Election of Representatives	5
Harley and Brown's Histological Demonstrations............	10
Hartwig's Harmonies of Nature............	8
——— Sea and its Living Wonders....	8
——— Tropical World	8
Haughton's Manual of Geology	8
Hawker's Instructions to Young Sportsmen............	18
Heaton's Notes on Rifle Shooting	18
Healey's Chess Problems	20
Helps's Spanish Conquest in America ..	2
Henderson's Folk-Lore	6
Herschel's Essays from Reviews	9
——— Outlines of Astronomy	7
Hewitt on the Diseases of Women	10
Hodgson's Time and Space............	7
Holland's Essays on Scientific Subjects..	9
Holmes's System of Surgery............	10

Hooker and Walker-Arnott's British Flora............	9
Hopkins's Hawaii	7
Horne's Introduction to the Scriptures....	14
——— Compendium of the Scriptures ..	14
Horsley's Manual of Poisons	9
Hoskyns's Occasional Essays	6
——— Talpa	18
How we Spent the Summer............	15
Howitt's Australian Discovery	16
——— Rural Life of England	16
——— Visits to Remarkable Places....	16
Hudson's Directions for Making Wills	20
——— Executor's Guide............	20
Hughes's (W.) Manual of Geography......	7
Hullah's History of Modern Music	11
——— Transition Musical Lectures	11
——— Part Music............	11
——— Sacred Music	11
Humboldt's Travels in South America....	16
Humphreys' Sentiments of Shakspeare....	11
Hutton's Studies in Parliament	6
Hymns from *Lyra Germanica*............	14
Ingelow's Poems	17
Icelandic Legends, Second Series........	17
Idle's Hints on Shooting	18
Jameson's Legends of the Saints and Martyrs	11
——————— Legends of the Madonna	11
——————— Legends of the Monastic Orders	11
Jameson and Eastlake's History of Our Lord............	11
Johnson's Patentee's Manual	12
——— Practical Draughtsman............	12
Johnston's Gazetteer, or General Geographical Dictionary............	7
Jones's Christianity and Common Sense ..	7
Jordan's Elements	8
Kalisch's Commentary on the Bible......	5
——— Hebrew Grammar............	5
Keller's Lake Dwellings of Switzerland ..	8
Kesteven's Domestic Medicine	10
Kirby and Spence's Entomology	9
Kuenen on Pentateuch and Joshua........	14
Lady's Tour round Monte Rosa............	16
Landon's (L. E. L.) Poetical Works........	17
Latham's English Dictionary	5
Lawrence on Rocks............	8
Lecky's History of Rationalism	2
Leisure Hours in Town	6
Lewes's Biographical History of Philosophy	2
Lewin's Fasti Sacri	13
Lewis on Early Roman History	4
——— on Irish Disturbances	4
——— on Observation and Reasoning in Politics............	4
——— on Political Terms............	4
Lewis's Essays on Administrations........	4
——— Fables of Babrius............	4
Liddell and Scott's Greek-English Lexicon	5
——— Abridged ditto	5
Life of Man Symbolised	11
Lindley and Moore's Treasury of Botany	9

NEW WORKS PUBLISHED BY LONGMANS AND CO.   25

LONGMAN's Lectures on History of England	1
LOUDON's Encyclopædia of Agriculture	13
——— Gardening	13
——— Plants	9
——— Trees and Shrubs	9
——— Cottage, Farm, and Villa Architecture	13
LOWNDES's Engineer's Handbook	12
Lyra Domestica	14
—— Eucharistica	15
—— Germanica	11, 15
—— Messianica	15
—— Mystica	15
—— Sacra	15
MACAULAY's (Lord) Essays	2
——— History of England	1
——— Lays of Ancient Rome	17
——— Miscellaneous Writings	6
——— Speeches	5
——— Works	1
MACFARREN's Lectures on Harmony	11
MACLEOD's Elements of Political Economy	4
——— Dictionary of Political Economy	4
——— Theory and Practice of Banking	19
McCULLOCH's Dictionary of Commerce	18
——— Geographical Dictionary	7
MACFIE's Vancouver Island	15
MAGUIRE's Life of Father Mathew	3
——— Rome and its Rulers	3
MALING's Indoor Gardener	9
MANNING on Holy Ghost	14
MARSHMAN's History of India	2
——— Life of Havelock	3
MARTIN's Commercial Handbook of France	19
MASSEY's History of England	1
MASSINGBERD's History of the Reformation	3
MAUNDER's Biographical Treasury	4
——— Geographical Treasury	7
——— Historical Treasury	3
——— Scientific and Literary Treasury	9
——— Treasury of Knowledge	20
——— Treasury of Natural History	9
MAURY's Physical Geography	7
MAY's Constitutional History of England	1
MELVILLE's Digby Grand	17
——— General Bounce	17
——— Gladiators	17
——— Good for Nothing	17
——— Holmby House	17
——— Interpreter	17
——— Kate Coventry	17
——— Queen's Maries	17
MENDELSSOHN's Letters	3
MENZIES' Windsor Great Park	13
MERIVALE's (H.) Historical Studies	1
——— (C.) Fall of the Roman Republic	2
——— Romans under the Empire	2
——— Boyle Lectures	2
MILES on Horse's Foot and Horse Shoeing	19
——— on Horses' Teeth and Stables	19
MILL on Liberty	4
——— on Representative Government	4
——— on Utilitarianism	4
MILL's Dissertations and Discussions	4
——— Political Economy	4
——— System of Logic	4
——— Hamilton's Philosophy	4

MILLER's Elements of Chemistry	9
MONSELL's Spiritual Songs	15
——— Beatitudes	15
MONTGOMERY on Pregnancy	10
MOORE's Irish Melodies	11, 17
——— Lalla Rookh	17
——— Journal and Correspondence	3
——— Poetical Works	17
——— (Dr. G.) First Man	8
MORELL's Elements of Psychology	6
——— Mental Philosophy	6
MOSHEIM's Ecclesiastical History	14
MOZART's Letters	3
MÜLLER's (Max) Lectures on the Science of Language	8
——— (K. O.) Literature of Ancient Greece	2
MURCHISON on Continued Fevers	10
MURE's Language and Literature of Greece	2
New Testament illustrated with Wood Engravings from the Old Masters	11
NEWMAN's History of his Religious Opinions	3
NIGHTINGALE's Notes on Hospitals	20
ODLING's Animal Chemistry	9
——— Course of Practical Chemistry	9
——— Manual of Chemistry	9
O'SHEA's Guide to Spain	16
OWEN's Comparative Anatomy and Physiology of Vertebrate Animals	8
OXENHAM on Atonement	15
PACKE's Guide to the Pyrenees	16
PAGET's Lectures on Surgical Pathology	10
PEREIRA's Elements of Materia Medica	10
——— Manual of Materia Medica	10
PERKINS's Tuscan Sculptors	12
PHILLIPS's Guide to Geology	8
——— Introduction to Mineralogy	8
PIESSE's Art of Perfumery	13
——— Chemical, Natural, and Physical Magic	13
PITT on Brewing	19
Playtime with the Poets	17
Practical Mechanic's Journal	12
PRATT's Law of Building Societies	20
PRESCOTT's Scripture Difficulties	14
PROCTOR's Handbook of the Stars	7
——— Saturn	7
PYCROFT's Course of English Reading	5
——— Cricket Field	18
——— Cricket Tutor	18
——— Cricketana	18
RAYMOND on Fishing without Cruelty	18
READE's Poetical Works	17
Recreations of a Country Parson	6
REILLY's Map of Mont Blanc	15
RIVERS's Rose Amateur's Guide	9

ROGERS's Correspondence of Greyson	6	TASSO's Jerusalem, by JAMES	17
———— Eclipse of Faith	6	TAYLOR's (Jeremy) Works, edited by EDEN	14
———— Defence of ditto	6	TENNENT's Ceylon	8
———— Essays from the *Edinburgh Review*	6	———— Natural History of Ceylon	8
———— Fulleriana	6	———— Wild Elephant	8
———— Reason and Faith	6	THIRLWALL's History of Greece	2
———— (E.) Fifth-Monarchy Man	3	THOMSON's (Archbishop) Laws of Thought	4
ROGET's Thesaurus of English Words and Phrases	5	———— (J.) Tables of Interest	20
RONALDS's Fly-Fisher's Entomology	18	———— Conspectus, by BIRKETT	10
ROWTON's Debater	5	TODD's Cyclopædia of Anatomy and Physiology	10
RUSSELL on Government and Constitution	1	———— and BOWMAN's Anatomy and Physiology of Man	10
		TROLLOPE's Barchester Towers	17
SANDARS's Justinian's Institutes	4	———— Warden	17
SCOTT's Handbook of Volumetrical Analysis	9	TWISS's Law of Nations	19
———— Lectures on the Fine Arts	11	TYNDALL's Lectures on Heat	8
SCROPE on Volcanos	7	———— Lectures on Sound	8
SEWELL's Amy Herbert	16		
———— Cleve Hall	16		
———— Earl's Daughter	16	URE's Dictionary of Arts, Manufactures, and Mines	13
———— Experience of Life	16		
———— Gertrude	16		
———— Glimpse of the World	16	VAN DER HOEVEN's Handbook of Zoology	8
———— History of the Early Church	3	VAUGHAN's (R.) Revolutions in English History	1
———— Ivors	16	———— (R. A.) Hours with the Mystics	7
———— Katharine Ashton	16	———— Way to Rest	7
———— Laneton Parsonage	16		
———— Margaret Percival	16		
———— Passing Thoughts on Religion	14		
———— Preparation for Communion	14	WALKER on the Rifle	18
———— Principles of Education	14	WATSON's Principles and Practice of Physic	10
———— Readings for Confirmation	14	WATTS's Dictionary of Chemistry	9
———— Readings for Lent	14	WEBB's Objects for Common Telescopes	7
———— Examination for Confirmation	14	WEBSTER & WILKINSON's Greek Testament	13
———— Stories and Tales	16	WELD's Florence	16
———— Thoughts for the Holy Week	14	WELLINGTON's Life, by BRIALMONT and GLEIG	3
———— Ursula	16	———— by GLEIG	3
SHAW's Work on Wine	19	WEST on Children's Diseases	9
SHEDDEN's Elements of Logic	4	WHATELY's English Synonymes	4
SHIPLEY's Church and the World	14	———— Life and Correspondence	3
Short Whist	20	———— Logic	4
SHORT's Church History	3	———— Remains	4
SIEVEKING's (AMELIA) Life, by WINKWORTH	3	———— Rhetoric	4
SMITH's (SOUTHWOOD) Philosophy of Health	20	———— Paley's Moral Philosophy	15
———— (J.) Paul's Voyage and Shipwreck	13	WHEWELL's History of the Inductive Sciences	2
———— (G.) Wesleyan Methodism	3	Whist, what to lead, by CAM	20
———— (SYDNEY) Miscellaneous Works	6	WHITE and RIDDLE's Latin-English Dictionaries	5
———— Moral Philosophy	6	WILBERFORCE (W.) Recollections of, by HARFORD	3
———— Wit and Wisdom	6	WILLICH's Popular Tables	20
SMITH on Cavalry Drill and Manœuvres	18	WILSON's Bryologia Britannica	9
SOUTHEY's (Doctor)	5	WINDHAM's Diary	3
———— Poetical Works	17	Wood's Homes without Hands	8
STANLEY's History of British Birds	9	WOODWARD's Historical and Chronological Encyclopædia	2
STEBBING's Analysis of MILL's Logic	5	WRIGHT's Homer's Iliad	19
STEPHEN's Essays in Ecclesiastical Biography	4		
———— Lectures on History of France	2		
STEPHENSON's Life, by JEAFFRESON and POLE	3	YONGE's English-Greek Lexicon	5
Stepping-Stone (The) to Knowledge, &c.	20	———— Abridged ditto	5
STIRLING's Secret of Hegel	6	YOUNG's Nautical Dictionary	19
STONEHENGE on the Dog	19	YOUATT on the Dog	18
———— on the Greyhound	19	———— on the Horse	18
STRANGE on Sea Air	10		
———— Restoration of Health	11		
Sunday Afternoons at the Parish Church	6		

www.ingramcontent.com/pod-product-compliance
Lightning Source LLC
Chambersburg PA
CBHW021149230426
43667CB00006B/322